Youth, the 'underclass' and social exclusion

The idea that Britain, the US and other western societies are witnessing the rise of an underclass of people at the bottom of the social heap, structurally and culturally distinct from traditional patterns of 'decent' working-class life, has become increasingly popular in the 1990s. Anti-work, anti-social, and welfare dependent cultures are said to typify this new 'dangerous class', and 'dangerous youth' are taken as the prime subjects of underclass theories. Debates about the family and single-parenthood, about crime and about unemployment and welfare reforms have all become embroiled in underclass theories which, whilst highly controversial, have had remarkable influence upon the politics and policies of governments in Britain and the US.

Youth, the 'underclass' and social exclusion constitutes the first concerted attempt to grapple with the underclass idea in relation to contemporary youth. The book begins by mapping the terrain of underclass debates and the socio-economic changes that have placed young men and women at the centre of underclass theories. The chapters focus upon unemployment, training and the labour market, crime and benefit fraud, homelessness, parenting and single-parenthood, and shifts in welfare and youth policy. In the light of all this evidence, youth underclass theories are found to be partial and politically malevolent, and, in conclusion, a new perspective on young people, their dangerous transitions and social exclusion is proposed.

Robert MacDonald is Senior Lecturer in Sociology at the University of Teesside.

For William and Patrick

Youth, the 'underclass' and social exclusion

Edited by Robert MacDonald

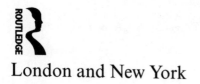

London and New York

First published 1997 by Routledge
11 New Fetter Lane, London EC4P 4EE

Simultaneously published in the USA and Canada
by Routledge
29 West 35th Street, New York, NY 10001

© 1997 selection and editorial matter, Robert MacDonald; individual
chapters, the contributors

Typeset in Times by Routledge
Printed and bound in Great Britain by TJ International Ltd,
Padstow, Cornwall

British Library Cataloguing in Publication Data
A catalogue record for this book is available from the British Library

Library of Congress Cataloging in Publication Data
Youth, the 'underclass' and social exclusion / edited by Robert MacDonald.
    p.   cm.
Includes bibliographical references and index.
1. Socially handicapped youth–Great Britain. 2. Urban poor–
Great Britain. 3. Hard-core unemployed–Great Britain.
4. Marginality, Social–Great Britain. I. MacDonald, Robert, 1962–
HV1441.G7Y65 1997
362.7'086'94–dc21   97–1608
                                                                        CIP

ISBN 0-415-15829-X (hbk)
ISBN 0-415-15830-3 (pbk)

Contents

Contributors

Debbie Baldwin is currently a research student in the Social Policy Department at the University of York. Her doctoral thesis – *Young people growing up in and outside of the Care System: an ethnographic approach to social policy issues* – is based on an in-depth study of young people leaving care in one local authority area in the North of England.

Shane J. Blackman is a Senior Lecturer in the Department of Applied Social Sciences, Canterbury Christ Church College. Shane has formerly taught at the University of Surrey and at the Institute of Education, University of London. He has undertaken qualitative research on schools, youth training, equal opportunities, workplaces, youth cultures, drugs, the police and currently on youth homelessness. He is the author of *Youth: positions and opposition – style, sexuality and schooling* (Avebury 1995).

Bob Coles is a Senior Lecturer in social policy at the University of York. He has a long-standing research interest in youth issues and in his most recent book, *Youth and Social Policy* (UCL Press 1995), he reviews research on vulnerable groups of young people. He is currently researching the needs of young people on social housing estates.

Steve Craine completed his doctorate – *Beggar's can't be choosers* – at the University of Salford in 1994. He is now an advocate and activist within the Mental Health Service User Movement and currently secretary to the US Network, mid-Wales representative for MINDlink, chair of the Ceredigion Advocacy Project and co-ordinator for Aberystwyth MIND.

Hartley Dean is a Reader in social policy at the University of Luton. His publications include *Social Security and Social Control* (Routledge 1991), *Dependency Culture* (with P. Taylor-Gooby, Harvester Wheatsheaf 1992), *Parents' Duties, Children's Debts* (editor, Arena 1995) and *Welfare, Law and Citizenship* (Prentice Hall/ Harvester Wheatsheaf 1996).

Tony Jeffs teaches in the Community and Youth Work Studies Unit, Department of Sociology and Social Policy at the University of Durham. He has written extensively about youth work issues and most recently has published *Informal Education* (with Mark Smith, Education Now 1996). He is a member of the editorial board of the journal *Youth and Policy*.

Gill Jones has been Assistant Director of Research at the Centre for Family Research, University of Cambridge since 1996. She was previously Senior Research Fellow at the Centre for Educational Sociology at Edinburgh University, where the study described in this book was based. She has published widely on issues of youth transitions including *Leaving Home* (1995) and, with Claire Wallace, *Youth, Family and Citizenship* (1992), both with the Open University Press.

Robert MacDonald teaches in the School of Social Science, University of Teesside. He has researched and written widely about youth transitions and about changing cultures of work. His doctorate on youth transitions in rural areas was followed by research on youth enterprise – co-authored with Frank Coffield as *Risky Business? Youth and the Enterprise Culture* (Falmer Press 1991) – and by studies of the informal economic activity undertaken by young people and adults in depressed local labour markets. He was on the editorial board of the journal *Youth and Policy* between 1992 and 1995.

Malcolm Maguire is a Principal Research Fellow at the Institute for Employment Research, University of Warwick. He has been undertaking research into aspects of employment, training and the labour market since 1975. In 1990, he co-authored *Restructuring the Labour Market: The Implications for Youth* (Macmillan), with David Ashton and Mark Spilsbury.

Susan Maguire is a freelance researcher. She previously worked as a careers adviser in schools, further education and higher education and has conducted research on the youth labour market, notably on recruitment and selection of young people, and the implementation of government training schemes. She is currently researching the youth labour market for a PhD at the University of Warwick.

Wendy Mitchell is a research student in the Social Policy Department at the University of York. Her doctoral research entitled *Leaving school: processes and routes taken by disabled young people in two local authorities* is based on the study of young people leaving special education in contrasting areas.

Ken Roberts is Professor of Sociology at the University of Liverpool. He is the author or co-author of *Black Youth in Liverpool* (Giordano Bruno 1991), *Careers and Identities* (Open University Press 1992), *Youth and Employment in Modern Britain* (Oxford University Press 1995) and *Poland's First Post-Communist Generation* (Avebury 1995).

Howard Williamson is Senior Research Associate in the School of Social and Administrative Studies, University of Wales Cardiff. He has written and lectured widely on youth questions related both to labour market and social welfare policies. He is vice-chair of the Wales Youth Agency.

Acknowledgements

This book was conceived at the *Youth 2000* conference held at the University of Teesside in the summer of 1995. Youth researchers were invited by the editor to contend with the popular, persistent but highly controversial idea that, in Britain and other late capitalist societies, young people now constitute a significant proportion of a new and dangerous underclass. I am grateful to all who were involved in a stimulating conference: the speakers who have suffered gracefully my editorial interventions and revised their papers for this volume; the audience for their pertinent questions and comments; and the organisations – Middlesbrough Borough Council, Middlesbrough City Challenge and the University of Teesside – who made the event possible.

Friends and colleagues have assisted me with the introductory and concluding chapters. I would like to thank Shane Blackman, Bob Hollands, Siobhan McAlister, Tracy Shildrick and Steve Taylor for their thorough, insightful and speedy critiques of these parts of the book. I hope that at least some of their useful advice has been included.

Most of all though, I would like to thank Jacqui Merchant for putting up with me and the book, and our sons, Patrick and William, for not becoming too delinquent in the (partial) absence of their father over the past six months.

Finally, to avoid confusion it is important to note that the writing of this volume concluded in the Autumn of 1996. On a number of occasions reference is made to the politics and policies of the current or recent governments. These allude to the series of Conservative administrations which terminated on 1 May 1997. It is of course too early to say whether these discussions of underclass formation and critiques of underclass policy will be more or less relevant to the period of the new Labour regime.

Robert MacDonald
Newcastle-upon-Tyne
November 1996

Chapter 1

Dangerous youth and the dangerous class

Robert MacDonald

INTRODUCTION

This book constitutes the first concerted attempt by British social scientists to grapple with the idea of the underclass in relationship to contemporary youth. It considers both how youth as a time of transition can be dangerous for young people themselves, leading to social exclusion, and how excluded youth – as a social category – has been constructed as dangerous and threatening for the comfortable majority of middle-aged, middle-class society. 'Dangerous youth' refers, then, both to processes of social exclusion that affect vulnerable young people and to the groups so excluded. The chapter commences with a review of the underclass idea – of the various debates and issues which shape contemporary theories of a dangerous class. It then shows how and why young people have become the prime subjects in discourses of the underclass, before describing the specific contributions to these debates made by the subsequent chapters.

THE UNDERCLASS: DEBATES AND ISSUES

The idea that Britain and other late capitalist societies are witnessing the rise of an 'underclass' of people at the bottom of the social heap, structurally separate and culturally distinct from traditional patterns of 'decent' working-class life, has become increasingly popular over the past ten years (e.g. Macnicol 1987; Smith 1992a; Robinson and Gregson 1992; Westergaard 1992; Morris 1994). Some claim to see the emergence of a class or stratum of people with quasi-criminal, anti-social, anti-work cultures of welfare dependency, who now threaten the happy security and ordered stability of wider society. Others are more reticent about the cultural content of this class but accept its likely existence given prevailing social structural conditions. For government ministers and their speech writers, for television documentary makers and the feature writers of the press, and for academics of different disciplines and political persuasions, the underclass idea in its various guises can describe and explain much about the state of our society as we approach the end of the century.[1] Academic and more populist discussions about the future of the welfare state, about family changes and the consequences of rising rates of single motherhood, about the gnawing attrition of the social fabric by rising crime, and about the extent, experience and social impact of the marginalisation of disadvantaged groups, have all become embroiled in arguments about an underclass.

Yet there is perhaps no other term in the contemporary social scientific lexicon that generates so much argument, ambivalence and passion as 'the underclass'. Indeed, despite its current popularity, some would argue that 'the concept of the underclass is a recurrent political and social scientific myth . . . because of its inherent theoretical, methodological and empirical flaws [it represents] a demonstrably false set of beliefs' (Bagguley and Mann 1992: 122, 125). There are, however, other points of view. Professors Giddens (1973), Dahrendorf (1987) and Runciman (1990), for instance, have each employed the concept, in different ways, to describe changes in the class structure and accompanying social and cultural developments, while Rex and Tomlinson (1979) use it to explain the situation of some ethnic minority groups in Britain. Runciman is as certain that there is an underclass as Bagguley and Mann are sure that there is not:

> that there is below the working classes an underclass which constitutes a separate category of roles is as readily demonstrable as that there is an upper class above the middle class in contemporary British society . . . the term must be understood to stand . . . for those members of society [who are] . . . unable to participate in the labour market at all.
>
> (Runciman 1990: 388)

Before considering the variety of positions which have been taken within the underclass debate it is necessary, at least tentatively and following on from Runciman, to attempt some definition of the phenomena to which the term refers. This is notoriously difficult.

Macnicol (1994a: 30) says that 'there are as many definitions of the underclass as there are sociologists' and this partly explains the uncertainty and ambiguity which befuddles the subject. Kirk Mann – one of the most avid critics of the underclass idea *in toto* – captures the confusion in underclass conceptualisations: 'the features of the underclass vary enormously . . . the disparate observers who claim to be able to witness an underclass are incapable of agreeing on what it is they have witnessed' (Mann 1994: 79–80).

Nevertheless, within British sociology (Mann was writing of the debate in the US and Australia as well) there is probably a greater and growing degree of consensus about what, for analytic purposes, might constitute this underclass and the processes which might define it. Later in this book, Ken Roberts (in Chapter 3) defines an underclass as follows: it should be beneath and disadvantaged relative to the lowest class of the gainfully employed population; this situation should be long-term and persistent for the individuals involved; crucially it should be typified by separate social and cultural outlooks and activities, as well as by economic exclusion, which serve as further impediments to joining the regularly employed workforce. Thus, at the centre of his definition, Roberts has the marginality of this group to regular employment, probably the defining feature of all sociologically oriented underclass theories in Britain. Whereas some (see Smith 1992b, for example) do not include reference to cultural factors (leaving these open to empirical investigation), Roberts's version is more useful for including these. If they are omitted from the definition we might simply re-label the long-term unemployed or economically inactive as an underclass (see Heath 1992). There is little analytic value in this, and such a definition would also limit sociological engagement with the powerful variants of the underclass thesis offered by the Radical Right (as we will see shortly). The long-term unemployed and economically inactive no doubt share similar objective relationships to production and consumption but, I would argue, for the socially and economically excluded to be properly understood as some sort of class – an underclass – they must also share some similar cultural outlooks, values and activities. My definition would be similar to Roberts' and it also attempts to encapsulate some of the diversity of underclass definitions within one working model:

> a social group or class of people located at the bottom of the class structure who, over time, have become structurally separate

and culturally distinct from the regularly employed working-class and society in general through processes of social and economic change (particularly de-industrialisation) and/or through patterns of cultural behaviour, who are now persistently reliant on state benefits and almost permanently confined to living in poorer conditions and neighbourhoods.

Of course, the notion of a 'dangerous class', defined and labelled in numerous ways, has a long and chequered history. It is impossible to read accounts of the underclass written in the 1980s and 1990s without hearing echoes of much older ideas about the poor and their social situation (Walker 1990; Buck 1992; Gans 1993. See Morris 1994 and Macnicol 1994a for detailed reviews of the aetiology and development of discourses of the dangerous class). Contemporary diatribes against an anti-social underclass mirror representations of the poor from previous decades and centuries (even into the Middle Ages, see Scott 1975); representations which persistently sought to divide the marginal, working-class poor into the deserving and undeserving (Mann 1992; Morris 1994). Malthus (1806), Marx and Engels (1848) and Mayhew (1950), for example, all described the burdensome, residual, pauperised, dislocated and redundant population newly to be found in the swelling urban centres of the industrialising world. The thriftless poor were regarded as parasitical upon the honest toil of the majority and threatened to morally corrupt the societies in which they moved. Although they occupied quite different political standpoints and provided quite different theories of poverty, unemployment and underdevelopment, these nineteenth-century social commentators were united in their moral condemnation of what they saw as the vagrancy, improvidence, idleness and irresponsibility of the 'dangerous class'.

The 'underclass' was first coined in 1918 to refer to the majority oppressed by the capitalist 'overclass' (Macnicol 1994a), but Myrdal (1962) is usually accredited with authorship of the *contemporary* underclass term and Auletta (1982) is seen as the first to popularise the concept (both of whom were writing of the USA). Myrdal's 'underclass' referred to an excluded minority left economically redundant through technological progress under capitalism, whereas Auletta focused upon the culturally as well as economically excluded, preferring to stress the inability of the underclass to assimilate into the American way of life. His underclass included drug addicts, drunks, drop-outs and drifters, bag ladies and released mental patients, street criminals and other hustlers, alongside the 'passive poor' and long-term welfare dependants. Auletta's work is typical of many preceding and subsequent views of the poor which, whilst making mention of how they have been made economically marginal, tend to emphasise the cultural characteristics of under-class members, seeking to label many of them as somehow personally culpable for their predicament and therefore undeserving of public sympathy or charitable support.

John Westergaard chose the underclass debate for his presidential address to the British Sociological Association in 1992. He, too, pointed to its long history and saw the re-emergence of a contempo-rary debate as evidence of the faddish nature of sociological concerns. However, Westergaard also argued that underclass theses were – at the same time – of critical sociological importance if they were correct in their view that 'the divide between this underclass and the majority is increasingly *the* most salient and challenging line of social division for the future, by contrast not least with the older divisions of class now said to be in eclipse' (Westergaard 1992: 576). He went on to identify different versions of the underclass thesis, and here four broad positions in the contemporary under-class debate are outlined.

First, there is what Westergaard refers to as the 'moral turpitude' thesis. This is the most well-known, politically influential and controversial argument. It posits that in America, Britain and other Western societies an underclass is either emerging or already fully formed which now threatens the social and moral order. This under-class is evidenced, it is claimed, by the anti-social actions, welfare dependency, moral irresponsibility and deviant cultures of a growing minority of the population (cultures which themselves have been fostered by prevailing, liberal welfare regimes). The underclass are regarded as the 'behaviourally poor' (Green 1992: 77). Elsewhere this perspective has been referred to as the culturalist, individualist or conservative approach and it has been championed by Charles Murray and others from the Radical Right in America and Britain.

The second perspective would concur with the first to the extent that it accepts that an underclass is here, or soon to be with us, but differs in the way that it explains its origins. Social structural factors are given precedence over cultural ones. As Robinson and Gregson observe, underclass theories hinge on the 'classic polarity between structuralist and behaviouralist approaches, between structure and agency' (1992: 42). Within this structuralist (sometimes called 'radical'), liberal Left perspective the underclass of Britain and America can be understood as an outcome of social and economic change, particularly of the movement towards a supposedly post-industrial economy. Westergaard calls this the 'outcast poverty' thesis. Economic change and government policy have combined to make a significant minority economically redundant. In the absence of legitimate employment, alternative, sometimes deviant under-class cultures may emerge. Despite the political opposition of the authors equated with them, these first two positions can elide into each other with some liberally inclined commentators seeing the structural influences on the growth of an underclass as antecedents to adaptive cultural behaviour which further entrenches the social exclusion of the group(s) involved.

Third, there is a more 'agnostic' view. This accepts the theoretical possibility of the existence of an underclass, or something similar, especially given the profound economic changes occurring in late capitalist societies, but argues that, as yet, there is not the evidence necessary to prove that such a controversial concept has an empir-ical reality. Here commentators tend to stress the need for further social scientific investigation of the underclass idea (Smith 1992a; Macnicol 1994a; Westergaard 1992).

Finally, there are those who reject the underclass thesis outright. They argue that there is no such thing as the underclass; that the concept is politically dangerous, empirically unsupported and theo-retically confused. This 'atheist' case has, in Britain, been best put by Kirk Mann and Paul Bagguley (Bagguley and Mann 1992; Mann 1992, 1994). It eschews discussion of the underclass as an empirical phenomenon and suggests that academic discussion of it simply serves the political interests of society's privileged, ruling classes. The underclass concept is an ideological red herring which diverts attention from the real causes of poverty and the real prob-lems faced by the poor.

The first two perspectives – culturalist and structuralist under-class theories – are considered in more depth in the following sections. The subsequent chapters collectively give a good example of the third perspective: they engage critically with the underclass idea and draw upon youth research to assess its theoretical value. Further consideration of the final, 'atheist' position in the under-class debate is reserved for the concluding chapter.

IDLE, THIEVING BASTARDS: CHARLES MURRAY AND THE RADICAL RIGHT

Charles Murray's writings on the underclass have been the most influential on both sides of the Atlantic over the past ten years. It is rare to read British accounts without coming across reviews of his thesis; reviews which are almost uniformly critical. Nevertheless, his distinctive, iconoclastic approach has invigorated sociological discussion in Britain of poverty, social exclusion and the cultural consequences of economic change. His impact has been even more profound in the political sphere. His thesis has shifted the political outlooks of both the Republican and Democratic Parties in the US and (at least sections of) the Conservative Party in Britain. The British Labour Party has also been keen to present itself as taking a less liberal, 'tougher' line on issues of welfare and crime in the light of the popularity of ideas such as those espoused by Murray.

In the US, the policy outcomes of Radical Right views of the underclass have included the Clinton administration's support – prior to the 1996 Presidential election – for state-level 'policy experiments' and national legislation which effectively demolish welfare for unmarried mothers (and so-called 'welfare queens'), institute 'workfare' programmes for the long-term benefit dependent and introduce ever more punitive approaches to offenders with the slogan of 'three strikes and you're out'.[2] President Clinton is reported as thinking that Murray is 'essentially right' and the Democratic Senator of Connecticut favours a shift in state funds from supporting teenage mothers to financing state orphanages in which their children might be raised (*Sunday Times* 29 May 1994). In a similar vein in this country the Institute of Economic Affairs has promoted calls for single mothers to give up their children for adoption and for single mothers to be confined to hostel accommodation so that their behaviour and the upbringing of their children can be monitored and supervised (*Independent* 5 March 1995).

In Britain policies attacking the underclass have not as yet been so far reaching. The early 1990s saw the Conservative government launch a moral crusade for a return 'Back to Basics' which stressed the 'traditional' values of marriage and family life (and which proved rather ill-fated as a number of Tory MPs were revealed themselves to be absentee fathers, adulterers or to favour sexual practices at odds with the sorts of 'Victorian values' espoused by Conservative Party Central Office) (Macnicol 1994a: 31). Single mothers, offenders, those on benefit and other members of the putative underclass continue to feature large in the demonology of the Conservative Party, however, and various policies have been, or are to be, implemented which attempt to police such people and regulate their behaviour more closely.

Given the enormous impact of Murray's thesis upon the politics and policies of governments and parties on both sides of the Atlantic, his ideas will be reviewed in detail – and in a neutral manner – in the following pages. The subsequent chapters of the book include extensive critique.

In 1984, Charles Murray published *Losing Ground*, which argued that US post-war welfare policy had encouraged the growth of a non-productive underclass dependent upon welfare payments (an argument which found an eager audience in the Reagan administration of the time). In 1989, at the behest of the *Sunday Times*, Murray visited Britain and produced reports later published by the Institute of Economic Affairs as *The Emerging British Underclass* (1990). This, and his 1994 update *Underclass: The Crisis Deepens* (also serialised first by the same newspaper), contain his account of the underclass in this country and are the references most frequently cited by British sociologists. Although Murray remains the chief protagonist, other right-wing British intellectuals – Patricia Morgan (1995) and David Green (1993), for instance – have authored further tracts which present a radical conservative reappraisal of welfare, the family, crime and unemployment.

In 1994, Murray wrote *The Bell Curve* with Richard Herrnstein, a volume even more controversial than its predecessors. Here, the authors revisited dusty debates about race and intelligence to argue that the disadvantage experienced by black Americans could be explained in part by the genetic inheritance of intelligence. Putting it simply (the book extends to several hundred pages), American society is claimed to be dominated by a powerful 'cognitive elite' who control an increasingly technological, information-based society.[3] Many of the social problems of the US have at their root low intelligence, and Murray and Herrnstein go on to argue that black people, on average, have lower IQs than whites and, because of their poor cognitive abilities, fall into a deprived and dangerous underclass. A fuller discussion of the black American underclass can be found later, and a review and critique of *The Bell Curve* in Fraser (1995) and Jacoby and Glauberman (1995). Of more immediate concern to us here is the British situation where the underclass problem has been constructed as one chiefly connected to issues of unemployment and the labour market (for example, Buck 1992). Field says there is 'no racial basis to Britain's underclass' (1990: 38), unlike in the US where it is largely conceived of as a black phenomenon (Silver 1993; Pilkington 1992; Heath 1992). Lash comments: 'in Britain the underclass would be overwhelmingly white, concentrated above all in the housing estates of Liverpool, Glasgow, Newcastle, and elsewhere. In the USA such concentrations of white urban poverty simply just do not exist' (1994: 171).[4]

In *The Emerging British Underclass*, Murray states his objective: 'as someone who has been analysing this phenomenon in the USA, I arrived in Britain a visitor from a plague area come to see whether the disease is spreading' (1990: 3). The title of this and *Underclass: the Crisis Deepens* make obvious his conclusions. But what *is* Murray's underclass? According to him, the US underclass is constituted by a particular type of poor people who are immersed in social problems:

> throughout the 1970s something strange and frightening was happening among poor people in the US. Poor communities that had consisted mostly of hardworking folks began deteriorating, sometimes falling apart altogether. Drugs, crime, illegitimacy, drop out from the job market, drop out from school, casual violence . . . showed large increases, focused in poor communities. As the 1980s began, the growing population of the 'other kind of poor people' could no longer be ignored and a label for them came into use. In the US, we began to call them the underclass.
>
> (Murray 1990: 2–3)

From his trips to 'poor communities' in the UK (to Easterhouse in Glasgow and to Liverpool, for example), he concluded that a similar underclass of this 'other kind of poor people' was also arising here. It had not yet grown to the size of its American cousin, but the social conditions necessary for its growth were established. Three inter-linked trends indicated its arrival: the rises in rates of unemployment, crime and illegitimacy that took place during the 1970s and 1980s. This is the 'unholy trinity' which gave rise to Bagguley and Mann's satirisation of Murray's underclass as just 'idle, thieving bastards' (1992).

In terms of crime, Murray compares England with the US concluding that in the late 1980s and 1990s in England, people are twice as likely to be burgled as in the US and that rises in the rate of violent crime are an 'early warning signal' that England may soon match the levels suffered in the US. He talks as well of the qualitative impact of lawlessness and how pseudo-careers of crime are now common, particularly amongst young underclass males. As in the US, the experience and fear of crime will hasten the flight of the respectable working-class from poor neighbourhoods, so hardening the geographical, as well as social, isolation of the residual underclass.

By 1994, he had attenuated his comments about crime (and unemployment). Murray now has most to say about illegitimacy and single motherhood. He charts the rise in illegitimate births and their concentration amongst the lowest social classes. This is 'a generational catastrophe. Illegitimacy produces an underclass for one compelling practical reason . . . namely communities need families. Communities need fathers' (1990: 7). Murray argues that 'revolutionary' changes in patterns of family formation – which have led to one in five British families with children being lone parent families (the vast majority of these being headed by lone mothers) – now threaten the orderliness and prosperity of society. Murray's numerous critics tend not to debate the facts of these statistical trends (although these are not as unproblematic as Murray would have it) but tend rather to argue about their sociological interpretation and implications (see Chapter 11). Murray (writing with Herrnstein in *The Bell Curve,* 1994: 519) adds in low intelligence to his account of the catastrophic problems engendered by 'incompetent' single motherhood in the US:

> the greatest problems afflict children unlucky enough to be born to and reared by unmarried mothers who are below average in intelligence – about 20 per cent of children currently being born. They tend to do badly socially and economically. They tend to have low cognitive abilities themselves. They suffer disproportionately from behavioural problems. They will be disproportionately represented in prisons. They are less likely to marry than others and will themselves produce large proportions of the children born to single women of low intelligence.

In Murray's eyes, the family is breaking down. However, this is not a universal trend. The institution of the family is undergoing renaissance within the British upper middle-classes, a cultural grouping he refers to as 'the New Victorians'. It is within 'the New Rabble' that families are undergoing terminal decline. For Murray, this cultural and moral division between the virtuous, respectable, industrious nuclear families of the New Victorians and the criminal, anti-social, feckless, single parent families of the New Rabble will become the major social dividing line in a new British class system (1994).

In Britain, ethical socialists (as they call themselves), such as A. H. Halsey, Norman Dennis and George Erdos, have joined the debate with some gusto. Their mission is to challenge what they see as a prevailing Marxist and feminist intelligentsia for forsaking the traditional, nuclear family. They challenge the permissiveness of an alleged New Left orthodoxy on single motherhood by reasserting the moral and social value, and indeed the superiority, of the nuclear family. Whilst expressing reservations about underclass terminology, they too decry the 'dismembering of the family' (Dennis 1993). To some extent, their intervention has shifted the academic argument in Britain from one about maternal deprivation and the problem with single mothers to paternal deprivation and the range of far-reaching social disadvantages said to subsequently face children from families without fathers (although policy responses remain targeted upon single mothers). Halsey condemns 'a situation where the man never *arrives* never mind *leaves*. There is a growing proportion of children born into single-parent families where the father has never participated as a father but only as a genital' (*Guardian* 23 February 1993).

For Dennis, the problems of rising crime and social disorder which have frequented Britain's inner-cities and outer estates can be traced back – not to poverty, unemployment or bad housing – but to the flight of fathers from the family. Dennis says that the Tyneside riots of 1991 'were characterized just as much by the statistical deficiency of stable families as they were by the statistical excess of the long-term unemployed' (1993: 113). The absence of fathers as disciplinarians and positive role models for male offspring has produced a failed generation of disorderly, disrespectful and delinquent youths doomed to reproduce down the generations the same dysfunctional families.

Unemployment is Murray's third underclass indicator:

if illegitimate births are the leading indicator of an underclass and violent crime a proxy measure of its development, the definitive proof that an underclass has arrived is that large numbers of young, healthy, low-income males choose not to take jobs.

(1990: 17)

He insists that much long-term unemployment is voluntary, that many of the unemployed, particularly the young, prefer to rely on what he regards as generous state benefits. The welfare state has served to deplete the work ethic, enterprise and self-reliance which previously characterised the British working class, replacing it with an idle and dishonest dependency culture (Green 1992; Marsland 1996); what the Minister for Social Security has termed 'a something for nothing society' (Lilley 1992). Murray talks of a 'lost generation' of young men who, in growing up in underclass locales, have lost a willingness to participate in training schemes or employment and who now seek easier livings through illicit means.

These three phenomena – crime, illegitimacy/single motherhood and unemployment – are woven tightly together by Murray to theorise the underclass. He suggests that its origins can be found *initially* in the way that society regulates and supports its citizens and provides 'incentives to failure' (1984); that is, it emanates 'more from the policy than the cultural context' (1990: 78). The criminal justice system and the welfare state have 'seduced people' into negative social behaviour and immoral outlooks at the expense of more decent ones (Murray 1990: 71). In terms of crime, the chances of getting caught, of being found guilty and of going to prison have all reduced dramatically since the 1960s and so more people commit crime (particularly as more of them now lack the moral guidance and discipline provided by fathers). For offenders, the personal consequences of offending have become too uncertain (Herrnstein and Murray 1994: 544). The provision of over-generous state support has encouraged idleness amongst the unemployed. Given the benefits accruing to single mothers, Murray regards their single parenthood as economically rational. Changes in the cultural climate have dispensed with the moral buffers which limited illegitimacy and have provided young women with the opportunity to take strategic advantage of local authority housing and social security benefits. Previously 'having an illegitimate baby was brutally punishing if you were poor', but with more liberal benefit regimes single motherhood 'went from "extremely punishing" to "not so bad" ' (1994: 29, 30). As young women need no longer rely on young men for financial support, young men need no longer commit themselves to what they may regard as low status employment, especially with the opportunity of a life on the dole enlivened and made more materially acceptable by hustling, benefit fraud and crime. As these young men become progressively marginalised from

– or as Murray would have it, make themselves progressively marginal to – the mainstream social and economic life of society, they become still more unattractive as marriage partners to young women. And so, according to Murray, illegitimacy, single mother-hood, unemployment and crime bind together in the cultural reproduction of the underclass.

So what does Murray say can be done about all this? His answer in 1990 was undeveloped and unclear. Then he suggested a dose of decentralised political autonomy for socially different neighbourhoods; apparently a form of social apartheid in which the unruly underclass could be left to get on with life in the way that it prefers, so long as it 'stays in its own part of town' (1990: 35) and is excluded (presumably by the repressive arms of the state) from the more decent and prosperous neighbourhoods of the moral majority (see Deakin 1990). By 1994, he favoured root and branch 'reform' of the benefit system central to which would be the complete elimination of benefits for unmarried women. He favours even more radical interventions to reduce illegitimacy in the American context (Herrnstein and Murray 1994). This is, for him, the only way that we can be rid of the central problem of the underclass: the rise of illegitimacy and single motherhood. In short, young women must not get pregnant outside of marriage (or, if they do, they must not expect state support). If young men insist upon sexual relations, young women must insist upon marriage and that men provide for them (thus regenerating young men's commitment to work and their families). Only in this way, he suggests, can we return to a society in which families function once again for the social good.

VICTIMS OF CIRCUMSTANCE: STRUCTURAL ACCOUNTS OF THE UNDERCLASS

Charles Murray and the Radical Right have made the intellectual running on the underclass issue. However, some from the liberal Left when they have chosen to engage with the topic (and there has been some nervousness about doing so given its recent political pedigree) have also found the underclass concept useful and have developed theses which stress the role of the economy, of govern-ment policy and of social structural inequalities in shaping an underclass. In short, members of the underclass are seen as victims of circumstance. Three writers – Frank Field, Ralf Dahrendorf and

William Julius Wilson – are used as exemplars of this more structural approach to understanding the underclass.

Frank Field, the Labour MP for Birkenhead in England, is one of the most widely quoted non-sociologists in the debate. The main thrust of his book *Losing Out* (1989: 2) is that 'the three hundred year evolution of citizenship as an incorporating force in British society has been thrown into reverse' as a result of the combined effects of government policy during the 1980s and the growing inequalities between those who did well out of the Thatcherite project and those who sank into deeper levels of poverty. Field regards those excluded from the material benefits of capitalism as an underclass:

> They increasingly live under what is a subtle form of political, social and economic apartheid. Indeed, the emergence of an underclass marks a watershed in Britain's class politics. Today the very poorest are separated, not only from other groups on low income, but, more importantly, from the working class.
>
> (Cited in Morris 1994: 106)

Field says the underclass is comprised of three groups. He agrees with Murray that the long-term unemployed might fall into it (but stresses the involuntary nature of their joblessness) and also agrees that single parents might be likely members (again, though, stressing the social rather than moral factors behind the rising trend). Field differs with Murray in that he also identifies the elderly poor as members of the underclass.

Field's argument is that in Britain the number and proportion of elderly people has increased steadily over recent decades. This elderly population is becoming more dependent upon dwindling state pensions which only provide for basic subsistence. Without an occupational pension, it is virtually impossible for older people to lead anything other than a restricted lifestyle. They become isolated in their poverty, unable to participate in the normal social life of their communities. Field suggests that pension-dependent elderly people suffer the same sorts of material deprivation and social exclusion as encountered by single parents and the long-term unemployed. For Field, the problem of the underclass is not primarily a problem of social order (of one class threatening another), nor is he claiming that this new underclass will share a common set of deviant, anti-social attitudes. His real purpose is to campaign politically for those groups who have been locked out of the affluence enjoyed by the comfortable majority.

Ralf Dahrendorf pursues a similar theme (1987). He, too, is concerned about the impact the growth of a socially excluded underclass might have upon social citizenship, but, like Murray, he is gloomy about the prospects for social order inherent in the underclass problem. Again, typical of Murray, Dahrendorf employs the imagery of disease and contagion to capture emotively this problem.[5] The underclass is a 'cancer which eats away at the texture of societies' (ibid.: 3) and, he argues, that 'whether it grows in size and hardens in separateness, or whether the boundary between it and the rest becomes more penetrable, is critical not only for the moral hygiene of British society, but also for its social and political stability' (ibid.: 11).

Dahrendorf, however, locates the origins of the underclass in the economic sphere. The 1980s phenomenon of jobless growth, wherein companies have been able to maintain profitability with fewer workers, has resulted in the economic redundancy of millions of unemployed in the UK and US. At the same time the deregulation of the labour market and employers' strategies for increased flexibility have generated a growing periphery of workers (under)employed in part-time and casual jobs, particularly in the service sector. These are the new working poor who, together with the unemployed, begin to form the underclass, in Dahrendorf's view.

He describes the underclass as suffering from 'a cumulation of social pathologies' (1987: 4) not just poorly paid work or unemployment. He mentions low educational achievement, illiteracy, teenage and single motherhood, miserable housing conditions in inner-city areas, the lack of useful role models for youth and so on. In Britain, he estimates that around one million people constitute this underclass, separated from the normal world of jobs and opportunities in self-sustaining ghettoes of deprivation. For Dahrendorf, the solution is a stake-holder society in which social policies (e.g. local community initiatives) are designed to tie back in those who are being excluded from social citizenship.

Yet Dahrendorf seems unsure about how exactly he wants to explain this phenomenon. He begins forthrightly enough by stating that the underclass is not 'at fault for its own condition', but the scathing language that he then uses as he describes this group (the 'laid back sloppiness' of 'mindless' underclass youth culture, for instance) implies their culpability (1987: 5). His position seems to be that, in the first instance, structural, economic factors are the cause, but subsequently there have developed styles of cultural behaviour which serve to sustain its existence. Thus, even macro-economic change, which might miraculously conjure up thousands of new jobs, would not now have much impact on the underclass. It has become a self-perpetuating sub culture (similar to Oscar Lewis's 'culture of poverty', 1966) set apart from the 'values of the work society' (Dahrendorf 1987: 5). Although Dahrendorf commences with a structural underclass theory, this soon slips into a cultural account not wholly different from that of Murray.

The most extensive structural account of the underclass emanates, like its conservative, culturalist counterpart, from the US. Here, we turn to the work of William Julius Wilson (1978, 1987, 1991). According to Wilson, the American underclass has resulted from social-class disadvantage even if the majority of its members are black. Race is important, but only in that it generates a particular constellation of social-class disadvantages. Combined with a decline in employment in working-class manufacturing jobs in the inner-city, have been socio-demographic changes (a growth in the population of poor black families in, and migration over the past three decades from the rural South to, the cities of the North-East and Mid-West) which have created a large pool of black youth with poor employment prospects (Morris 1994). Alongside this concentration and impoverishment of the black ghetto poor has been an improvement in the career opportunities for the better educated, black middle-class. Thus, in the 1970s and 1980s, the proportion of black people in unemployment *and* in professional jobs grew, which Wilson cites as evidence for the primacy of a class, rather than racial, explanation of the underclass phenomenon (Morris 1994).

This social mobility has been accompanied by geographical mobility wherein the better-off (both whites and blacks) have fled to the suburbs. In taking businesses and job opportunities with them they leave a poor black underclass stranded in the inner-city. Wilson's argument is clearly a structural one but he also addresses the supposedly degenerate cultures which Murray sees as now typifying the black ghetto poor. *The Truly Disadvantaged* (1987) represents the most important left-of-centre analysis of the interplay of structural and cultural change in the reproduction of the US underclass (see Mann 1994 for a useful critique). Wilson extends his class analysis of underclass causation into an explanation of the cultures of the ghetto poor (cultures which Murray wrongly takes to be the cause of the underclass). In respect of the apparent taste for welfare and distaste for legitimate employment said to typify the underclass, Wilson says two things. First, black workers may be disinclined to seek standard employment because of repeated rejection in the job market. This is the 'discouraged worker' effect reported in the British sociology of unemployment (Marsh 1988). Second, a legacy of the black consciousness movement may be an attitude which sees low-paid and menial jobs (i.e. the sort usually available to the black working-class) as demeaning and to be rejected as further evidence of society's racism.

Wilson also explains black single motherhood in terms of cultural adaptation to social structural factors. Rather like Murray he suggests that the weakened labour market position of young black men has made them less attractive as marriage partners to young mothers who instead seek welfare support. In terms of the alleged criminality of this black underclass, Wilson stresses not the inherent pathology of a black culture of poverty but rather the combined cultural impact of structural changes, particularly the social isolation that shifts in the black population have ensured. The black inner-city poor become disconnected from more prosperous, middle-class families now resident in the suburbs. Young black men in the ghetto become distanced from job networks and deprived of positive images and role models of black people in their neighbourhoods who have succeeded within the American system.

The ghetto poor now live in a 'commercially abandoned locality where pimps, drug pushers and unemployed street people have replaced working fathers as predominant socialising agents' (Kasarda 1989, cited in Morris 1994: 90). Lash (1994), following Wacquant (1991), describes these locales as 'hyper-ghettoes' which have been emptied of the regulating institutions of civil society.[6] In their absence, alternative criminal sub cultures develop. Jeffs and Smith (1996a) report that one in four African-American males between the ages of 20 and 29 are currently incarcerated, on probation or on parole. Lash (1994) suggests that drugs now form the centre of an alternative economy for a significant proportion of young black men and the associated gang violence has speeded the 'white flight' from the inner-city to the safety – albeit safety underwritten by the 'armed response' of private security – of bourgeois suburban enclaves (Davis 1990). The gang cultures of young, black ghetto males (which, ironically, have become global cultural commodities through the marketing of films, music and street style and which have provided an escape from poverty for a few) are for the majority only illusory, 'magical' solutions (Hall and Jefferson

1976). The image, argot and demeanour typical of such black sub-culture, Wilson notes, alienate potential employers and further distance young black men from job opportunities.

In summary, in the US there is far less scepticism about the existence of an underclass, which is defined as a primarily black phenomena (see Jencks and Peterson 1991). Wilson's work has fed a burgeoning underclass industry of research projects, conferences and journals dedicated to unravelling the relationships between the underclass and race, class and poverty (Mann 1994; Morris 1994). Indeed, Fainstein suggests that the 'underclass' has become 'the reigning hippopotamus' in the jungle of discourses about class and race in America; it 'takes up much space and eats up resources within academic disciplines, the media and government' (1993: 320–1). The focus of these American underclass debates tends to be upon the question of causality. Like Dahrendorf, Field and others in this country, Wilson prefers a broadly structuralist explanation. Although Wilson does not necessarily dispute the picture of the underclass painted by Murray, he does dispute its causation, regarding these aspects of black culture as long-term cultural adaptations to class disadvantage (see also Katz 1993). In turn, many have criticised Wilson's stress on the primacy of class over race in explaining the underclass (e.g. Iniss and Feagin 1989). Finally, we should note that Wilson has come to agree with Gans (1990) that the term 'underclass' has become so imbued with the politics and meanings of the Radical Right that it should now be dropped. Wilson now favours 'the ghetto poor'. Whether this will help cleanse discussion of the distasteful politics that have sometimes been associated with 'the underclass', as Wilson hopes, and whether a change in terminology might serve to clarify debates about poverty and social exclusion, are questions returned to in Chapter 11.

DANGEROUS YOUTH

Whereas Gans (1990) suggests that in the US 'the underclass' has become a 'racial code-word', a sub-text to much British underclass commentary concerns the supposedly parlous condition of *youth*. In the nineteenth century, societal fears about the dangerous class revolved around 'the twin concerns of the labour market behaviour of males' (particularly the perceived idleness of young males) and 'the reproductive behaviour of young females' (their alleged promiscuity and disregard for responsible parenting) (Macnicol 1994a: 32).

The key figures in the landscape of modern, conservative accounts of the underclass are again the irresponsible, welfare-draining single mother and the feckless young man. Murray does not conceal his view of young men as 'essentially barbarians' (1990: 23). The three social developments he highlights are ones which mainly concern the situations and activities of teenagers and young adults – rather than children, the middle-aged or elderly. In quasi-structural accounts, too, there is emphasis on the youthfulness of the protagonists. Dahrendorf, for instance, implies that it is the young who must be inculcated into the work ethic and extended social citizenship if they are not to be sucked into a dangerous, disorderly underclass (1987). Marks says 'one has a suspicion that they [underclass theorists] invent a social class all of whom are under the age of 25' (1991, cited in Mann 1994: 86).

Furthermore, many of the numerous policies which have been suggested or enacted to deal with underclass phenomena have been ones directed at youth (as the following chapters reveal). These include the reduction of benefits to single mothers, the withdrawal of unemployment benefits for under-18-year-olds, punitive policies on young offenders, authoritarian restrictions on young people's cultures and social lives – such as the proposal for night-time curfews for teenagers (Jeffs and Smith 1996a) and the outlawing of activities associated with the dance/rave culture (Redhead 1991) – and the growing clamour for citizenship or workfare programmes for the young unemployed (John Major announced at the Conservative Party Conference in 1996 that pilot workfare projects were to be extended to cover up to 75,000 unemployed people (*Guardian* 8 October 1996)).

Finally, a central tenet of underclass theses (an idea that would need to be substantiated for them to have real value) is that the young people of underclass locales are being socialised into the deviant cultures of their economically side-lined parents; that a distaste for work and traditional patterns of family life and a taste for crime and welfare dependence are being inculcated into the young so that the underclass reproduces itself down the generations (see Chapter 3). For these reasons, I suggest that the underclass debate is in large part a debate about youth, even if some writers are less than explicit about the fact that their prime suspects (or subjects) are young people. Debates about the existence of an underclass (or about its causation or about social policies to counter its development) must consider, primarily, the situation of young people in society.

What is it about the social condition of youth in Britain today that has led them to be considered as key members of this alleged underclass? To answer this we need to appreciate the way that the process of becoming adult has changed over the past thirty years. Young people now grow up in social, economic and political conditions radically different to those encountered by their parents' generation in the post-war years of relative economic prosperity and social cohesion. The following chapters document the transformations in family life, the institutions of education and training, patterns of leaving home and housing, the criminal justice system, state welfare systems and in social citizenship which have all reshaped the worlds of youth. But the primary transformation which has so altered the social situation of youth has been the rapid collapse of employment opportunities for school leavers and young people. Whilst youth sociologists now take family and housing transitions more seriously (see Chapters 6 and 7, for instance), their chief concern remains the economic transition from school into the labour market and the unequal occupational opportunities that befall young people as they progress towards adulthood. A wealth of studies have charted career trajectories and the ways these are shaped by social structural factors (e.g. social class, education, gender, ethnicity and locality) and, to a lesser extent, the active 'choices' made by young people (e.g. Coles 1988; Banks et al. 1992; Bates and Riseborough 1993).

This focus upon the economic situation of youth is understandable. The world of work that now greets young women and men would have been unrecognisable thirty years ago. Until the mid-1970s, the clear majority of young people could make what are regarded now as successful, secure and normal transitions to work, to social independence and to economic security in adulthood (albeit ones structured by class and other structural inequalities). The economic crises of the 1970s and the recessions of the 1980s and 1990s generated wide-scale industrial restructuring and mass redundancies which changed all this. In 1980, youth unemployment rose by more than it had in the previous ten years put together (Coles 1988). The collapse of the youth labour market and the more general transformations which have affected British labour markets over the past two decades (see Chapter 11) have left the economic position of youth severely weakened (particularly those already disadvantaged by ethnicity, class, qualification, locality or disability). This is described in detail in Chapters 2 and 3.

One dramatic example, from Teesside, a once prosperous conurbation of heavy, manufacturing industry in the north-east of England, can be given here. In 1974 when Paul Willis's 'lads' (1977) were stepping from school into manual, working-class jobs their counterparts in Teesside were doing the same; finding apprenticeships and jobs at British Steel, ICI or the docks. Then, 55 per cent of Teesside's 16-year-olds left school for employment.[7] Within twenty years, the movement of the area's school leavers into work has virtually ceased. In 1994, 4 per cent got jobs; the lowest figure ever recorded. Youth Training now soaks up about a quarter of the age cohort (with only around one-third of these finding employment afterwards). Further education has become the dominant structure through which post-16 transitions are made: in 1994, 57 per cent 'stayed on' compared with 28 per cent in 1974. In 1994, 16 per cent of the cohort were 'unemployed'. These are the young people not in education, employment or training (and probably not in receipt of benefit) characterised in Chapter 5 as 'Status Zer0' youth, a group which in Teesside has grown from 11 per cent of the cohort in 1987.

. Numerous studies have described the effects of this disintegration of traditional routes of transition to adulthood and the resultant social exclusion of vulnerable youth. Bates and Riseborough (1993), for instance, see Britain as typified by sharpened social divisions and deepening inequality which are faced nowhere more directly than in youth, and Williamson argues that:

> young people already disadvantaged become more vulnerable to processes which disadvantage them further . . . more fortunate young people, with supportive family networks, find themselves propelled onto a more constructive path, whereby educational achievement opens doors to better quality training and employment futures, which in turn provides the resources to find routes into restricted housing markets, and thereby to personal, social and financial independence. For a growing minority of young people, however, the process of transition is destructive and debilitating. Policies directed at young people have increasingly worsened the opportunities and possibilities for this age group.
>
> (Williamson 1993: 43)

Thus, middle-class youth can still, in the main, trade on their cultural capital and carve out relatively successful paths through education into middle-class jobs (even if these transitions are themselves becoming riskier). But youth sociologists in the 1990s began to wonder whether, for some working-class young people from poor localities of persistently high unemployment and for other groups of vulnerable youth, one outcome of these structural processes of social exclusion and economic marginalisation might be the creation of some form of dispossessed, economically surplus youth underclass. Wilkinson's study of Sunderland in the north-east of England described a 'drop-out society' and suggested that the youth under-class nationally might now include 100,000 people (1995). Wilkinson and Mulgan (1995) call the youth of underclass neighbourhoods 'underwolves' (like underdogs but more ferocious). On the other hand, Holman (1994/5) and Kinsey (1993), both drawing upon Scottish research, have argued that the underclass thesis does not capture the true attitudes and behaviour of such young people.

In the main, though, British youth sociology has mirrored the wider discipline in its hesitation to deal with underclass theories. Ambivalence and undeveloped scepticism tends to mark most forays into this terrain. Accounts of the way that youth have suffered the consequences of economic decline, structural unem-ployment and unjust government policy have not been few in number and yet there has been a reticence about engaging more fully with the underclass debate.[8]

But underclass theories will not go away, no matter how much we ignore them. Societal anxieties about 'dangerous youth' and 'dangerous classes' are powerful and persistent ones; as we approach the millennium they will continue to set political agendas and inform policies which to do much to determine the quality of young people's lives (see Chapter 10). Youth sociologists have a responsibility to contend more directly with underclass theses and, if they are found wanting, to offer alternative, more useful explana-tions of the social exclusion of disadvantaged youth.

The contributors to *Youth, the 'underclass' and social exclusion* have this task. They investigate how economic and social transfor-mations have impacted upon the transitions and experiences of young men and women in the late 1990s. They critically engage with underclass theories, interrogating them with evidence drawn from a diverse selection of recent studies of youth in Britain.

In Chapter 2, Malcolm and Susan Maguire chart the changes which have beset the youth labour market. Despite increases in post-16 participation in education, the Maguires point to the growth of a group of low-skilled and marginalised young people who comprise a significant proportion of 16- to 19-year-olds. Whilst the authors report some research which would suggest that this group may be becoming an unskilled, excluded underclass, they stress that the complex and diverse developments which are taking place in the youth labour market disallow any easy predictions about the formation of such a group. Whether we are seeing the emergence of a youth underclass, or more temporary social exclusion, is an issue Ken Roberts takes up in Chapter 3, where he disaggregates the key elements of underclass theses. Unlike some of the subsequent contributions, Roberts is more tolerant of the underclass idea and argues that, contrary to the received academic wisdom, extant youth research does not disprove it.

Chapter 4 is more critical of the underclass idea. It is written by Hartley Dean who extends his previous critique of the underclass thesis (Dean 1991) by examining changes in social security policies in Britain in the 1980s and 1990s and the effects on young people of the curtailment of their welfare rights. The increased risk of poverty amongst young people, resulting from social security 'reforms', might have a negative impact upon their sense of social citizenship and their feelings of obligation to the state, as suggested by some underclass theorists. He investigates this idea with the aid of recent research on the 'dependency culture' and social security benefit fraud. The responses of young people consistently excluded from welfare provision and education, training and employment is a theme taken up by Howard Williamson in Chapter 5. He reports research from Wales on 'Status Zer0' youth: those not in education, training or employment nor entitled to social security benefits. Their social and economic marginalisation has been taken to be emblematic of the underclass of the future and whilst Williamson also rejects overly pessimistic predictions he concludes that Status Zer0 youth may be the first generation for whom the underclass becomes a social reality rather than a political and ideological device.

Debbie Baldwin, Bob Coles and Wendy Mitchell argue, in Chapter 6, that underclass theories oversimplify the complex processes of social exclusion which lead heterogeneous groups of vulnerable youth (such as care leavers and those with special needs and disabilities) along unsuccessful transitions. For the authors, the underclass idea is simplistic and politically dangerous and more coherent social policies which recognise this are advocated. One of the key processes of youth transition, they note, concerns housing careers. In Chapter 7, Gill Jones draws upon her own extensive research to examine the usefulness of the underclass thesis in understanding patterns of youth homelessness. She seeks to replace right-wing representations of the underclass with a more sociological analysis of the interplay of structure and agency in shaping the risky housing transitions faced by youth.

Shane Blackman's chapter follows. It takes a closer, ethnographic look at the everyday cultures of unemployed, homeless young people in Brighton, in the south-east of England. He demonstrates the usefulness of ethnography in exploring the rituals, meanings and outlooks of marginal youth and their cultures of survival. This group certainly experienced the plethora of 'social pathologies' that Dahrendorf sees as indicative of the underclass, yet Blackman questions the value of this label. Chapter 9 is also qualitative in nature. Steve Craine is one of the few to have recently conducted longitudinal ethnographic research with young people, tracking the outcomes of difficult, early transitions. His sample grew up in the 1980s in a high unemployment area of Manchester in the northwest of England. He shows how alternative careers in crime and informal enterprise became rational, given the restricted opportunities of poor-quality training schemes and dead-end jobs (the 'black magic roundabout').

In Chapter 10, Tony Jeffs discusses youth policy and youth work with marginal and supposedly 'underclass' youth. He examines how, in recent years, an emergent and wide-ranging set of government policies to control 'dangerous' youth has been inspired by underclass ideology. In particular, a new authoritarianism now characterises much youth work practice: a philosophy which negates the democratic and educational approaches which historically have underpinned more progressive traditions of work with young people.

The final chapter provides a conclusion to the preceding ones. It summarises their key findings in respect of youth underclass theses, outlining areas of consensus and disagreement, and assesses the usefulness of the underclass concept in understanding the dangerous transitions experienced by young people. The final pages of the book discuss the future of the underclass debate, suggesting how, as we approach the millennium, we might better understand the social exclusion of youth.

NOTES

1 Recent journalism has, for instance, identified a 'skills training underclass' (*Guardian* 9 June 1992), a 'literacy underclass' (*Guardian* 27 April
1993), an 'electronic underclass' (*Guardian* 4 April 1996), a 'housing
underclass' (*Daily Telegraph* 8 June 1994), an 'internet underclass'
(*Guardian* 22 October 1996) and even 'a genetic underclass' of people
unable to get insurance because of inherited medical disorders (*Observer*
15 September 1996), as well as the usual welfare and criminal varieties.

2 As reported in the following, for example: *Guardian* 9 March 1995 and 6
May 1996; *Daily Telegraph* 25 July 1996; *Observer* 25 August 1996.

3 In an interesting parallel, the Chief Constable of West Mercia police has
warned of the growth of an 'electronic underclass' in the UK, denied
access to new technology and excluded from education and wealth,
adding to problems of crime and disorder (*Guardian* 4 April 1996).

4 However, Murray has also written of a 'coming white underclass' in the
US if illegitimacy rates continue to rise (1993).

5 David Sibley, in his fascinating book *Geographies of Exclusion* dissects
the metaphors of disease which we find in underclass theories. Although
Murray's work is not referenced, his analysis of this discourse is particularly pertinent:

> Disease in general threatens the boundaries of personal, local and
> national space, it engenders a fear of dissolution . . . of social disinte-
> gration . . . Disease is a more potent danger if it is contagious. The
> fear of infection leads to the erection of barricades to resist the
> spread of diseased, polluted others. The idea of a disease spreading
> from a 'deviant' or racialized minority to threaten the 'normal'
> majority with infection has particular power.
>
> (1995: 24–5)

6 Lash identifies, together with the cities of America, the outer estates of
Tyneside in north-east England as 'hyper-ghettoes'.

7 These and following statistics from Teesside Training and Enterprise
Council (1995a, b).

8 This is partly explained by the disciplinary and sub-disciplinary boundaries which continue to dog British academia; most of the underclass
debate in Britain has taken place within the realms of social policy and
the sociology of (un)employment and labour markets. Only recently
have youth sociologists become more alert to the possibilities and problems of the underclass thesis.

Chapter 2

Young people and the labour market

Malcolm Maguire and Susan Maguire

INTRODUCTION

The significance of employment in providing not only the necessary income on which to live, but also social status and psychological well-being, has long been established. A series of studies by Marie Jahoda has been seminal in this respect (1979, 1982). Jahoda's contention that 'work plays a crucial and perhaps unparalleled psychological role in the formation of self-esteem, identify and a sense of order' (1979: 312) has been confirmed in other writings (Hayes and Nutman 1981; Sayers 1988). As far as young people are concerned, Wallace (1987) asserted the relevance of Jahoda's findings and, on the basis of her study of young people on the Isle of Sheppey in the early 1980s, referred to 'a growing divergence between the mainly employed and the mainly unemployed as they enter adulthood: in other words, a form of social polarisation . . . what seemed to be emerging were new divisions based upon whether young adults had access to a job or not' (ibid. 221–2).

Any discussion of the notion of an emerging youth underclass must, therefore, incorporate an understanding of the labour market context with which young people are currently confronted, and that which is likely to face future cohorts of young people. Thus, this chapter will consider trends in the industrial and occupational distribution of young people since the early 1980s, and particularly those factors which are currently affecting, and are likely to have a continuing significant impact on, the demand for youth labour. It will then focus on key issues which require attention in order that the problematic features of the youth labour market may be identified, investigated and better understood. Among these issues are the rising levels of participation in education of 16- and 17-year-olds, changes in the routes into the labour market for young people, the notion of the existence of a group who are effectively excluded from conventional statistics, and the debate concerning employers' demand for youth labour.

TRENDS IN THE DEMAND FOR YOUTH LABOUR

Over the last twenty years, there has been a transformation of the labour market opportunities available to school leavers, with the attendant changes resulting in a less easily identifiable and distinctive youth labour market. It is important to assess the impact of these changes in order to understand the nature of the process of what Coles (1995: 8) regards as one of the three 'main transitions of youth . . . the transition from full-time education and training to a full-time job in the labour market (the school to work transition)'. Research conducted during the late 1970s and the first half of the 1980s suggested that, because young people were effectively excluded from recruitment to sections of the adult labour market, while at the same time having points of entry in which they were sheltered from competition from adults, there existed a separate youth labour market (Ashton, Maguire and Garland 1982). This market was characterised by the concentration of entrants to the labour market in a restricted number of industrial and occupational sectors, by a propensity for high proportions of 16-year-olds to leave school at the minimum school-leaving age, and by the relative lack of skills and qualifications of those entering employment. Thus, in 1979, 81 per cent of employed 16-year-old males were located in five industrial orders: Distribution (31 per cent), Metal Goods (15 per cent), Other Manufacturing (15 per cent), Construction (11 per cent) and Other Services (9 per cent). Similarly, females were concentrated in just three industrial categories: Distribution (41 per cent), Other Manufacturing (21 per cent) and Financial Services (17 per cent). As far as the occupational distribution was concerned, 24 per cent of 16-year-old males were in Metal and Electrical Processing and Machining occupations and 17 per cent in Other Processing and Machining, while 83 per cent of females were in just four occupational orders: Clerical (28 per cent), Selling (25 per cent), Catering (16 per cent) and Other Processing and Making (14 per cent). Not only have events since that time radically reshaped the number and pattern of opportunities for young people, but it is now questionable whether there is a distinct youth labour market.

The *Youth in the Labour Market* project (Ashton et al. 1982) also highlighted the importance of local labour market variations in determining the structure of job opportunities for school leavers and the significance of firms' internal labour markets, wherein systems of internal promotion provide avenues for career progression to meet the requirements of the organisation. One conclusion of the study was that the youth labour market was composed of a number of broad occupational segments, which determined the structure of opportunities available to young people, the quality and length of training they were likely to receive, and the likelihood of future occupational mobility and career progression (Ashton, Maguire and Spilsbury 1990: 19). Most importantly, this analysis pointed to the first destination of the young person after leaving school being crucial as an indicator of their future career trajectory. While one of the consequences of entering an inappropriate segment might be restricted career opportunities, the implications for young people who are unable to gain entry to any form of employment could be calamitous.

The significance of the concentration of 16-year-old entrants to the labour market in a restricted number of industrial and occupational sectors at the time of this study is that subsequent trends have severely reduced the opportunities in the occupations in which they were concentrated. Since the early 1980s, the demand for youth labour has declined dramatically. Among the reasons for this decline are: drastic reductions in the numbers employed in labour-intensive industries, notably in manufacturing, which had formerly relied heavily on school leavers as a source of labour; the impact of technology; increased business competition which, notably in parts of the service sector, has reduced the demand for routine clerical workers; organisational restructuring; and the repackaging of jobs to make them more suitable for people wishing to work part time.

A consequence of this process of change has been a marked reduction in the demand for the labour of relatively unqualified 16-year-olds. Thus, overall, a significant number of jobs which were traditionally open to young people have disappeared, and in others, young people face stiffer competition from other sections of the labour force.

While the sources of change outlined above have been readily identifiable, it has been argued that a series of underlying processes are likely to have a more profound effect on the operation of youth labour markets internationally in the future (Ashton 1992). Among the processes identified by Ashton are: first, the growth of multinational corporations, whose impact, as far as the United Kingdom is concerned, has resulted in the loss of manual jobs in the manufacturing sector through the relocation of some labour-intensive industries overseas; the emergence of transnational trading blocs, such as the European Economic Community (EEC), the Association of South East Asian Nations (ASEAN) and that effected by the North American Free Trade Agreement, which profoundly affect the operation of labour markets, including the youth labour market, within their spheres of influence; second, new forms of organising production, such as the introduction of 'flexible specialisation' (Piore and Sabel 1984); third, organisational restructuring, often incorporating a reduction in the layers of management (delayering) and in the size of the workforce (downsizing), as part of a drive to create 'flatter' organisations (Kanter 1990). As a result, employers are now often seeking different qualities in recruits than was formerly the case, commonly encompassing aspects such as problem-solving skills, conceptual ability and a commitment to the values of the organisation. Crucially, however, there is, ultimately, the need for a more highly skilled workforce; fourth, the growing importance of firm internal labour markets, wherein skills which are specific to the firm are required for progression, as opposed to occupational labour markets, which have usually involved the recruitment of school leavers and the provision of training. Firm internal labour markets tend to place less reliance on school-leaver recruitment, as the firm-specific skills are often composed of knowledge of the organisation, its production system and organisational goals as well as particular technical expertise.

While the existence of these trends is undeniable, and it would clearly be foolish to ignore not only their impact so far, but, more importantly, the potential effect they will have on job opportunities in the United Kingdom in the future, there is a danger of becoming seduced into believing that jobs for people with few qualifications or low-level skills will disappear completely. This would be an exaggeration, for not all firms operate in the way described above. Indeed, a large proportion of firms continue to operate in a manner which requires only low-level skills and places few demands on the workforce. In considering the impact of new technology on skill levels in the United States, Baran contends that 'in the face of heightened competition and little organised labour resistance, managers may well choose the immediate benefits to their bottom line that deskilling strategies promise' (Baran 1988: 704). Nonetheless, while some job opportunities for relatively unqualified and unskilled young people will continue to become available, the overall reduction in these opportunities could contribute to the emergence of significant numbers of young people who are effectively excluded from participation in the labour market.

PARTICIPATION IN EDUCATION

In the wake of numerous publications which pointed to deficiencies in the skills and qualifications of the British workforce posing a threat to the country's future international competitiveness (Wiener 1981; Barnett 1987; CBI 1989; Porter 1990; Hutton 1995), initiatives to address this problem have arisen from different sources. Notable among government policy initiatives have been the introduction of *Investors in People*, and the establishment of *National Targets for Education and Training*. Moreover, the debate has grown from a concentration on vocational training to encompass a concern with increasing participation in processes of learning of the population as a whole. The concept of lifelong learning is now firmly entrenched in Department for Education and Employment (DfEE) policy and plays a significant part in the activities of Training and Enterprise Councils (TECs). It is also central to the Economic and Social Research Council's (ESRC) *Learning Society* initiative, and the Royal Society of Arts' (RSA) *Campaign for Learning*. In terms of young people, it became accepted that the relatively high proportions leaving school at the minimum school-leaving age constituted a problem; it was posited that if increased participation in post-16 education could be achieved, the UK would be more competitive internationally.

What has happened since the mid-1980s is that there has been a dramatic rise in the proportions of 16-year-olds continuing to participate full time in education, with less steep, but still significant increases for 17- and 18-year-olds. Thus, for 16-year-olds, the participation rate rose from 48 per cent in 1987 to 75 per cent in 1993, while that for 17- and 18-year-olds rose from 33 per cent to 55 per cent (in 1992/3) and from 18 per cent to 34 per cent respectively. Interestingly, however, due to the declining size of annual cohorts, the numbers involved did not increase significantly.

A number of factors have contributed to this increase in participation. David Raffe (1992) has shown that there has been a compositional effect, with increasing proportions of recent cohorts of 16-year-olds coming from middle-class families, among whom participation rates in education are commonly higher. There has also been a combination of other factors, including: the reduction in the number of jobs available for 16- and 17-year-olds, notably as a result of the onset of the recession in 1990; the withdrawal of entitlement to unemployment benefits to 16- and 17-year-olds in 1988; the impact of GCSEs in recognising a wider range of attainment, and rising levels of attainment; the imposition on both schools and further education colleges of the necessity to generate greater numbers within these establishments, emanating from changes in funding arrangements, which has led to them giving more encouragement to 16- and 17-year-olds to remain within the system; a perceptible rise in young people's educational aspirations; and increased attractiveness of the vocational route.

John Gray has suggested that employers' requirements have impacted on staying-on rates in that:

> (a) certain (expanding) sectors of the economy (notably parts of the service sector) have lifted the stakes as regards the qualification levels being sought from potential recruits; (b) certain (declining) sectors of the economy (such as traditional manufacturing industries) have decreased their insistence on early entry (at 16+) and introduced more flexible strategies and/or simply failed to recruit young people to the same extent as before.
>
> (1992: 2)

Such increases in participation rates would appear to represent an appropriate response to the clamour for developing a more highly qualified and highly skilled labour force. Whatever the underlying reasons for this substantial rise in participation rates, it has not, of itself, effected any sort of instant solution, either to the skills deficiencies of the British workforce, or to difficulties encountered by young people in entering appropriate employment. Indeed, concerns have been expressed about some of the facets of this participation. The *Learning for the Future* project, which has been undertaken jointly by researchers from Warwick University and the Institute of Education at London University, points out that between 1987 and 1993 increases in levels of participation were twice as great as gains in levels of achievement. This is supported by research undertaken during this period by Ken Spours in Tower Hamlets in London, which suggested that, while participation had increased, through the effects of the recession and an increase in pupil and parent aspirations, significant proportions of those staying on at sixteen were subsequently leaving the education system at seventeen with little or no enhancement to their qualifications. Other research has pointed to many young people staying on in order to remain with their friends and peer group, in the absence of any acceptable alternatives and in preference to possible unemployment or government schemes (Unwin 1993).

Other problems identified in the *Learning for the Future* report are the lack of progression of those who stay on to the next level of learning, and in particular between NVQ levels 2 and 3 courses, and the high rates of drop-out and failure rates, of the order of 30 per cent, which have been found to be characteristic of post-16 courses (Audit Commission/OFSTED 1993). Furthermore, participation rates appear to have peaked and are now showing slight falls. For example, the UK Heads of Careers Services annual survey 'recorded the first decline in the proportion entering full-time further education in the seven years that the survey has been conducted – down to 67.6 per cent in 1995, from 68.1 per cent in 1994' (Industrial Relations Services 1996: 6). At the same time the work-based route is becoming more popular, partly through the introduction of Modern Apprenticeships and the spread of Youth Credits. However, if these initiatives are successful, they may lead to a further marginalisation of those with few or no qualifications. Maclagan has warned of the dangers of the Modern Apprenticeship initiative becoming elitist: 'it offers some young people higher quality opportunities by implicitly devaluing or marginalising what is available to the less favoured' (1996a: 16). As far as Youth Credits are concerned, Deakin (1996) points out that young people who are disadvantaged in some way, and may be harder to train, will be considerably less attractive to employers and training providers unless the value of their 'credit' is higher than average. Thus, the creation of a market system with few checks, balances and regulations is likely to be detrimental to the interests of those who are most disadvantaged in the labour market. In another significant development, sizeable numbers of young people are becoming employed in temporary or part-time jobs, which are increasingly characteristic of a casualised labour market (see Chapter 11; MacDonald 1997).

Overall, then, there is no substantial body of evidence to suggest that recent increases in rates of participation in full-time education post-16 are symptomatic of deep-seated shifts in cultural attitudes, which reflect a desire to strive for high-level qualifications in order to secure positions in the high-skills economy of the future on the part of 16- and 17-year-olds. The complex combination of explanations of these trends may, indeed, serve to introduce greater confusion into the policy-making process (Fergusson and Unwin 1993). The picture is further complicated by the apparent lack of emphasis given to qualifications by employers during their selection of applicants. For example, research carried out for the Employment Department in 1990 indicated that vocational qualifications were ranked only eighth out of nine attributes that employers sought in school leavers (Employment Department 1991). Even at the higher occupational levels, in the recruitment of graduates, it has been found that the applicant's 'cultural capital', which is closely related to their social-class background, and the status accorded to the university they attended, is often more important than the degree classification, or even the subject discipline (Brown and Scase 1994).

CHANGES IN THE ROUTES INTO EMPLOYMENT

The impact of the multiple sources of change identified above can be found in the dramatic changes which have occurred in the patterns of post-school destinations of 16-year-olds in recent years. Thus, the number of 16- to 17-year-olds who entered the labour market had fallen from 608,000 in 1984/5 to 276,000 in 1992/3. As a proportion of the age cohort, those 16-year-olds entering employment fell from 62 per cent in 1975 to 49 per cent in 1979, declined rapidly to 22 per cent in 1983, remained relatively constant to 1990, when it was 18 per cent, but then dropped dramatically to only 9 per cent in 1992. Over this same period, the introduction of Youth Training and its antecedents was clearly important, accounting for 6 per cent of 16-year-olds in 1979, rising to 26 per cent in 1987, before falling again to 14 per cent in 1992.

The destination statistics of those who left YT between April and December 1994 show great regional and local variations in both unemployment rates and early leaving rates. For example, 72 per cent of trainees in Sunderland left before completing, compared to 37 per cent in Hertfordshire (Maclagan 1996b). Overall, 50 per cent of trainees in England and Wales achieved a qualification, with high rates of early leaving being identified as a cause for concern.

Although differences between males and females, in terms of achievement, were not great, trainees from ethnic minority groups were markedly less successful in achieving qualifications. Of those leaving between July 1994 and June 1995, 58 per cent entered employment, while 50 per cent gained a qualification (Labour Market Quarterly Report 1996).

However, reservations have been expressed about the quality and accuracy of the data on which our understanding of these patterns, and subsequently policy decisions, is made. Reliance is placed on destination data, collected nationally by the Department for Education and Employment and locally by the Careers Service. This data identified whether the first destination of school leavers has been remaining in full-time education, entering employment or YT, or becoming unemployed. Two significant limitations about the current methods of collecting data are: first, little is known about what happens to young people within and between these broad categories; second, there remains a residual group whose destination is 'not known'.

As far as the first point is concerned, some meaningful data does exist at an institutional level, although this is not collected or collated systematically at a national level. It is well known, for example, that large numbers of young people move from their first destination category within six to eight weeks. There is also considerable movement between courses within FE. Furthermore, the current destination categories are only related to 16-year-olds. Given the fact that greater numbers of 17- to 18-year-olds are staying on, there would seem to be a strong case for introducing a more systematic process of collecting accurate data on their progress. This lack of detailed information makes the development of appropriate responses and strategies difficult to achieve.

Another issue of great concern has been the identification of significant numbers of young people who fall outside the official statistics. The work of Williamson and his colleagues at the University of Wales (Istance, Rees and Williamson 1994) which is dealt with in greater detail in Chapter 5, has been pathbreaking in this respect. Other studies have also pointed to this phenomenon being more widespread than is officially acknowledged. In the preface to a report of one such study in the north-east of England, Coffield states:

> These young people are not so much caught up in a 'vicious circle of alienation' as sliding quickly down a spiral of official

neglect and intensifying poverty. If the problems so powerfully portrayed in this book were to be confined to Sunderland and the North East, then perhaps we could console ourselves with the comforting fiction that only a few hundred young adults lead such precarious lives. But this is not a local, regional or even a national problem . . . Youthaid put the total number of such 'drop-outs' to be around 100,000 in the UK.

(Wilkinson 1995: viii)

EMPLOYERS' DEMAND FOR YOUTH LABOUR

As intimated earlier, much of our thinking in relation to employers' future demand for youth labour is predicated on the assumption that an ever-increasing majority of jobs will require high levels of skill, which has been formally accredited. A government publication asserts that 'the number of higher skilled professional and managerial white collar jobs will continue to increase (1.7 million extra by 2001), with demand for low skill manual occupations continuing to fall by more than half a million' (Employment Department 1994: 5). This will be accompanied by an increase in the skills being demanded within occupations. This is clearly in line with assertions which have been made about the need to prepare ourselves for the creation of a high-skills economy.

That such broad trends are in train, and will continue to generate a demand for more qualified and skilled entrants to the labour market is difficult to deny. Nonetheless, some commentators are more sceptical about the all-embracing nature of these forces. Keep and Mayhew (1994) contend that the level of skills demanded by employers may not be rising as quickly as has been suggested. Part of their argument is supported by Institute for Employment Research projections which show that the fastest growth rate for any occupational area will be among Personal and Protective Service occupations, which include catering, travel, child care and beauty occupations, as well as health service workers such as nursing auxiliaries, hospital orderlies and ambulance staff (Wilson and Webb 1995). These occupations cannot be said to be at the leading edge in terms of high-level skills. Furthermore, Keep and Mayhew point to evidence from studies carried out by the National Institute for Economic and Social Research which have repeatedly shown that significant proportions of British employers effectively choose to adopt strategies which are based on low-quality, low-skill, price-based competition. While the continuation of such strategies may be regrettable in the long term, it could be argued that, in the short term, the availability of low-skill jobs in considerable numbers is essential to sustain a comparatively unskilled labour force and to meet the demands of a nation which has one fifth of Europe's poor (Commission on Social Justice 1993).

CONCLUSION

This discussion has pointed to a fundamental transformation of the youth labour market since the beginning of the 1980s. Furthermore, projections about occupational trends and the future demand for labour would suggest that there will be an ever-dwindling number of opportunities for young people (or any job-seekers, for that matter) who lack the higher level skills which are increasingly being recognised and demanded. A conclusion could be drawn that there will be no opportunities at all at the lower levels of the occupational hierarchy. This is self-evidently not true, for, as the expansion in certain parts of the service sector has shown, the very process of industrial expansion generates jobs at lower levels. Also, even if we are to swallow whole some of the more extreme prognostications, a number of important issues need further debate and elucidation before appropriate policy responses can be contemplated with any degree of confidence.

First, there is a need to gain a far better understanding of employers' current and likely future demand for youth labour. In particular, we need to know more about: the added value to young people of staying on at school or entering further education, in terms of enhancing employability; employers' selection criteria when recruiting young people for training places; the structure and range of employment opportunities for young people; local labour market variations in the structure of opportunities; the extent to which employers are providing low-level, part-time, unskilled jobs; the effects of wage rates on employers' decisions about recruiting young people; and the extent to which a boosting of the supply of skills and qualifications will, of itself, lead to increased demand for, and usage of, skills in the workplace.

Second, it is clear that our present mechanisms for monitoring the position of young people during the years immediately following leaving school are inadequate. As far as existing data are concerned, they tend to provide patterns of destinations which fail to identify or convey any depth of understanding about young people's experiences between destinations, some of which may only loosely be termed progression. It may be better, therefore, to supplement current data-gathering mechanisms with a series of longitudinal profiles of individuals from a variety of first destinations. This would enable policy decisions to be formulated on the basis of a better understanding of young people's post-16 choices and experiences.

It was stated at the outset that it was now questionable whether there remained an identifiable youth labour market. Some credible commentators have suggested that this is no longer the case. For example, Skilbeck et al. (1994: 234) acknowledge that:

In a segmented labour market, there will no doubt remain limited opportunities for full-time paid youth employment, but these are likely to be in jobs which are short term or of limited significance for purposes of long-term career development.

Furthermore, they contend that:

the most profound structural change . . . is not to be found in the design and development of new programmes and organisations to deliver them but in the decline, temporary revival, and now, it seems, final collapse of the youth labour market.

Certainly, the parameters of the youth labour market, and even its very existence, would seem to be far less clear-cut than was previously thought. In addressing the vexed question of whether a distinct youth labour market exists, it may be advisable to jettison the notions which may have been appropriate in the 1970s and early 1980s, that is of 16-year-old school leavers obtaining direct entry to the labour market. Rather, in the 1990s, we should consider the possibility of there being a much broader-based youth labour market which encompasses young people who enter the labour market at different ages (say from 16 to 21), from a variety of educational settings (schools, further education, university) and training programmes (YT, Modern Apprenticeships), with a multitude of vocational and academic qualifications (including GCSEs, A levels, NVQs, HNDs, degrees), and face a similarly broad range of opportunities.

In the 1970s, when delineating the characteristics of a distinct youth labour market, emphasis was placed on the influence of local labour market conditions in determining the nature of opportunities for young people entering the world of work. Recent years have seen government initiatives, notably through the introduction of the TECs, seeking to strengthen this influence and placing responsibility on local bodies to make decisions about the training and employment opportunities which are to be encouraged and supported. This would suggest that the importance of local labour markets in shaping the structure of opportunities for young people has grown. There is a danger that this process has detracted from our ability to identify and understand, at a national level, significant trends, and to obtain an accurate overview of what is going on. While information collected at a local level is of great importance for local decision-making, there is a need for something more than a series of disparate local snapshots. What is needed is a coherent mechanism whereby information collected locally is able to be aggregated and interpreted at a national level, so that we are able to construct as complete a picture as possible of the scope and range of opportunities which exist for young people, and, crucially, of the routes taken by young people into the labour market.

However, a focus on local labour market conditions is vital if we are going to confront the very real threat of the emergence of an underclass of individuals excluded from participation in the labour market through insufficient demand for the type of labour they can offer. Current labour market trends, notably the reduction of job opportunities requiring only low levels of skill or qualifications, could exacerbate the likelihood of the creation of an underclass of disaffected young people. The evidence from studies in Wales and the north-east of England suggests that this process is well under way.

The social costs of neglecting the relatively unskilled and unqualified in the headlong rush to create conditions whereby Britain is able to compete effectively in global markets, and in the production of high value added goods and services, may eventually become too high a price to pay. Long-standing debates about the relationship between unemployment and crime continue to be aired, even in a report by the Audit Commission which states that 'policies to reduce crime by young males are unlikely to succeed while large numbers continue to be economically redundant. Participation in work is fundamental to young people's sense of identity, belonging and self-esteem' (quoted in the *Observer* 3 November 1996: 1).

Chapter 3

Is there an emerging British 'underclass'?

The evidence from youth research

Ken Roberts

UNCONVINCING REFUTATIONS

Claims that their country has an emerging underclass have been repudiated by a series of British sociologists (see specifically Byrne 1995; Gallie 1994; Mann 1992; Marshall et al. 1996; Morris 1992, 1994; Morris and Irwin 1992). Some of its critics, who are represented in other chapters of this book, would clearly like to consign the underclass concept to oblivion. This is unlikely to happen because the quality of the critics' evidence and arguments does not match their quantity and ferocity. The underclass is likely to remain one of British sociology's most hotly contested issues for many years. It is an issue on which many protagonists have feelings as well as ideas. This generates an atmosphere in which misunderstandings easily arise. So it may be useful to point out that the above sentences do not support the underclass hypothesis; judging the denials unconvincing is not the same as joining the other side of the argument. Most of those prepared to countenance the idea of an underclass, including the present author, claim no more than that its creation is probable given broader socio-economic trends and conditions.

The underclass hypothesis has become a casualty of a broader attenuation or fragmentation of class analysis. Some analysts compare broad economic aggregates and look for class outcomes. For example, they compare the political partisanship of manual and non-manual workers, or those currently in jobs with those out of work (Gallie 1994). Other investigators focus upon class processes within specific groups. For instance, they study the effects of economic recession among the residents in selected localities (Byrne 1995; Morris 1992, 1994). Representatives of each approach have been accused of failing to engage with the other's evidence (Crompton 1996). Arguments about the underclass are just one example (see Morris and Scott 1996). Some micro-studies unearth supportive evidence while macro-comparisons point towards a different conclusion. Each party sticks to its own evidence and the debate sinks into an impasse.

Reasserting some normal rules of inference may aid the underclass debate. First, demonstrating that x is not present in one section, or even several likely sections, does not prove that it does not occur anywhere in a given population. So showing that the unemployed, or even just the longer-term unemployed in places a, b and c, or young homeless people (see Chapter 7), or those with backgrounds in statutory care (see Chapter 6), do not exhibit the features of an underclass can never be sufficient to dismiss the claim that such a stratum exists somewhere unless the analysts have looked in all possible locations, which, as argued below, remains far from the case. Second, it can be simultaneously true that all members of a group possess characteristic z while only a tiny proportion of those with z belong to the group in question. This means that showing that overwhelming majorities of representative samples of the unemployed, or residents in districts with especially high unemployment in particular towns, regions and even throughout the UK, do not resemble an underclass does not discredit the hypothesis that typical underclass members are not in employment.

One should expect members of an underclass to be under-represented in any samples which are researched using conventional survey methods. We know that the least educated are the least likely to return questionnaires (for an example in a study of young people see Banks et al. 1992). Given their alleged lifestyles (Murray 1990; Wilson 1987) one would expect the underclass to be under-represented on electoral registers and other common sampling frames. One would expect them to be over-represented among persons with no fixed address and those temporarily withdrawn from normal social circulation into institutions such as prisons. The whereabouts of young adults who are normally 'out-of-contact' is discussed at greater length in Chapter 5. It is known that Britain's ten-yearly censuses fail to count all citizens. In 1991, it was believed that a larger number than on previous occasions were missing. Tens of thousands were believed to have 'gone to ground' and left their names off electoral registers and similar records in order to avoid the 'poll tax'. In the 1960s, John Goldthorpe and his colleagues (1968) could claim that they had sought bourgeois manual workers in a place (Luton) where such people should have been well represented, if they were present anywhere. Similar claims on behalf of British critics of the underclass theory are less convincing (see below). It would probably be necessary to search thoroughly in the most likely places to discover an underclass, if such a stratum exists, since those who argue the case do not believe that this class, as yet, comprises more than a minority even among groups such as the unemployed and the poor. Attacking straw men is easy but ultimately pointless. No one has claimed that unemployment, even long-term unemployment, is a sufficient cause of underclass membership or creation, or that all or even most of the unemployed are members of an underclass. This is despite unemployment being among the factors that all underclass theories incorporate in their explanations.

Certain underclass theories definitely offend current standards of political correctness. The best-known (American) versions of the theory implicate single parents in the creation and reproduction of the underclass (Murray 1990, 1994; Wilson 1987). Murray's explanation also implicates over-generous welfare. All sociological versions suggest that the values and lifestyles of underclass members play a part in preventing their social and economic ascent. Frank Field (1989), a Labour Party politician, has chosen to describe as an underclass a variety of groups who are extremely poor. Most sociologists (see Chapters 1 and 11) would prefer to describe such groups as simply 'poor' unless they are also distinguished by their attitudes, values and social patterns. Many contemporary sociologists dislike appearing to suggest that the disadvantaged are partly to blame for their disadvantages, but the fact that a proposition seems distasteful, or might be misused by some politicians and their apologists, is never sufficient reason for declaring it false. The fact that a 'culture of poverty' may originally have been a consequence of material deprivation which the victims did not choose will not prevent the culture becoming another cause of the condition's perpetuation. Likewise, it may be the case that the majority of single parents do not originally choose the status. Some may never have chosen the situation; it may have been created for them through desertions by their partners. In cases where the status is chosen, this is likely to be because, for those directly involved, single parenthood is preferable to the even less attractive alternatives that are available to them (see Cieslik 1996). But none of this disproves, or even reduces, the likelihood of single parenthood disadvantaging the children *vis-à-vis* those reared by two parents.

The same applies when parents become welfare dependent through no fault or choice of their own. It may be that Britain's current welfare regime ensnares dependants in poverty not because the payouts are over-generous, but because they are not generous enough to act as a 'helping hand' (Dean and Taylor-Gooby 1992). It can still be the case that the regime fosters lifestyles and attitudes which themselves reduce the likelihood of those concerned ending their dependency. Demonstrating that the underclass theory is ideologically beneficial for the privileged, that the latter have always harboured if not actively propagated unattractive views of the 'lower orders', and that in earlier historical periods these beliefs had little basis in fact (Bagguley and Mann 1992), is insufficient to disprove that an underclass exists today. Belief in such a stratum may be both ideologically convenient for the privileged and factually true. At a minimum, this is a possibility that deserves serious consideration.

To repeat, none of the above proves or even argues that contemporary Britain does have an underclass; only that the proposition is so far not convincingly disproven.

DEFINITION

Whether an underclass exists and, if so, why, is hotly contested (see Westergaard 1992). Fortunately the protagonists appear to agree on some of the matters that they are arguing about. This is not a pseudo debate. All sides seem to agree that before the underclass label can be properly applied four conditions should be met (see also Connolly et al. 1991).

First, the stratum should be disadvantaged relative to, and in this sense beneath, the lowest class in the gainfully employed population.

Second, for the individuals and households involved, this situation should be persistent, in many cases for the duration of their entire lives and, indeed, across the generations.

Third, the underclass should be separate from other groups in social and cultural respects as well as in its lack of regular employment. For example, its members might live in separate areas, belong to separate social networks, and have distinctive lifestyles and values. In other words, the underclass should be a socio-cultural formation as well as an economic aggregate. This is the crucial difference between an underclass and people who are simply unemployed or poor.

Fourth, the culture of the underclass, whether developed initially as a response to, in order to cope with, to adjust to or resist economic exclusion, should have become another impediment, and sufficient in itself even if other obstacles were removed, to significantly reduce its members' likelihood of joining the regularly employed workforce. Such a culture will distinguish an underclass, if one exists, from a 'reserve army' who are excluded from employment purely by lack of opportunity and take jobs when their labour is in demand.

Youth researchers are in a privileged position to assess whether Britain does in fact have an underclass. Young people are a critical group for judging whether an underclass has formed or is emerging. From their backgrounds, experiences, attitudes and ways of life it should be possible to establish whether cultures that separate an underclass from the employed population are being transmitted down the generations and discouraging some young people from joining the regular workforce.

RESTRUCTURED TRANSITIONS

Over the last twenty years, the entire process whereby young people make their transitions from compulsory education into adult employment has changed substantially as the Maguires have explained in Chapter 2. The most appropriate adjective – substantially, radically, profoundly, dramatically – may depend on the comparison. The changes have been momentous compared with the relative tranquillity in Britain during the 1950s and 1960s, but even the post-1970s scene in Britain has been calm compared with recent developments in East–Central Europe (Roberts and Jung 1995). However, in Britain, young people's transitions have been prolonged and have become more complicated than formerly. Their destinations while in transit have become less certain, and all their steps have become more risky. Yet contrary to earlier fears and forecasts, school leavers *en masse* have not been thrust into a never-ending limbo. Despite the analogies with broken bridges and suchlike, transitions have been restructured rather than destroyed. Unemployment has been a common experience, but one with which the majority of young people have coped (see Banks et al. 1992; Brown 1987; Furlong 1992; White and McRae 1989). Indeed, despite the talk about *youth* unemployment being especially damaging, young people have proved better able to cope than their elders (Daniel and Stilgoe 1977; Kelvin et al. 1984; Warr 1983). This is not to say that the young unemployed suffer no ill-effects let alone that they 'opt' for the situation. Rather, the crucial facts of this matter are that, compared with adults, young people's episodes of unemployment are generally shorter, this age group improves its labour market situation as individuals grow older, family support usually prevents their impoverishment, and it has proved relatively easy to develop alternative roles (students and trainees) that preserve young people's well-being (see Roberts 1995 for a review of the relevant evidence). It is also the case that young people whose first choice would be 'good jobs' may regard the 'trash jobs' that they are able to obtain as intolerable for long unbroken periods. However, these same young people usually consider long-term unemployment at least equally detestable (see Roberts et al. 1982a). Claiming that young people cope does not mean that they 'thrive on', but that most 'survive', unemployment, and, in the majority of cases, emerge with their futures unscathed and their motivations intact (see Elder 1974; Furlong and Spearman 1989; Travers 1986).

The relevant studies show that the majority of the young people who have coped have often owed much to the support of their families (see Hutson and Jenkins 1989) and this fact is of crucial relevance in the underclass debate. This support is typically simultaneously financial, social and emotional. Communities whose industries have been destroyed have typically striven to maintain standards, and parents have encouraged their children to do likewise (Wright 1994). When the adult members of such communities have taken undeclared 'fiddly jobs' while claiming benefit, this is more likely to have been evidence of their desire to work than a preference for 'something for nothing' (MacDonald 1994). Such parents have usually insisted that their children do their best to obtain decent jobs, and have done everything possible to prevent them surrendering their futures (see Allatt and Yeandle 1991).

An inescapable question that follows is what happens when the support systems that, up to now, have assisted most young people when coping with unemployment are themselves undermined by this condition? The same studies that have highlighted the support that parents normally offer when their children are unemployed have drawn attention to how unemployment places family relationships under strain (Allatt and Yeandle 1991). What happens when the parents of the young unemployed are themselves long-term unemployed? Up to now most young people have coped and survived with the help of their families and, in many cases, the moral support of the surrounding communities (see Coffield et al. 1986). But some young people have not coped and recovered, and there are grounds for predicting that, if unemployment persists at the levels that have been normal in the UK throughout the 1980s and 1990s, their numbers will increase.

INDICATORS

Several developments that the underclass theory would lead us to expect have in fact become evident among out-of-school youth.

Long-term youth unemployment

As explained earlier, most youth unemployment is short-term. Since the 1970s, levels of unemployment among young people have been higher than among adults, but young people's out-of-work spells have been shorter (see Roberts 1995). This is partly due to young people's higher rate of job changing which helps to spread unemployment around, and also to the training schemes for which the under-25s have usually been priority cases; these have broken-up what would otherwise have been longer spells of uninterrupted joblessness.

Unemployment rates among young people in specific districts can reach 30 per cent before long-term unemployment begins to rise steeply (Roberts et al. 1981). Lower levels of unemployment are mostly absorbed in sub-employed careers in which spells between jobs, or between schemes and jobs, or between leaving school and entering a job or scheme, become common. However, there have been many parts of Britain, such as Liverpool, where particularly disadvantaged groups of school leavers, the least qualified whites and members of some ethnic minority groups, have faced persistent unemployment levels well in excess of 30 per cent since the 1970s (see Connolly et al. 1991). Even Britain's economic booms have not eradicated the structural inevitability, due to a straightforward shortage of jobs, of long-term unemployment among the most disadvantaged school leavers in Britain's unemployment black spots. In Liverpool, a fifth of all young people have been reaching their twenties without ever establishing themselves in, or, in some cases, even experiencing, regular jobs, and this situation has persisted since the 1970s (see Roberts et al. 1987). Among Liverpool's young blacks, the unemployment rate has been above 60 per cent and long-term unemployment has been as common as continuous employment (Connolly et al. 1991). This is not to say that some of the long-term young unemployed do not find and settle in jobs in their twenties, but by then many have begun rearing a further generation of children with prospects (see below) as bleak as their parents'.

Britain's ethnic minorities will be over-represented in any emerging underclass, but in this country the term 'underclass' is not a euphemism for ethnic minority groups. Britain differs from North America in this respect. In the USA, where the present-day under-class debate began, the alleged members are the black and Hispanic inner-city ghetto populations who have been left behind and cut adrift from other sections of their own ethnic groups as well as from the mainstream white society (see Chapter 1). In the USA, since the 1960s, many blacks have taken advantage of the opportunities that America offers to its citizens, often assisted by anti-discrimination legislation and positive action programmes. However, some sections of the minority groups have failed to benefit due to a combination of (with the stress varying according to the theorist), and the inter-action between, the extent to which their neighbourhoods have been stripped of jobs, the welfare regime, and the disadvantaged groups' own cultures which, it is alleged, condone rather than condemn single parenthood and certain types of criminality (see Murray 1984; Wilson 1987). All the American theorists acknowledge that the disadvantaged starting points of underclass members were created, at least in part, by America's history of racial discrimina-tion. However, the underclass theorists claim that it is no longer racial barriers that keep the groups 'under'. Hence, the description of the groups as an underclass. There are poor whites in America, but they are not usually categorised as underclass. They are more likely to be regarded as individual deviants or victims of multiple disadvantages rather than the kind of class which, it is believed, has been created in ethnically homogeneous urban ghettos.

In the 1970s, there were some forecasts of Britain's immigrant minorities becoming an underclass as second and subsequent gener-ation settlers remained disadvantaged and developed their own responses to their treatment by the wider society (see Rex and Tomlinson 1979). However, the British underclass that is now alleged to be emerging is not composed mainly of ethnic minorities. Britain's minorities are a smaller proportion of the total population than America's non-whites. Since the 1970s, Britain's minorities have had diverse experiences. Some have experienced collective socio-economic ascent. Others, mainly with Afro-Caribbean origins, remain heavily disadvantaged. In this sense they resemble North America's underclass, but are different in so far as the rise in unemployment in Britain has spread the relevant disadvantages throughout many sections of the white population. Most of Britain's long-term unemployed are native-born whites. Ethnic minority groups generally have above-average unemployment rates. But because, even in combination, they amount to only around 5 per cent of the total population, they comprise only a minority of the unemployed. The same applies to the poor, single parents, convicted offenders and all the other groups from which any underclass is likely to be drawn. Britain's blacks are over-represented among all these groups but dominate none. This is a crucial difference between the types of underclasses that are likely to be formed in America and those in Britain. The British version will be the more diverse ethnically and, therefore, it might be inferred, less likely to be as cohesive and as segregated from the wider society as North America's ghetto minorities.

Out of the system

We know that by the time they leave school some young people are already effectively 'out of the system'. They include the persistent truants whose effective schooling ends well before the statutory school-leaving age. Beyond the age of sixteen, they may join the 'Status Zer0' group who are not in education, training or employment. At any point in time, a significant number of 16- and 17-year-olds, recently estimated at over one in seven in South Glamorgan (Istance et al. 1994 and Chapter 5 of this book), occupy this status. Many are Status Zer0 only temporarily – before long they rejoin 'the system' – but a hard core appear to remain permanently 'lost'. The withdrawal of most 16- and 17-year-olds' social security entitlement in 1988 greatly reduced their incentive to register. Actually, most of those who remain outside education, training and employment for long periods are known to other parts of 'the system'. They are usually known to local authority social services departments, the police and the courts. Many are from single parent and reconstituted families, and built up records of non-attendance when they were supposed to be in full-time education (Istance et al. 1994).

It is difficult to quantify precisely the number of young people who are homeless at any point in time, and the larger number who experience homelessness at some time or another (see Hutson and Liddiard 1994; Jones 1995a; and Chapter 7 in this book). Homelessness is usually temporary, like Status Zer0. However, we know that at any time most British cities have young people who are sleeping rough and begging for cash. Without an address or acceptable appearance, not to mention lacking any record of employment or training, re-entering the workforce is always difficult.

This also applies when young people are compulsorily withdrawn from 'the system' into judicial custody. During the post-war decades of full employment, Probation Service and other after-care officials treated employment as a necessary first step in the successful rehabilitation of offenders. At that time, employment was a realistic aim even for the least advantaged groups. Subsequently, given the intense competition for jobs from young people with reasonable records in education and training, the prospects for stigmatised groups have become extremely bleak. Employers are now able to demand 'character' as well as qualifications (see Dench 1993; Hunt and Small 1981; Jenkins 1982).

Unemployable

This term is widely used by Job Centre and Careers Service staff even though it is never used in government reports. The term is ideologically loaded but realistic in suggesting that some unemployed individuals are unlikely to be recruited by any employer. The reasons why individuals become unemployable, for all practical purposes, include limited physical or mental capacities, and personality traits and lifestyles which involve, for example, persistent drug use or heavy drinking.

Whether a particular type of person is employable or not always depends, at least in part, on the balance between labour market demand and supply. In times of full employment, lack of qualifications, a history of chronic job instability and even a criminal record may not be barriers to further employment (see Baxter 1975; Parker 1974). In contrast, when employers can pick and choose when hiring unskilled labour, as has been the case in most parts of the UK since the 1970s, would-be workers at the back of the queue can be unemployable for all practical purposes. This will apply irrespective of whether jobs have become more demanding due to a combination of technological change and competitive pressures which, some argue (Gallie and White 1993), oblige employers to insist on higher standards thereby raising the threshold of employability.

Hustling

The name varies from time to time and place to place, but in high unemployment areas there is always a generic term for remunerative activity which involves some breach of the law (see Roberts et al. 1982a). The breach may be undeclared income while claiming benefit, or non-payment of tax and national insurance contributions. Alternatively, or more likely in addition, the activity may involve theft or handling stolen goods; or the trade may be more serious – for example, in drugs. Most young people must have some contact with hustlers if, as recent research suggests, the majority are offered illegal drugs at some time or another (Measham et al. 1994; Parker et al. 1995). Whether a young person has used/abused drugs is irrelevant to the issue of underclass membership. The point is that some users are also sellers (dealers) and a minority generate significant incomes in this manner. This must be the case, given the scale of use of cannabis and Ecstasy-type products, which normally cannot be obtained legally.

Most hustling is undoubtedly part time, even opportunistic, but for some young people it is their normal way of earning. Exactly how many is beside the present point. Ethnography (see Craine 1994 and Chapter 9 in this book) is vastly superior to questionnaire surveys for establishing that some young people develop hustling as their main long-term occupation. The negative reference groups of the 'respectable' unemployed working class, old and young, have a basis in fact (see Howe 1994). And it seems reasonable to assume that, as unemployment has risen, as most types of property crime have become more common, and as drug use has become increasingly widespread, hustling must have increased. Unemployment may be neither a sufficient nor a necessary cause of crime, but, in a context of other criminogenic pressures, it can hardly avoid increasing the risks. Joblessness leaves young people with time on their hands, short of cash, and with another neutralising vocabulary of motive.

Unconventional families

All the relevant studies show that young people with unemployed parents, and those not reared by two parents, are less successful at school and have higher rates of subsequent unemployment than other members of their age group (Bosman and Louwes 1988; Davies 1993; Dennis 1993; Dronkers 1994; Spruit and de Goede 1995). Indeed, nowadays the life-chance inequalities associated with

these circumstances are as stark as the gradient between the middle
and working classes (Roberts et al. 1987). The processes whereby
unemployment in a family, and single parent situations, become
disadvantageous remain open to dispute, but the relationships
themselves are not in doubt. Indeed, family composition and
employment histories are our best predictors of whether young
people will become part of all the groups described above – the
long-term unemployed, those who disappear from 'the system', the
'unemployable' and hustlers.

It is also the case that unemployed teenagers are more likely to
become teenage parents, nowadays typically single parents, than
either full-time students or contemporaries who are in employment
(Payne 1987; Penhale 1989). Again, the reasons for these relationships are open to debate. They are likely to include the shortage of
potential male 'breadwinners' in the social networks of the young
women who become single parents, the fact that early parenthood is
a long-established norm in the relevant social strata, and also, in
some cases, a means whereby adulthood can be demonstrated and
welfare rights claimed (independent accommodation, for example).
Whatever the responsible processes, the point is that young people
from unconventional families, especially where unemployment is
also part of their family backgrounds, tend to repeat the cycles with
their own children, and during the last thirty years the number of
households in this particular cycle has risen sharply.

THE STRUCTURE OF THE UNDERCLASS

At the beginning of the twentieth century, social researchers
routinely identified Britain's 'lower orders' using terms which today
sound condescending, derogatory and even offensive – criminal
classes, loafers, and suchlike. The reasons why such terms lapsed
from social research are not only that investigations became more
scientific. By mid-century, the lower orders had all but disappeared
as a result of full employment and welfare legislation which had
made standards of living, health care, education and housing, not
greatly inferior to those enjoyed by the employed working classes,
into rights of citizenship.

During the last twenty years these earlier trends have been
reversed, and an expected result must be the re-creation of 'lower
orders' or excluded groups of some description. The gap between
social security benefits and typical earnings has widened. Some

down-market council housing estates have been deserted by all but households who receive Housing Benefit (see Jordan and Redley 1994). The only alternative accommodation for Britain's new poor is provided by the private sector landlords who cater for tenants who are 'on the social'. Alongside these trends, health inequalities have widened (Townsend et al. 1988) and low educational standards have become endemic in 'sink schools' located in districts with particularly high unemployment (Byrne 1995).

Given what its theorists actually claim, it is less appropriate to ask whether a fully-fledged underclass already exists ready-made than whether one is being formed. Charles Murray's claim is only that there is an *emerging* British underclass. This remained the case in 1994 when Murray found evidence of a 'deepening crisis' and the formation of a 'new rabble'. If an underclass comes into existence, it is less likely to be an instant consequence of unemployment, particular family patterns, welfare regimes or anything else. Like the working class and the bourgeoisie, it will be formed over decades and generations, rather than in months and years.

These processes may still be too immature to justify declarations that an underclass exists and can therefore be 'discovered', but it is possible to point to current trends and conditions which locate underclass formation somewhere between the possible and the probable. For two decades now, in Britain's most disadvantaged social strata, significant numbers of young people have left school and become long-term unemployed. Some disappear or are withdrawn from 'the system' for varying periods of time and, for all practical purposes, given the prevailing labour market conditions, easily become 'unemployable'. For some, hustling becomes a normal way of making a living. The individuals concerned tend to be from the kinds of households – and themselves tend to form these same kinds of households – wherein children are heavily disadvantaged. Some young people already appear to fit the underclass definition: they are not part of the employed working class; they remain in this condition for long periods of time; lifestyle factors, in addition to their lack of work, separate them from the employed; and their culture will act as an additional impediment to their absorption into the working population. The strength of their desire to enter the available jobs helps to explain which unemployed people regain work or obtain it for the first time (Dawes 1993; Honess 1989). We know that some of the long-term unemployed are simply 'not interested' in the jobs that they are likely to be offered (Full Employment UK 1990). All of this is fully documented.

Given the economic polarisation that has occurred in Britain since the 1960s, we should expect sociology's older class schemes to need revision. We should expect there to have been fundamental changes in the class structure as a result of the emergence of new configurations of market and work situations. New classes should have formed or old classes should have changed in a fundamental way. The formation of a stratum beneath the employed working class does not need a new theory of class formation; the development is predictable from sociology's standard theories and has indeed been predicted by perfectly conventional class theorists (Giddens 1973; Runciman 1990). These theories *must* lead us to predict an underclass of some description, given the trends in Britain's economy and labour markets over the last twenty years. Whether an underclass will exist at some time in the future, if recent trends and conditions persist, seems less contentious than its likely character and, indeed, whether 'underclass' is the most appropriate label.

'Underclass' is not the same kind of label as 'working-class' and 'middle-class'. The latter terms are parts of the self-identities of most members of the named groups. The underclass is more like the capitalist class and the service class; these labels are far more likely, possibly only likely, to be applied to, rather than adopted by those concerned to identify themselves. However, those labelled underclass cannot really be bracketed with capitalists and service-class members as equally vulnerable victims of sociologists' concepts. The latter groups are far better placed to ignore others' opinions and promote their own interpretations of their social roles. Members of the alleged underclass are far more vulnerable, and if the term enters general social usage it is likely to contribute to their social exclusion. There is a real dilemma here for politically sensitive sociologists. The take-up of the terminology may well depend on a predisposition; the public does not invariably adopt sociological jargon. Nor will it abandon it at the request of sociologists. There is plenty of evidence that members of other strata will grasp any easy opportunity to distance themselves from the least advantaged (see Howe 1994). In the absence of sociological jargon, other terms can be, and are being, coined. If 'excluded groups', 'ghetto poor' (see Wilson 1992), 'dispossessed working class' (Byrne 1995) or other alternatives to 'underclass' were promoted successfully by sociology, the alternatives would surely acquire equally derogatory connotations once the subjects were known. So there is probably no point in sociology hesitating to use the term 'underclass' for socio-political reasons. Sociological denials of the existence of an underclass are unlikely to save the least advantaged from everyday abuse. The underclass is not coterminous with the poor or the unemployed. Nor is the underclass synonymous with a reserve army. The latter are ready to be employed when their services are required. In the interim, they typically struggle to maintain standards and respectability (see Byrne 1995; MacDonald 1994). The underclass, if one is being created, will be recruited from the above groups, but this will not prevent the 'parents' rejecting the offspring even when all concerned continue to reside in the same districts.

A British underclass is unlikely to be culturally homogeneous let alone solidaristic. This is a safe forecast given the variety of ways in which young and older people can be set apart from, and beneath, the employed workforce. In Chapter 6, Debbie Baldwin, Bob Coles and Wendy Mitchell draw attention to the variety of ways in which young people can become socially and economically excluded. The ways in which young people respond to prolonged unemployment are just as diverse as their reasons for facing the predicament. Hustlers, the homeless, and young single mothers do not share a common way of life. Welfare dependants who need to know their rights develop quite different skill repertoires to drug dealers. But this does not necessarily invalidate the underclass concept. After all, members of the so-called 'service class' enter in a variety of ways. Roughly as many ascend as are born there. Some who rise enter directly via educational success while others rise during their employment careers (Goldthorpe et al. 1987). There are lifestyle differences within the 'service class' (see Butler and Savage 1995) and the manual working class (see Goldthorpe et al. 1968). Sociological custom and practice can justify the use of the underclass concept even if its members share no more in common than being economically, socially and culturally different from, and less esteemed than, not just the lowest stratum of the employed population, but respectable sections of the non-employed.

Class formation among the new lower orders, if such processes occur, is most likely to take the form of mutual tolerance and support born from mutual interests that stem from their common experiences of exclusion from, and rejection by other strata, and having no one else to whom to turn. The normally state-dependent may become involved in occasional opportunistic hustles. Drug dealers and individuals with other criminal businesses may fund, support and protect each other. Steve Craine offers evidence of these processes in Chapter 9.

Class is a relational concept, and it is through relationships with equals, efforts to usurp the more privileged, and the exclusionary strategies of the latter, that all classes come into existence, then stabilise or change. These are processes that youth researchers can investigate. Rather than simply affirming or denying the current presence of an underclass, youth researchers need to acknowledge that the conditions have arisen in which underclass formation is at least possible, if not probable – that already some groups of young people have biographies, behaviour patterns and attitudes that are consistent with underclass formation – then begin investigating the processes whereby, over time, the creation of such a fully-fledged class may be effected.

Chapter 4

Underclassed or undermined?

Young people and social citizenship

Hartley Dean

I would there were no age between ten and three and twenty, or that
youth would sleep out the rest; for there is nothing in between but
getting wenches with child, wronging the ancientry, stealing, fighting.
(William Shakespeare, *The Winter's Tale*, Act III: Scene iii)

Youth has always been regarded as a dangerous age. Single parenthood, contempt for authority, theft and violence amongst young
people are not recent phenomena. Shakespeare's lament mirrors
that of contemporary neo-conservative commentators, some of
whom associate the tendencies of youth with the emergence of an
even more dangerous phenomenon: the 'underclass' (see Chapter 1).
What is perhaps new is the attempt by writers like Murray (1990,
1994) to link youth with the existence of an imagined 'dangerous
class' and, in the process, to portray the rights of welfare citizenship
as a corrosive rather than an enabling force in the lives of young
people. The purpose of this chapter is to argue, first, that both
'youth' and the 'underclass' are symbolic social constructions;
second, that attempts to undermine young people's rights of citizenship may be profoundly counterproductive – a point I will illustrate
using a study of social security fraud.[1]

DANGEROUS YOUTH: AMBIGUOUS CITIZENSHIP?

'Youth' is that ill-defined stage between the states of 'childhood'
and 'adulthood'; between dependence and independence. It has
been argued that 'The idea of "youth" . . . like that of "retirement"
is not simply a reference to some objective natural state of being, it
is a social construction which has its origins in the capitalist division of labour' (Lawrence 1982: 55). Our understanding of youth

has been conditioned by the changing political economy of the household and the labour market.

In medieval times, childhood as a stage of dependency upon parents would have ended at the age of seven (Gittins 1993: 8). Thereafter, young people were full participants in productive processes within the household or as servants or apprentices in other households. With the coming of the wage labour system, the nature of the demand for young people's labour changed until, in the nineteenth century, factory legislation began to curtail young people's hours of work (and hence their earning power) and compulsory education ensured that young people remained dependent upon their parents for longer. The offspring of a household became increasingly an economic burden, rather than an asset. Childhood as a period of dependency has continued in the course of the twentieth century to extend. Correspondingly, 'youth' as a period of transition has been collapsed or become increasingly ambiguous.

The 'civilising' influences of protective legislation and compulsory education were associated with new preoccupations for child welfare. In the nineteenth century, welfare reforms sought to rescue the destitute children of the 'perishing' classes, while the criminal justice system sought to contain the delinquent children of the 'dangerous' classes (Morris et al. 1980; see Jeffs in Chapter 10). During the course of the twentieth century, institutions such as the juvenile court have attempted to combine both concerns, and the debate about 'welfare' versus 'justice' continues to this day (Kroll and Barrett 1995). 'Childhood', it would seem, is the term appropriate to the needy and disturbed; 'youth' is the term for the disruptive and dangerous; though the young person to whom the terms apply may be one and the same, depending on the context. A child may be constituted as a legitimate object of welfare intervention and, for all the debate about the 'rights of the child' (Franklin 1986), it is not supposed that a child can have full citizenship status. A youth, on the other hand, is a subject of the welfare state, though the extent of his or her citizenship status is circumscribed.

Because youth may be held culpable for its misdeeds, it is assumed to be morally competent, though ironically this also implies that youth enjoys the rights as well as the responsibilities of citizenship, including the rights of social citizenship. The high point of social citizenship in western capitalist democracies – that period from the end of the Second World War until the global economic crises of the 1970s – coincided with a time when youth and youth culture 'came to embody the promise of modernity within the ethos of social democracy' (Mercer 1990: 52). In the 1980s and 1990s, by comparison, the ascendancy of the Radical Right has largely succeeded in recasting the welfare state as an encumbrance from the past and in reconstituting youth in terms of its threatening qualities rather than its promise for the future.

THE DANGEROUS CLASS: A FAILURE OF CITIZENSHIP?

I have argued elsewhere that the term 'underclass' does not so much define a tangible phenomenon as symbolise socially constituted definitions of failure (Dean 1991). The imprecision of the concept makes it useless for analytical purposes, but its significance lies in the manner of its construction and debate (Mann 1994).

At the root of contemporary debate lie different notions of what it is that is threatened by the disparate phenomena which are variously supposed to constitute the underclass. All sides might agree that extremes of social polarisation, rising crime, high unemployment and rapid diversification in family and household structures represent a potential threat to a normative social order in which individuals are expected peaceably to coexist, while sustaining themselves through paid employment and maintaining each other within families. The argument is about the basis for that order and the nature of citizenship.

The underclass of the Radical Right is characterised in cultural terms through the deviant behaviour which members of that class exhibit. It is an effect created by social rights of citizenship which are in reality a 'mirage' (Hayek 1976). Those who fail in society do not have rights against those who succeed. Giving effect to such rights through taxation and state interference is a violation of 'real' (i.e. property) rights (Nozick 1974). What is worse, according to Murray, the provision of welfare benefits to unemployed youngsters, of housing to young single mothers and social work support to young offenders, rewards rather than punishes their failure: he explicitly concedes, 'I want to reintroduce the notion of blame, and sharply reduce our readiness to call people "victims" ' (1990: 71).

In contrast, the Fabian Left's underclass (for example Field 1989) is characterised in structural terms through the social disadvantage which members of that class experience. Social policy academics and the poverty lobby have claimed that those who invoke the underclass concept to make the case for the restoration of full citizenship rights to the poor are 'playing with fire' (Lister 1990: 26), yet the perceived hazard stems primarily from the pejorative connotations of a particular word, not the contention that 'the poor' may be systematically excluded from full citizenship. For the Fabian Left – whether they speak of 'the poor' or 'the underclass' – the problem is that of the failure of the social rights of citizenship (Roche 1993).

At stake is the question of whether capitalism needs not only civil and political liberties, but social rights as well. The question which T. H. Marshall (1950) originally posed has been reformulated as a debate about a socially constructed underclass. Are citizens failing because they have been given too much by way of social rights or because they have been given too little? In particular, do social rights cause failure by making young people dependent on the state, or do they mitigate such failure by allowing young people to be independent of their families and/or of exploitative employers?

These questions have been explored in recent research into the attitudes of British working-age social security claimants (Dean and Taylor-Gooby 1992). That research had been prompted by the introduction of changes to the British social security system which were intended to reduce state dependency. Some of those changes, as will be explained, had borne with particular severity on young people, though their general intention was to increase work incentives, to encourage greater family dependency, and to reduce benefit fraud. The research found no evidence of a distinctive or uniform 'dependency culture' among social security claimants. Claimants subscribed by and large to mainstream values, attitudes and prejudices. They needed little encouragement to work, since they aspired to the security and dignity of respectable employment, and they resisted the idea that they should increase their dependency upon their immediate families, feeling there were proper limits to such dependency.

Most claimants expressed some degree of anger or sense of unfairness at the way they were treated by the social security system and, in this context, a surprisingly high proportion, when asked, said they would be prepared to 'fiddle' the system to get extra money (if they knew they could get away with it). It is possible that, by diminishing the social rights of citizenship and undermining citizens' expectations, changes to the social security system are undermining people's sense of obligation as citizens, and diminishing the duties they feel they owe in their dealings with the state.

UNDERMINING YOUNG PEOPLE'S RIGHTS

In the 1980s and 1990s, the rights of people in Britain beneath the age of twenty-five were significantly eroded. A primary purpose of the government had been 'to transfer power and responsibility wherever appropriate from the state to the family' (Bottomley 1994). What this entailed was an attempt to roll back the age at which children, through the acquisition of social rights, become adults. The consequences for some young people were far-reaching. As Andrews and Jacobs put it:

> It is hard to escape the conclusion that the young have been deliberately selected as easy targets in the assault against benefits. Unemployment, poverty and homelessness have become for a minority of young people, tragically linked as their rights to independent income and housing benefits have been lost.
>
> (1990: 74)

It would be perverse to portray this minority of young people as an 'underclass'. One housing minister said of unemployed homeless youngsters: 'many of these people are children, and our first advice to them is, therefore, to go back to their parents' (*Hansard* 24 January 1990: col. 884). 'These people' have become a problem, not because they have claimed their independence prematurely, nor because they are thereby socially distinctive. They have been constituted as a problem because the government is seeking through its social policies to redefine childhood; to defy the process by which our ideas of childhood, youth and adulthood are socially constructed (see Chapter 10). Pivotal to the attempt has been an implication that the transition to adult citizenship is not a function of age, but of employment and dependency status.

Evidence of this intention could be divined from a raft of changes to the social security system which had already begun in 1980 (Allbeson 1985). The process began with changes which delayed school leavers' entitlement to social assistance benefits, while extending their parents' entitlement to child benefit. Rules were introduced which made it difficult for students in further and higher education to receive independent benefits. At the time that housing benefit was introduced in 1983, the social assistance benefits of 16- to 17-year-olds were reduced by the amount of the notional 'rent contribution' which they were supposed to pay their parents, and this sum was effectively transferred to parents (since the housing benefit paid towards rental costs is not reduced on account of 'child' dependants within a household in the way that it is for 'adult' non-dependants). The following year this principle was extended to 18- to 20-year-olds and now it applies to all under-25-year-olds. Also at this time, the Youth Training Scheme was introduced which, though not compulsory, was associated with benefit penalties for young people who unreasonably refused or abandoned training places. In the mid-1980s the government introduced a series of rule changes to limit board and lodging additions to basic social assistance benefits and so prevent unemployed young people living away from home.

Major changes came in 1988, when 16- to 17-year-olds finally lost the right to social assistance, being required, if they were not in full-time education or employment, to undertake compulsory job training. Young people aged 18 to 24 became eligible for a reduced level of social assistance. The abolition of the householder's addition made it more difficult for young people to live independently, as did the replacement of special needs payments by the social fund. Special needs payments had in some circumstances provided grants towards the costs of setting up home, while assistance from the social fund is discretionary, budget limited and is in most circumstances given by way of a loan. For 16- to 17-year-olds discretionary severe hardship payments were introduced as a concession to meet the needs of especially vulnerable youngsters who cannot live at home.

The new youth training arrangements failed to provide enough places for the young people required to take them, leaving substantial numbers dependent on short-term 'bridging allowances' (currently just £15 per week). For youngsters who obtain placements, youth training persists by and large in providing low-level or redundant skills, so failing to equip trainees for a rapidly changing labour market (see Chapter 9; Ainley 1993; Craig 1991). By the early 1990s, the economic activity rate for young people was falling rapidly (see Chapter 2). The number of young people receiving special hardship payments increased from 17,921 in 1989 to 76,957 in the first nine months of 1992, although the number of young people left with no income at all also rose during the same period from 70,000 to over 97,000 (Maclagan 1993). As the cost of severe hardship payments continued to rise (reaching £40 million per year), the government eventually invoked a clamp down and is now demanding more evidence from youngsters claiming to be estranged from their parents (Strickland 1995).

It is striking that none of the major social policy texts on poverty feature youth poverty as an issue. Other dimensions of disadvantage are systematically discussed – gender, ethnicity, disability and old age – but youth is not. It is youth homelessness that is more generally identified as a 'social issue' (Hutson and Liddiard 1994), and it is as causes of homelessness that such issues as youth unemployment are generally discussed (e.g. McCluskey 1994). The poverty of 'grown up' children living in the parental home and young women who become lone parents is recognised usually in the context of 'family' poverty. The poverty of young 'adults' in work is recognised usually in the context of low-pay issues. As a social policy issue in its own right, 'youth' is perhaps only visible when it is not at home and not at work (see Chapter 8).

The status of 'youth' has been squeezed by a systematic attempt to deny young people access to independent housing and to depress their earning power. The main thrust of government housing policy in the 1980s and 1990s was to promote owner-occupation, a form of housing tenure which is not a realistic option for the vast majority of young people. Other options were curtailed: local authority housing stock was reduced by a third; housing associations, some of which had specialised in meeting the needs of young people, were forced to take over from local authorities the role of main social housing provider and to give priority to the statutorily homeless (so excluding young people without children of their own); access to the private rented sector was made more difficult because of deregulation, which limited security of tenure and increased rents to an extent for which housing benefit entitlement does not necessarily fully compensate. Labour market deregulation ensured that young people who did get jobs tended to be concentrated in insecure and poorly paid employment. Such initiatives as the Young Workers Scheme (introduced in 1982 directly to subsidise employers for taking on young low-paid labour) and the subsequent removal of young people from Wages Council protection in 1986 (a move preceding the eventual abolition of Wages Councils) were portrayed as job creation measures. By 1992, the level of wages for full-time 16- to 17-year-old males stood at just one third of that for all full-time male workers but, in spite of this, young people still faced higher unemployment than their elders: in January 1993, the unemployment rate for 18- to 24-year-old males was 24 per cent, compared with an overall unemployment rate of 14.5 per cent (Hutson and Liddiard 1994). Low wages do not guarantee young people independence through the labour market.

The tendency resulting from prevailing policy is such as to require young people to remain in the parental home and to accept low wages. For young people whose parents are themselves on benefits, this is not an easy option. Young people over eighteen who live in the parental home and (in 1995/6) earn £145 per week or more are presumed to make a rental contribution of £30 per week, and this sum is deducted from their parents' housing benefit entitlement.[2] If young people pay the contribution, they impoverish themselves; if they don't, they impoverish their parents. Young people from affluent families may be enabled to buy their independent status without the need for social rights of citizenship. The diminution of the social rights of citizenship has undermined the status of those young people who are poor, confronting them with a choice between acute dependency upon parents and exploitative employers, or the vulnerability of homelessness and unemployment.

RATIONALITY AND CITIZENSHIP

If young people are denied the rights of citizenship, why should they observe the obligations of citizenship? This is one of the questions the author has sought to address through an investigation of the attitudes and motivations of people involved in social security benefit fraud.[3] The study mainly involved those, including young people, who were claiming social security benefits while failing to disclose earnings from work in the 'informal' economy. In one sense, what such people do makes economic sense: it is a rational response to the ways in which casualisation in the labour market interacts with complexity and rationing in the benefits system (Jordan and Redley 1994). At another level, however, such behaviour is significant for what it tells us about the ways in which people experience and apprehend the rights and responsibilities of citizenship.

The research, conducted in 1994/5, was based on in-depth interviews with a small sample (thirty-five respondents) drawn from the Luton and London areas. Respondents were contacted through professional and community 'gatekeepers', informal contacts and 'snowballing'. The focus of the study was individual or 'petty' social security fraud – or what is colloquially referred to as 'fiddling' – as opposed to more organised forms of fraud. What emerged from the study may be encapsulated as three principal findings (for fuller accounts see Dean and Melrose 1995, 1996).

First, social security claimants who fiddle are not exercising a life style choice. They tend not to be informed by a sophisticated understanding of the social security system and only seldom by any degree of systematic planning. Most are highly motivated to work and anxious to maintain a reasonable standard of living. Almost all cite economic deprivation or hardship as the primary reason for their behaviour and, although many are anxious about the risks involved, the worry of living on a low income is for them a bigger worry than the prospect of getting caught for fraud. The thing which would dissuade virtually all such claimants from fiddling would be a 'proper' job: employment, that is, with reasonable pay and status. This much is broadly consistent with findings from other research (Cook 1989; Evason and Woods 1995; Hessing et al. 1993; Jordan et al. 1992; MacDonald 1994).

Second, the claimants interviewed had ambivalent conceptions of citizenship. Most believed they had a right to claim social security – not least because they, their families or forebears had paid contributions and taxes – although this was not a right which was highly prized. They were generally uncomfortable with or felt stigmatised by their status as claimants. At the same time, members of this sample were unclear about the nature of their obligations as citizens. Some thought of these only vaguely in terms of 'being a good person', or 'obeying the law', though others felt they had no particular obligations.

The third main finding was that there is no one type of fiddler. There was considerable diversity amongst the claimants interviewed with regard to age, gender and class and the very different ways in which they approached fraudulent claiming. However, for the purposes of this chapter, it is age differences which are of interest. Given the size of the sample and the qualitative nature of the research, no claims are made as to the statistical significance of patterns within the data. Nonetheless, the evidence gathered is sufficiently persuasive to suggest certain tendencies.

The older people in our sample, by and large, were more anxious about fiddling than the younger people. Younger people, though they shared similar expectations with regard to the rights of citizenship, seemed less supportive of the welfare state than were older people. Young people seemed less likely than older people to blame social security fraud upon economic circumstances, and were more inclined to apportion at least some of the blame to the perpetrators of fraud. Possibly, therefore, it is not so much the case that people become more anxious about fiddling as they become older, but that younger people are in some ways more individualistic and instrumental in their approach to risk and morality. Certainly, the evidence suggests that it may be much harder to deter people under the age of thirty-five from social security fraud than it is those over thirty-five.

There were important differences between those within the sample aged sixteen to twenty-five and those aged twenty-six to thirty-five. It was the older group which tended to exhibit the most 'hard-nosed' and amoral attitudes. The twenty-six to thirty-five age group had been the 'youth' of the 1980s, during the period of greatest change in young people's social rights of citizenship. Arguably, it is they who will have experienced an undermining of the expectations with which they might have grown up. Within this group, a number of claimants had previously been involved in other more 'serious' criminal activity (such as burglary). They were the group most likely to feel that there are no obligations attaching to citizenship and to feel that the rights of citizenship should be conditional on a person's nationality, residence or 'race'.

In contrast, the sixteen to twenty-five age group (of whom there were five, aged from nineteen to twenty-four) exhibited rather more principled and tolerant attitudes. They appeared, however, especially preoccupied with sustaining their life style and with the extent to which they were only doing what they believed other people did. This group will have 'come of age' after most of the changes described above came into effect and, significantly, they were proportionately the least likely of any of the age groups to think they had an automatic right to social security. No member of this group expressed positive feelings about the welfare state.

Of these five young people (three male and two female), two lived with their parents, two with partners and one lived alone. Four of them had had legitimate short-term employment from which they had been made redundant and were now or had until recently been claiming income support while doing undeclared 'informal' work (in three cases, with the direct collusion of their employers). The fifth member of this group had recently fiddled her claim for family credit (once again, with the collusion of her employer). If we are to believe Murray, these young people are representatives of a greedy, hedonistic rabble that is ruthlessly exploiting the welfare state. However, the evidence reveals five quite different individuals.[4]

John, who was twenty, figured ostensibly as one of the least scrupulous members of our sample. When asked, 'How much longer do you think you'll stay on [social security] benefit?' he replied, 'As long as I can . . . there's no point in me coming off it.' He made no bones about the fact that he 'just liked to have money', yet clearly he was not 'work-shy'. He was working full time for a demolition company which gave him time off every other Wednesday to 'sign on'. In the four years since he had left school, he had been twice made redundant and the only reliable employment he could obtain was with an employer who expected him to top up his wages from social security. Nor did John have any strong sense that social security was a right of citizenship: he couldn't see that it was a right because 'they give you their money when they want to . . . They take their time'. His experiences of the welfare state had left him with no sense that he had any entitlement and, in such an uncertain world, it is perhaps not surprising that he should have had no correlative sense of obligation.

Greg, who was nineteen, had also had two spells of legitimate employment since leaving school. He had stopped fiddling at the time of the interview, but had recently spent a period working in a pub while continuing to claim benefit. Greg might well be described as a hedonist. The reason he fiddled was: 'Extra money. Enjoyment'. The problem with living on benefits was: 'Well you walk down the street and you see someone with a nice posh motor, and its like, why can't I have that?' At the time he was fiddling, he said he didn't worry about whether it was wrong because: 'I was too busy enjoying myself. Working my guts out during the day, then enjoying myself in the evening.' Since then, however, Greg had set up home with a partner and he didn't think he would fiddle again because, if he was caught: 'it's gonna affect your partner as well. And that's just blatant unfairness.' In Greg's case, there may perhaps be some truth in the proposition that a permanent relationship can be a 'civilising' influence (cf. Murray 1990). It does not, however, resolve unemployment. Greg told us: 'at the moment I'm basically applying for jobs that I just don't want to do.' He believed he did have a right to the benefits he was claiming and he acknowledged there had to be rules. What he resented were 'restrictions'. In particular, he felt his dignity to be undermined by conditions compelling him to observe job-seeking rituals which were manifestly meaningless in the context of actual labour market conditions.

James, who was twenty-two, was claiming income support while doing occasional roofing work, cash in hand. If, however, he is representative of the 'New Rabble', the striking thing about him is the extent to which it is the doctrines of the Radical Right which he has taken to heart. James struggled inarticulately to explain why he thought the right to social security was not the same as other rights, and why universal entitlements were an obstacle to the proper exercise of discretion in favour of the deserving (amongst whom he would not have numbered himself!). He asserted his belief in 'moral standards' and 'back to basics', but then, referring to his own fraudulent behaviour, he said with disarming candour: 'I'm not proud to do it, but I'm greedy.' Contradictions arose because, for James, there is a difference between the world as it ought to be and the world as it is:

> There's fraud everywhere in the world. Government, they're all at it, so why shouldn't the lower classes have their own little bit.[5] . . . If the wages were higher and we had a minimum wage, then obviously people wouldn't have to go out and commit fraud, especially young mothers and people like that.

James bears the marks of a 'Thatcherite' culture, but the orthodoxy of his attitudes is tempered by his first-hand experience of poverty and exploitation. Having been unable to keep up with the cost of his own accommodation, he had experienced a spell of homelessness, which he found traumatic. He had recently reluctantly returned to live with his parents. He was plainly impressed by the virtues of independence, but it had been systematically denied him.

Ann was twenty-four. She once held a reasonably paid clerical job and had her own flat but, since being made redundant, had given up the flat and returned to live with her mother. She was claiming income support but, to pay off the debts she has built up, was doing two part-time jobs – one as a cleaner, the other as a shop assistant. So far as Ann was concerned: 'They took enough money out of me, so I'm just getting some back.' The problem, however, was:

> social's not giving you the money for the standard of living now, today. They're not doing it, so the only other choice is either to work [i.e. while claiming] or crime, innit? . . . I think it's a damn cheek really to say £75 I can live on every two weeks . . . No, it's not right . . . so I'm not gonna like go by the rule.

Ann's preoccupation was with finding a job that would pay as well as the one she had before. Fiddling social security was not what she wanted to do: 'If I found a full-time job now that paid me enough, I wouldn't sign on because it's a waste of time, a waste of money.'

Ruth was a 24-year-old mother of two. In so far that she was married and lived with her husband she might not count as a member of Murray's underclass, but, as a member of a household that had been dependent on social security benefits for some three years, she would most certainly count as a member of Field's underclass. Ruth had previously transferred from income support (the main social assistance benefit) to family credit (a means-tested in-work benefit) while she took a part-time job. To qualify for family credit (which is more generous than income support) she would have had to work not less than sixteen hours per week, but in fact she only worked ten. It was her employer who had suggested and facilitated a false declaration to the social security office. Born of middle-class parents, Ruth stayed on at school to do A levels and would have left at about the time of the 1988 social security reforms. In spite of this, she appeared to retain some faith in the idea that the welfare state provides a 'safety net', though her attitudes were essentially conservative:

> I think you need to show a bit of initiative yourself about getting off and doing something for yourself . . . if benefits were put up to whatever you would say a decent standard of living was, then it would be seen as encouraging [16-year-olds coming out of school] to choose that life.

This conservatism was contradicted by a sense of resentment that stemmed from a lessening of expectations. Commenting on her experiences at the hands of social security officials she acknowledged that she may have 'lowered [her] standards about what [she is] prepared to accept from them.' When speaking about the 'right' to social security she explained: 'We pay our contributions when we do work and the money that's meant to go into pensions doesn't any more, so you're not going to get a pension out of it.' This lowered sense of expectation was not unrelated to her fiddling episode: 'because you have to work so hard to get anything out [of social security] to start with then, in a way . . . getting more than you should do is, you know, a way of sticking your fingers up.'

Most revealing was Ruth's concept of citizenship. This was expressed in response to a set piece question in which the interviewer mentioned that, according to social attitude data, most people think social security claimants are made to feel like 'second-class citizens': we then asked what respondents supposed a 'first-class citizen' to be.[6]

If you're talking about 'the system' supporting you, then it's rather similar to still being at home with your parents and having to ask for handouts, and it does make you feel like a child ... The 'second class' comes from this original sense of failure ... You have to go down to the Post Office and queue up with all the other poor sods that have to do the same thing every two weeks to get your handout ... The 'first-class' citizen on that basis would be someone who can support themselves, have their own house, have this supposedly ideal existence, yes? ... This is what you need to have in order to be a successful, happy, fulfilled sort of person ... I can see how they [people on benefits] feel: that they have no rights because they don't know how to work the system, except for to do minor frauds on it.

Here is a young woman whose sense that she is an adult enjoying full rights of citizenship has been undermined by her experiences. She detects a relationship between the materialistic conception of citizenship which she feels prevails in Britain and the incidence of social security fraud.

CONCLUSION

I have argued that the terms 'youth' and 'underclass' are inherently problematic. The concepts are socially constructed and ideologically loaded. For all that, we must be aware that discourses of 'youth' touch upon a range of critical issues associated with the processes of transition from childhood to adulthood, and that discourses of 'underclass' touch upon a range of equally critical issues associated with the ways in which we understand failure in relation to work and family relationships.

What has bound 'youth' and 'underclass' together in contemporary discourses has been an attack upon the social citizenship of young people. Debates about 'youth' and 'underclass' intersect with normative debates about the nature of citizenship and the extent to which citizens should enjoy enforceable social rights as well as the civil and political liberties appropriate to a democracy. Social rights guarantee substantive independence and they afford to young people a status which is not conditional upon employment or family circumstance.

It may be said that young people need protection, not as children, but as citizens: the social rights of citizenship enable them to resist exploitation by unscrupulous low-paying employers and the freedom to establish a household (or a family) upon their own terms. The 1980s and 1990s, however, have been dominated by a political agenda which regards the social rights of citizenship as potentially damaging to the independence and self-discipline of young people and as an unwarranted encroachment upon free labour markets and the natural responsibilities of the family.

Using benefit fraud as a window on to the perceptions of young people living at the margins of citizenship, this chapter has argued that recent reductions and qualifications to the social rights of citizenship are undermining young people's sense of independence and adulthood. With this comes the risk, not of some isolated underclass, but a more widespread impoverishment of the very meaning of citizenship. It is not only that some young people may have internalised a Thatcherite scepticism towards the idea of social rights, but that none but the most privileged can feel their capacity to function as independent persons is guaranteed. Their dependency, if it is not on their parents, is upon the vicissitudes of market forces. The measure of their independence is not responsibility, but consumption. The danger is that eroding young people's social rights of citizenship may also corrode their sense of responsibility as citizens of the future.

NOTES

1 The author would like to acknowledge the assistance of Margaret Melrose and David Barrett, who contributed ideas for this paper and helpfully commented upon an earlier draft.
2 In 1995/6 those earning less than £145 per week but at least £111 per week were presumed to make a contribution of £14 per week; those earning less than £111 per week but at least £74 per week were presumed to make a contribution of £10 per week; those earning less than £74 per week, unless they were under twenty-five and in receipt of income support, were presumed to make a contribution of £5 per week.
3 The project, *Welfare Citizenship and Economic Rationality*, was undertaken at the University of Luton by the author and Margaret Melrose and was funded under the Economic and Social Research Council's Economic Beliefs and Behaviour Programme: grant reference no. L122251010.
4 The names used here are not the young people's real names.
5 The interview took place at the time the news media were highlighting the so called 'sleaze factor' in Parliament (see, for example, *Sunday Times* 9 April 1995).
6 In the 1993 British Social Attitudes survey, 55 per cent of respondents either agreed or strongly agreed with the proposition 'People receiving social security are made to feel like second-class citizens' (see Jowell et al. 1994, Appendix 3: 218).

Chapter 5

Status Zer0 youth and the 'underclass'
Some considerations

Howard Williamson

INTRODUCTION

There are growing assertions that more and more young people are being systematically propelled to the edges of conventional and legitimate pathways to adulthood (Aspire Consultants 1996; Wilkinson 1995; Williamson 1993). Quite *who* these young people are, and *how* they are being excluded and marginalised remains open for discussion; it is easy for the academic debate – in order to serve particular objectives – to slip into the same kinds of rhetorical and polemical devices for which politicians who do the same are rightly criticised. Both 'youth' (specifically allegedly 'disaffected' youth) and the assumed 'underclass' have remained powerful metaphors for societal decay and the focus for 'respectable fears', often with limited, or mythical, justification (Davis 1990; Pearson 1975, 1983).

It seems timely, therefore, to examine the position of supposedly 'marginalised' young people within the context of the wider debate on an emergent 'underclass' and to explore whether or not such young people are, somehow, emblematic of the underclass of the future. To do this, evidence will be drawn from a widely reported study of 'Status Zer0' youth: those young people aged sixteen and seventeen who are not in education, training or employment.[1]

There would seem to be a prima facie case that Status Zer0 young people, failing to participate (for whatever reason) in post-school training structures which, at minimum, provide a symbolic rite of passage to the labour market (see Clarke and Willis 1984), are already being consigned (or consigning themselves) to marginalised economic futures – a situation which has often been held to represent the central identifying feature of those within the underclass. Yet it will be argued, in line with some positions expressed in relation to the underclass debate itself, that such determinism is premature. Although such prospects for Status Zer0 young people may well materialise, they are certainly not inevitable for even many of those who have an extended experience of Status Zer0, but what is urgently required is an informed and rigorous policy debate so that provision and practice is restructured in order to enable those young people to find a 'way back' into mainstream education, training and labour market processes.

THE UNDERCLASS DEBATE

The 'underclass' debate has, simultaneously, a long history and a contemporary spontaneity, stimulated by the political polemic of the New Right. Yet it was as vigorously contested in the Victorian era and, indeed, throughout the 1960s (see Chapter 1). From the 'residuum' (Stedman-Jones 1971) and the 'savage, semi-criminal class of people' (Booth, in Thompson and Yeo 1973) of the nine-teenth century to those trapped in 'cycles of disadvantage' and 'cultures of poverty' (Lewis 1966; Rutter and Madge 1976; Valentine 1968) during the 1960s, there has been a continuing clustering of 'respectable fears' (Pearson 1983) around those at the margins of the labour market and the lifestyles and behaviour patterns associated with them: crime, job instability and social disorganisation.

The term 'underclass' was first coined as a *descriptive* tool to depict those who had become economically marginalised by the growth of post-industrialism (Myrdal 1962). It has, however, subsequently become co-opted, notably by Charles Murray (1984, 1990) as a *moral* category, to inform policy analysis, to influence the political direction of state activity in relation to the poor and, in particular, to withdraw what are argued to be the counter-productive measures of the welfare 'nanny' state.

The debate has slid seamlessly between political, economic, cultural and moral contentions, comprising a plethora of theoretical assertions (often suiting particular political perspectives) but rarely generating persuasive empirical substantiation. Even Smith's (1992b) minimalist definition of the underclass in Britain – that is, long-term or frequent claimants of income support – has only found limited empirical support (Smith 1992a). Although there is little dispute that three key groups fall into this category – the long-term unemployed, unskilled workers in erratic employment and younger single mothers – there remains little consensus that they can be linked together in any systematic way to justify positioning them in the firm conceptual 'class' of the underclass. And if the 'underclass' debate is far from resolved, then the relationship of 'Status Zer0' young people to it clearly remains open to further interrogation.

However, it is useful to consider Dahrendorf's (1992) question of whether or not the underclass is a 'hard' or a 'soft' category, for the latter provides more scope for debate. As a 'hard' category – a solid, fixed group of people with their own culture – no convincing theoretical criteria for membership has yet been established, even if descriptions of those who *might* fit within it are plentiful. As a 'soft' category – a condition with permeable boundaries, with some moving out and some dropping into it – it is a more persuasive possibility. For, although there is seemingly little evidence of complete dissociation from societal opportunities, there *is* evidence of people dropping through the net for some reason, either because they want to or because they find it difficult to comply with the dominant value systems, expectations and opportunities in society. Status Zer0 young people might possibly fall into such a category.

THE PHENOMENON OF STATUS ZER0

Twenty-five years ago, the problem of young people getting 'lost' in the transition from school to work was not an issue. What was at issue then was the 'problem' of apparently unrealistic aspirations (requiring strategies for 'cooling out') and the 'problem' of recurrent job changing in the early years after leaving school (Cherry 1976; Maizels 1970; Roberts 1968; Veness 1962).

Escalating youth unemployment during the latter part of the 1970s created massive forms of state intervention designed to provide work experience and a 'bridge to work' (Holland 1977; Rees and Atkinson 1982). Young people not continuing in education and unable to find employment went on to government training programmes designed explicitly for this purpose. Only during the early 1980s, after the initial 'youth opportunities' programme had become discredited through the poor quality of training and vocational preparation provided and decreasing job placement success (see Jones et al. 1983), did evidence emerge of 'sub-employment' amongst some young people, especially black young people (Roberts et al. 1981). Roberts et al. depicted a 'revolving door' of training schemes and unemployment and a tendency for young people having that experience to find alternative means of survival, usually through work in the informal (and sometimes illegal) economies (see Chapter 9).

The reconstructed training initiative (Department of Employment 1981; Manpower Services Commission 1981), in the guise of the new Youth Training Scheme (established in 1983), led to renewed hope that improved quality would provide the necessary incentive to participate, despite the fact that the 'social engineering' objectives of earlier programmes had been abandoned. Yet, one in ten minimum-age school leavers continued to reject such training opportunities (Horton 1985). That such young people were opting to remain unemployed (and, at the time, receiving supplementary benefit) was deemed politically unacceptable. By 1988, 16- and 17-year-olds no longer had the 'option' of unemployment. The 1988 Social Security Act withdrew their eligibility for state income support, instead *guaranteeing* them a youth training place.

Despite this, it has been estimated that some 30,000 young people each year 'vote with their feet' and refuse to participate in YTS (British Youth Council 1992). Moreover, since the Training and Enterprise Councils (TECs) took over responsibility for youth training following the 1988 *White Paper on Employment* (Department of Employment 1988), there have been repeated allegations that they are unable to provide sufficient youth training places to meet demand, and thereby to meet the government's commitment to a training 'guarantee' (Maclagan 1992). Methods of counting those awaiting a 'guarantee' place have been altered (ibid.) and, despite persistent political assertions that there *is* a training place for all those who require it, this is countered by evidence that well over 100,000 young people aged sixteen and seventeen are not in education, training or employment, of whom three-quarters have no visible means of support (see, for example, Convery and Chatrik 1994; Shakespeare 1995). What is more, the numbers in receipt of Severe Hardship Payments (the safety net for young people in certain dire circumstances) have steadily increased over the last few years (Maclagan 1993), although more recently there have been renewed efforts to restrict its availability, particularly through the use of new guidelines on estrangement (Chatrik 1996).

The original research on Status Zer0 young people – young people aged sixteen and seventeen who are not in education, training or employment, despite the fact that unemployment for this age group is no longer an 'option' – has been widely reported elsewhere (Istance, Rees and Williamson 1994; McRae 1994; Williamson 1994) and is simply summarised here. Although based on a study of a local area, it was methodologically innovative and generated both summative and formative data, the former arising from a systematic study of the routes taken by one cohort of school leavers over two years and the latter developed through more in-depth qualitative work with a small number of Status Zer0 young people.

The analysis of routes taken by a one-in-four sample of 1991 school leavers (using only one source of data – Careers Service records – to avoid any risk of double-counting, but which were subjected to various forms of analysis) indicated that some 16–23 per cent of those who left education at the minimum age are in Status Zer0 at any one time. So few young people found employment they are almost immaterial to the analysis. For the purposes of this paper, one critical finding was that two-fifths of these young people experienced Status Zer0 for six months or more (an arbitrary cut-off point, but a pertinent one nonetheless, since it represents a quarter of the full course of a youth training programme). This does not include the one-third of young people who were 'missing' from Careers Service records throughout the two years, and whom we have assumed (correctly, we believe, since the detailed contentions on this front which informed the analysis have not yet been rebutted) to have been in Status Zer0 throughout. Taken together, almost three-quarters of the school leavers in our study experienced Status Zer0 for six months or more.

Admittedly, some of these young people had intermittent spells in Status Zer0, interspersed with other experiences (in education or training). However, the scale of the phenomenon of Status Zer0 *per se* and long-term (i.e. six months plus) Status Zer0 in particular rendered the qualitative study of young people in this situation all the more important.

Although the initial intention was to trace (through the Employment, Careers and Probation services and, most productively, through existing informal networks) young people who had been in Status Zer0 for all of the time since they left school (not necessarily, yet, for a full two years, but usually for at least one year), some respondents had had fleeting contact with the infrastructure of youth training. Few, however, had 'lasted' much more than a week or so. Thus, the case-study work was focused on a small group of young people whose *predominant* post-school experience was of being in Status Zer0. There is no claim that the twenty-six young people interviewed were necessarily representative of young people in Status Zer0 but, as young people at perhaps the extreme end of the Status Zer0 experience, they do illustrate – and illuminate – the fate that might befall any young person who is unfortunate to experience being in Status Zer0 for any length of time. It is sufficient to outline here their *current* lifestyles and behaviour, before turning to their attitudes, backgrounds and prospects in the context of the underclass debate.

Two common threads run through the current behaviour of these Status Zer0 young people: short-termism and opportunism. Their lives were about living from day to day: few, if any, aspects of their lives, had any stability (see Chapter 8). Money was a constant preoccupation (see National Children's Homes 1993) as, often, was securing a roof over their heads. Relationships with family and friends were tenuous. Perhaps the key finding, however, was the fact that all had slipped, or were slipping steadily along a continuum of 'income generation': from benefit fraud (if it was possible), through casual employment and opportunistic petty crime, to more calculated and organised criminality. Only a few, however, were as yet firmly entrenched in committed and regular offending. The daily round for all was characterised by lying in bed until late, wandering around shops (and possibly shoplifting), hanging around in the evenings (and possibly using drugs and drinking) and staying up until the early hours – not a routine that would lend itself easily to the time structures of formal training or work. But where 'work' (casual, informal or illegal) needed to be done, they were usually on hand to do it. This is consistent with MacDonald's work on 'fiddly jobs', where both young people and adults were keen and entrepreneurial in their search for (quasi) work (see MacDonald 1994).

When asked why they had not availed themselves of the youth training 'guarantee', there was a mixed, sometimes muddled, response. Many alluded to the low level of the training allowance which, it is important to note, has remained static for 16-year-olds since 1989 and 17-year-olds since 1986 and is now on a par with income support levels; had it kept pace with average wages it would now be some three times greater (Maclagan and Convery 1994). Others commented on their perception of youth training as 'slave labour' which led nowhere, a 'fact' often corroborated by their peers, even those who were participating on the programme. It appeared particularly unattractive to those who did not believe they would be offered training places which squared with their occupational aspirations – a retracing of the old debate about unrealistic or inappropriate expectations, particularly when contemporary youth training provision is meant to be compatible with future local labour market forecasting. Many of these young people wanted to be motor mechanics (young men) or hairdressers (young women), for which few youth training possibilities are available.

STATUS ZER0 YOUNG PEOPLE AND THE 'UNDERCLASS'

In a crude way, then, as suggested initially, there appears to be a prima facie case that at least some Status Zer0 young people lie within a broad conceptualisation of the 'underclass'. Their behaviour and lifestyles apparently fit well with Booth's nineteenth-century notions of 'occasional labourers, loafers and criminals' (Booth 1904: 37, quoted in Thompson and Yeo 1973: 108) and with Murray's contemporary ideas about ne'er-do-wells who contaminate those with whom they come into contact (Murray 1984).

But their *present* behaviour conceals the very different backgrounds and former expectations of those who are currently in Status Zer0 (see Chapter 6). It would still be relatively convincing to argue that many of their family and educational backgrounds were symptomatic of belonging to the underclass. Many *did* come from divided families; many *did* have fragmented and partial schooling histories, having dropped out completely from school long before the statutory leaving age. Furthermore, some had been involved in criminal activity from an early age, following on in the local cultural traditions of 'ducking and diving' and 'making out' in whatever way they could. All this is consistent with 'underclass' ideas about disorganised communities, broken homes, lack of ambition and aspiration, and cultures of crime and deviancy. *But, on the other hand, many did not.* There are major problems here of attributing causality when even clear correlation is contentious. Some of these young people *never expected* that they would be experiencing Status Zer0. Some had been anticipating staying on at school or going on into further education. Some had very clear ideas about what they *would like* to be doing within the mainstream training and labour markets. Some had even firmer views about what they were definitely unwilling to be doing. But, in their terms, something had happened, beyond their control, which had almost propelled them into Status Zer0, and their current confusion and material need to 'live for the moment' was disabling them from any real rational consideration of how to get out (see Chapter 8).

What had happened varied from individual to individual. Parental friction and separation, physical assault, an apparent lack of interest or follow-up by purportedly 'concerned' professionals, unexpected homelessness, an 'unfulfilled' meeting with a careers official, even a miserably negative first day on a YT scheme – any one of these independently, or in some combination, had disrupted even the very tentative 'plans' they had made. These past experiences may well be viewed as a 'tangle of pathologies': non-school attendance; fractured childhoods as a result of 'broken homes'; at least temporary homelessness; brushes with the law; sexual and physical abuse and other forms of violence; drug misuse. These were then often compounded by an alleged lack of interest amongst those professionals with whom they came into contact. The majority of these young people displayed a sense of low self-esteem, and uncertainty and disorientation about the future. They were, from their point of view, being thrust from pillar to post with little sense of having much control over what was happening to them.

Meanwhile, with very limited access to state income support, they were having to get by using whatever means possible. This does not mean that they were somehow committed to a life of theft and crime. Indeed, many apparently regretted having to behave in this way, but felt that they had little alternative – they had no option but to be 'pragmatic and resourceful'. In some respects, their arguments fall in with criminological theories about 'techniques of neutralisation' (Sykes and Matza 1957). Beyond the few who were 'persistently deviant' and, to a large extent, conforming to local cultural norms, the rest rationalised their present deviant behaviour in 'Robin Hood' terms, taking from the better off to give to the less well off – themselves. In contrast to earlier studies of youth in transition, in which young people tended to blame themselves for their predicament (and thereby confirm the prevailing individual 'deficit model' attributed to unemployed, unemploy*able* young people – see Atkinson et al. 1982), these young people seemed to believe quite genuinely that they had been let down by others: politicians, professionals, parents. Few had any clearly articulated political stance, but they were more inclined to blame family, educational or social circumstances than themselves.

Most, as we have noted, held strongly negative views about youth training, but only the 'persistently delinquent' and one or two 'political refuseniks' ruled it out completely. For the former, the level of the allowance was a joke when compared to the money they made from crime; when £29.50 a week was mentioned, the common retort was 'you can't even buy a decent pair of trainers for that'. The latter who, on any criteria but particularly given their family backgrounds and educational qualifications, were clearly *not* members of the underclass, wanted no part in Thatcher-inspired 'exploitative' labour market initiatives. We have depicted both these groups as conveying 'policy problematics' for youth training policy (if not for other areas of social and youth policy).

The remainder were still, provisionally, willing to consider youth training. We have suggested that these Status Zer0 young people represent 'policy possibilities' for youth training, but it will require greater flexibility and imagination in the current structure of provision to coax them back into participation.

Thus, while 'Status Zer0' serves as a powerful metaphor for young people who currently count for nothing and appear to be going nowhere, there is little indication that they display firmly-grounded values and experiences which may be equated with a culture of poverty and the underclass. Gallie (1994) makes a similar point about the values of the long-term unemployed. Certainly, they currently exhibit disdain for dominant values and structures of opportunity (or the lack of it). Certainly, their current lives are governed by *ad hoc* expediency and short-term self-interest, but this is hardly illustrative of some alternative 'way of life'. Most still subscribe to dominant *goals*, but either don't know how to get there, think it is impossible to get there, or are exploring different ways of getting there!

AN ALTERNATIVE VIEW

Green (1992) has argued that the underclass question cannot be divorced from the debate about the proper role of the state. There are clearly debates to be had and dilemmas to be addressed about the appropriate response to the Status Zer0 phenomenon. The current political response is to assert that, as the only country in Europe to offer a youth training guarantee, the UK is ahead of the field. If young people choose not to avail themselves of such opportunities that is their choice (and their problem). That is yet another implicit reference to one version of the underclass argument.

The underclass debate, given credence and some 'autonomy' and validity through being subjected to academic enquiry (Bagguley and Mann 1992), has always – and continues to be – penetrated and permeated by both moral and ideological polemic. This has weakened the rigour with which the concept has been explored *theoretically* by both Left and Right since, to some extent at least, the theoretical argument follows, rather than precedes, recommended social policy measures. It is the justification (for either cultural attacks or structural redistribution away from the poor), not the explanation. The situation of Status Zer0 young people lends itself to precisely the same '*post hoc* rationalisation' for particular political and policy preferences. Hence, the recalcitrance of government in failing to consider alternative youth training policy measures: these *types* of young people would not take part, however it was constructed. The evidence from the early Status Zer0 research would suggest otherwise.

But first a different explanatory framework is required. Turning away from the vast literature on vocational preparation and training, it is informative to look to two pieces of criminological work from the 1960s. David Matza (1964) argued that young offenders were prone to *drift* into delinquency, as they evaluated the pros and cons of alternative courses of action, a point which was made more firmly in relation to the structure and processes of juvenile justice by Williamson (1978). Cloward and Ohlin (1961) maintained that various sub cultural formations developed in response to different structures of opportunity, depending on the extent to which individuals subscribed to the dominant goals of society and whether or not they possessed the legitimate means to achieve them. Their argument would, it is perhaps significant to note, fit comfortably with those 'culture of poverty' perspectives which maintain that poverty sub cultures are a response to structural circumstances.

A version of these ideas may be applied to many, if not all, Status Zer0 young people. Their behavioural characteristics are often a product of 'drift' and a response to their structural predicament. The youth training allowance now offers little more than a component income to a larger household income; it cannot provide for independence, if it ever did. The quality of much youth training remains questionable. The capacity of youth training to provide opportunities 'relevant' to young people's interests and aspirations is in doubt (see Mizen 1995). The prospect of youth training obviously connecting young people to real employment opportunities clearly diminishes as recessions deepen and the youth labour market contracts (see Lee et al. 1990). Even when there may be some general economic resurgence, this is *decreasingly* reflected in the youth labour market, so still leaving more than a residuum of young people on the edge. Thus the *structure of opportunity* in post-school transitions, even if their form is apparently much the same, has altered dramatically during the last ten years (see Chapter 2). In response, young people have developed a range of strategies to deal with it, one of which *may be* a 'culture of survival' for those who, for many reasons, find themselves experiencing Status Zer0. Only by restructuring post-school opportunities – including in particular the framework, remuneration and internal flexibility of youth training – will a different balance of possibilities be presented for consideration by young people. Such a balance will need to incorporate some response to personal and social needs, as well as training and labour market imperatives, for, as we have seen, it is those factors which often propel young people into Status Zer0 and sometimes make it difficult for them to contemplate making their way out. To view the phenomenon of Status Zer0 as a product of personal choice, or some kind of cultural determinism, is both naive and ill-informed.

CONCLUSION

Bernard Davies (1986) detected that during the 1980s, in many areas of youth policy, there had been a steady shift away from the 'winning by consent' approaches of the post-war democratic consensus to a Thatcherite approach based on the 'coercing of compliance' (see Chapter 10). The former does, of course, present possibilities for debate, experimentation and constructive change; there is little evidence that the latter does anything more than displace a public issue from one policy area to another.

The 'underclass' is a convenient ideological tool for either abandoning any commitment to the poor and disadvantaged, or cultivating popular support for more coercive measures. The irony, in our view, is that either of these measures is in fact likely to create and solidify an underclass. It becomes a self-fulfilling prophecy. Only by developing policy approaches based on debate and broad consensus, which maintain the 'permeable boundaries' between the labour market and those outside it (and, indeed, between the training market and those in Status Zer0), will some sense of social integration be sustained and dangerous forms of social exclusion – whether termed an 'underclass' or something else – forestalled.

Clearly, the jury is still out on the concept of the 'underclass'. Yet it is not an issue to be side-stepped. There are observable long-term changes in the structure of the labour market which tend to increase the social polarisation captured by the underclass idea (Smith 1992b). There is probably an increase in the salience of educational qualification as a determinant of employment prospects, and a concomitant decline in the opportunities available to those without skills or qualifications (see Chapter 2). Minimum-age school leavers who subsequently experience long-term Status Zer0 clearly have a precarious relationship with formal labour market opportunities, a relationship which is likely to worsen if no effort is made to accommodate their needs. There is a risk of scaremongering about the wider social consequences (in terms of, for example, homelessness, drug misuse and criminality) arising from such long-term marginality to mainstream structures of economic opportunity, but that does not mean they will not materialise.

To date, even the 'long-term' unemployed usually have a predominant history of *employment*. Even in the areas of highest unemployment, more people are usually in employment than out of it. As Buck has noted, the long-term unemployed of the 1980s 'were not so much stable members of an underclass as unstable members of the working class' (Buck 1992: 19).

The current problem with the debate about the underclass is that the concept attempts to encapsulate considerable heterogeneity in experience, attitude and orientation (Heath 1992; and see Chapter 6). The same applies to our qualitative analysis of Status Zer0 young people. The concept of the underclass is, therefore, not yet a coherent explanatory idea. However, while there is limited evidence of an emergent underclass, there is equally little to counter the view that such an underclass may be *in emergence*, through the changing structures of families and employment. There is evidence that some people do move between non-employment and precarious jobs, casual or part time, and become trapped in a low-income cycle from which it is increasingly difficult to break out (Cornford 1992; and see Chapter 9). Status Zer0 young people, if renewed effort is not made to integrate them into training and labour market structures, may be the first generation for whom the underclass is a social reality rather than a political and ideological device.

NOTE

1 'Status Zer0' has proved to be a contentious term. The original research report (Istance, Rees and Williamson 1994) was intended to be titled 'Status Zer0'. During the fieldwork, 'status 0' was simply a technical concept to depict the status of those young people not in education, training or employment and to distinguish them from those in education (status 1), training (status 2), and employment (status 3). It was felt, however, that 'Status Zer0' represented a powerful metaphor for young people who appeared to count for nothing and be going nowhere. This terminology, however, created a political furore at the local level and references to 'status 0' in the research report were replaced by 'status A'. As questions concerning young people not in education, training and employment have entered the political and policy arenas, their categorisation has been sanitised yet further; it is alleged that at high levels of central government they are referred to as NEET young people: those Not in Education, Employment or Training.

Chapter 6

The formation of an underclass or disparate processes of social exclusion?

Evidence from two groupings of 'vulnerable youth'

Debbie Baldwin, Bob Coles and Wendy Mitchell

This chapter will argue that allegations of the formation of a youth underclass in Britain in the late twentieth century (Murray 1990) should be regarded as at best conceptually muddled and at worst as politically mischievous and ideologically dangerous. On both counts the use of the term 'underclass' contains the seeds of misconceived social policy interventions in the management of youth transitions. Whilst addressing some of the issues raised by allegations of the development of a youth 'underclass', this chapter is based upon a conceptualisation of youth around the interrelationship of three main transitions or career lines. The chapter further seeks to apply this theoretical framework to two main groupings of young people largely ignored by mainstream youth researchers: disabled young people and young people 'looked after' in the public care.

The central argument of the chapter is that the study of these two groupings of young people highlights the fact that social exclusion occurs in a variety of very different ways. Whilst it may be true that the young people discussed may eventually share some similar social and economic characteristics – no involvement in full-time paid employment, dependence upon benefits, susceptibility to homelessness and problematic relationships with their families – the routes to these statuses are manifestly different. It is the argument of this chapter that the use of the term 'underclass' masks diversity (see also Jeffs in Chapter 10), replaces complex analysis with simplistic slogans, and apportions blame without the research evidence to understand the complex transitions of 'vulnerable youth'. What must be understood, therefore, is the range of complex processes of social exclusion, under what circumstances these are most likely to occur and what can be done to throw these processes into reverse. Only with a deeper sociological understanding of the transition processes which define 'vulnerable youth' can we build a more informed social policy for such young people.

YOUTH AS A SERIES OF INTER RELATED TRANSITIONS

In order to understand the changing nature of youth in the late 1990s, we must understand youth as a series of inter related transitions. Elsewhere these have been described as involving three main career lines: education, training and labour market careers (the school-to-work transition); domestic careers (from families of origin to families of destination); and housing careers (from living with families or surrogate families to living independently of them) (Coles 1995). Each of these three transitions must be understood as constructed through the interplay of decision-making by both young people and their families or surrogate families *and* those charged with responsibility for the social and economic context in which they grow up. It is important to understand *both* sides of this equation. Only by doing so can one begin to appreciate either the micro-patterns of individual career development or the macro-patterns of 'youth' as a general and socio-structural phase within the life-course. So, for instance, the 1990s have witnessed a rapid expansion of post-16 and post-18 education which has fundamentally reshaped the transitions of many young people (Coles 1995; Courtnay and McAleese 1993, 1994; Gray et al. 1993). To understand this, we need to understand not only young people's 'choices' of options at school or college but also the policy environment within which these 'choices' are made. The latter include the changing shape of the youth labour market and increasing competition between schools and colleges following the 1988 Education Reform Act (Department of Education and Science 1988). We also need to recognise the inter dependence of all three transitions rather than treating one (the school-to-work transition) as predominant and pivotal to the other two. Much of the sociology of youth in the last decade has concentrated upon the school-to-work transition (Banks et al. 1992; Bates and Riseborough 1993; Jones and Wallace 1992). The young people discussed within this chapter help us to recognise that, although the movement from school to work is important, for some groups their housing careers and family relationships are of equal (and for some paramount) importance (Jones

1995a, b; and Chapter 7). It is also important to recognise that families themselves are undergoing considerable change. The number of lone parent families more than doubled between 1971 and 1991, and by the age of sixteen nearly a quarter of young people will have experienced the divorce of their parents and many will be living with step-parents (Burghes 1994; Haskey 1994). All this adds to the complexity – and, some would argue, the brittleness – of family relationships at the very time when government policy assumes family dependency for longer and longer (as described by Dean in Chapter 4).

DISABLED YOUNG PEOPLE

We first examine disabled young people for a number of reasons. First, they are highly likely to experience processes of exclusion in childhood (through forms of special education) which can have long-term consequences for later youth transitions. Second, whilst disabled young people will increasingly experience protracted transitions involving a variety of different forms of post-16 education and training, they are unlikely to obtain full-time employment and are highly likely to be dependent in the long term on welfare benefits. Third, because they are unlikely to be in receipt of a living wage, this calls into question the predominance of the school-to-work transition in determining the course of the transition to adulthood. Fourth, the consideration of disabled young people raises awkward questions for youth underclass theorists. For whilst they may eventually share many of the charactersics of the underclass, they are much more difficult to castigate and blame. Indeed, their social exclusion can be shown to be as much a result of the actions of policy makers and practitioners rather than any characteristic they might share with other members of an alleged underclass.

Disabled young people do not constitute a homogenous group. Included within this broad heading are those defined as having 'special educational needs', those with impairments and disabilities, and those with 'learning disabilities'. Being defined as having 'special educational needs' is specifically reserved for those for whom special educational provision is made available. This is influenced, of course, by the willingness of authorities to make resources available, as well as the recognition of 'need' (Coles 1995). Following Warnock (1978), it might be claimed that approximately one in five young people has a 'special educational need' at some time in their life. However, almost two-thirds of these are defined as such, not because of any medical impairment, but because of some temporary learning disability or emotional and behavioural problem. A much smaller grouping (around 2 per cent) can be identified by the issuing of a 'statement' (or 'record' in Scotland) (Department for Education 1994). Yet, it is also known that Afro-Caribbean boys in particular are hugely over-represented in this group, which has raised the issue as to whether 'statementing' is used as an instrument of social control (Tomlinson 1982). The term 'disability' is also far from clear-cut. Some legislation (for example, the 1986 Disabled Persons Act (Department of Health and Social Security 1986)), defines 'disability' predominately in terms of medical impairment, which restricts the numbers so defined to approximately 3 per cent of young people under the age of sixteen (Bone and Meltzer 1989). Yet even this term is open to interpretation and can be inconsistently applied by different authorities (Middleton 1992).

The process of definition is political and an important part of the mechanism of social and cultural marginalisation and exclusion (Abberley 1991; Barnes 1991; Oliver 1990). For young people, this most obviously occurs in decisions taken either to issue a 'statement' or, perhaps more critically, to recommend attendance at a 'special school', though this means that some children are excluded from mainstream school lessons and, as Brisenden argues, restricted to an educational diet which can have a profound impact upon their life-chances and self-perceptions. At its worst, the segregated education system can be regarded as 'a conveyor belt of judgements weighing disabled people down with low expectations', rather than extended 'self development at every stage' (Brisenden 1989: 218). He suggests that *can't yet do* may become institutionalised as *shouldn't be expected to try* and internalised as *can't possibly do* in a self-fulfilling prophesy. This is not to say that teachers in mainstream or special schools do not attempt to do their best for the young people in their charge or attempt to encourage positive self-perception. Clearly, as Mitchell's ongoing research documents (1996), many teachers are committed to the education and development of disabled young people and, as teachers, are well regarded by the disabled young people they teach. We are certainly not arguing here for the closure of all special schools or the presumption that all special education is second class. Rather, what must be recognised is the complexity of issues surrounding segregated provision, whilst simultaneously acknowledging that special education does operate within structural constraints. These can have both immediate effects and long-term consequences on youth transitions.

Barnes (1991) has argued that young people attending special schools often have to travel long distances, which can thus lead to young people being socially separated from their peers within the community in which they live. He also points out that often special schools also cater for children as young as 2 years old and young adults as old as nineteen, an age distribution which can perpetuate the myth of disabled young people being 'eternal children'. Necessarily, given their size and the age group for which they cater, special schools have fewer specialist teachers. So that, whilst some schools may attempt to embrace the national curriculum as an 'entitlement curriculum', many young people are restricted in the range of subjects provided and the levels of attainment they achieve (Barnes 1991). This does not, of course, add up to an argument that all special schools should be disbanded but rather that the allocation of pupils to them should be carefully and parsimoniously carried out. Even when disabled young people attend mainstream schools they may not be integrated within them. Swann, for example, found that some young people spent as little as 3 per cent of their time in the same classroom as their able-bodied peers (Swann 1988, in Barnes 1991: 50).

Much recent legislation (the 1989 Children Act and the 1993 Education Act, for instance) and the accompanying guidelines and codes of practice are concerned to stress the need for regular, multi-professional reviews of young people's needs and 'transition planning' as those with special educational needs approach minimum school-leaving age (Department for Education 1994). Many disabled young people now stay on in some form of education and training at the age of sixteen. Research on the post-16 transitions of disabled young people has been limited (Armstrong and Davies 1995; Tisdall 1996; Todd 1995). One notable exception is a recent series of studies by Ward, Thomson and Riddell focusing upon young people with recorded 'special educational needs' leaving school in Scotland. Their 1991 study follows 618 young people and found that for those who could be traced almost half (47.2 per cent) stayed on at school post-16 in the late 1980s. The three most frequent first post-school destinations were also likely to be in segregated placements, training centres and sheltered workshops (28 per cent), work training/experience (24.3 per cent), and special further education (18.8 per cent) (Ward et al. 1991).

Special further education has been significantly expanded in recent years, yet a number of worries remain about the type of provision and its long-term impact upon the young people involved. Much provision continues to perpetuate social segregation, isolation and exclusionary practices. Furthermore, as more and more young people become accredited through post-16 courses of education and training, Tomlinson and Colquhoun point out that there is a real danger that young people perceived as 'special' will be left even more stigmatised as 'deficient' or 'less competent' (1995: 200). Similarly, in later life as a result of the 1992 Further and Higher Education Act, it is those adults with the most severe learning disabilities who are potentially in danger of exclusion from continuing education (National Institute of Adult Continuing Education 1996).

Concern has also been expressed about the course content of special further education, particularly on courses such as *Preparation for Employment*. Corbett and Barton (1992) argue that these courses often focus on individual adaptation, individual flexibility and personal attributes. For those perceived as being *unlikely* to obtain employment, however, courses frequently focus on social and life skills which again emphasise adaptation to 'normal' society. The presupposition is that young people can be appropriately assessed, defined and channelled. There is also the associated danger, especially in the courses surrounding employment, that this becomes both another version of a 'self-fulfilling prophecy' and a means of providing an individualising solution to a structural and economic problem. Thus, courses identify the difficulties that disabled young people face rather than addressing the wider socio-political context from which the problems evolve (Corbett and Barton 1992). In terms of employment, the net effect may be to turn the lack of jobs into a belief about personal inadequacy in the competition for employment, and the exclusionary (and often discriminatory) practices of employers into an internalised belief about unemployability. Macro-economic problems are thus transformed into personal inadequacy (Corbett and Barton 1992; Tomlinson and Colquhoun 1995).

Most studies of the youth transitions of disabled young people reveal that, however the sample is defined, relatively few obtain open employment. By the age of 22 or more, fewer than one in five of the Scottish sample studied by Thomson and Ward (1994) were in either open or sheltered employment. In a study of disabled young people as defined by the Office of Population and Census

Surveys at the end of the 1980s, Hirst and Baldwin (1994) found that only around a third had obtained work (compared with over two-thirds of their able-bodied contemporaries). Given this, often both training and education courses are geared towards transitions to 'adulthood' or 'independent living' rather than training for jobs. Hirst and Baldwin, for instance, examined not only the institution-based status transitions (as in the transitions between school, college training and work), but also the attainment of personal qualities of autonomy and control over various aspects of everyday living and social relationships. They conclude that, although one cannot say that *all* disabled young people experience transition problems or do not obtain an independent 'adult' status, compared to young people in general, a 'sizeable minority' can, and do, experience significant difficulties achieving adult independence. More specifically Hirst and Baldwin argue that disabled young people were often less empowered and relatively more dependent upon their families both socially and emotionally. Disabled young people experienced relatively less enriching and varied social relationships and, in this sense, they become less and less prepared for, and uncertain of, moving towards independent living. Disabled young people also frequently experienced lower levels of independence in the use of their own money and, even when in employment, earn less than their able-bodied peers by an average of around £7 per week (Hirst and Baldwin 1994). All this means that they are less able to afford a social life through which social and relationship skills, autonomy and self-efficacy might be developed.

Ultimately, one cannot perceive all disabled young people's transitions in a wholly negative light. Positive outcomes can and do occur, as some case studies have suggested (Thomson and Ward 1994; Ward et al. 1991). For example, in Mitchell's ongoing research, one young person currently undergoing youth training in catering is looking forward both to continuing this career and living independently. His youth training is being undertaken after a period of independence training at residential college. Others also have clear aspirations for their future in terms of employment and/or independent living. However, patterns of support for youth transitions vary. Whilst, in one of the authorities being studied, attendance at residential college is a relatively common occurrence, in another it is much less so. What this emphasises is the complexity of youth transitions and the numerous determinants involved. What is less clear-cut is the degree to which the state of the local economy, proactive work with local employers, good practice in 'transition planning', the type of further education or training provision, or, for some, the degree of impairment, can determine the eventual outcome. This requires further research and analysis. But what is clear is that it is far too simple to dismiss the whole diverse grouping with a label which presupposes their social exclusion or assumes their long-term unemployability and benefit dependency.

The evidence does, however, strongly suggest that many disabled young people do experience prolonged transitions and ones which often result in exclusion from the labour market and continued dependence within and upon their families. The second main grouping upon which this chapter focuses experience the transitions of youth in a remarkably different way. For them, the transitions are short, sharp and early. Whilst, like disabled young people, they are unlikely to experience an illustrious educational career equipping them with the requisite qualifications to promote a successful employment career, they are highly likely to be dumped out of their surrogate families and expected to live independently by the ages of sixteen or seventeen.

YOUNG PEOPLE IN AND LEAVING CARE

Each year in the United Kingdom approximately 8,000 young people leave the public care system. It is a system in which the state acts *in loco parentis* or, as is more commonly understood, the state is the corporate parent; a responsibility devolved to local authority social service departments. These 8,000 young people account for less than 1 per cent of their age group. Yet, they are arguably the most vulnerable and disadvantaged group within their age cohort. Drawing on a variety of recent studies, Barnardo's (1996a) reports that: amongst young people leaving care more than 75 per cent have no academic qualifications; between 50 per cent and 80 per cent are unemployed; and at least 13 per cent of young women leaving care are pregnant or are already mothers. Furthermore, Barnardo's notes that 38 per cent of young prisoners, 30 per cent of single young homeless people, and 10 per cent of 16- to 17-year-old claimants of severe hardship payments have been in care. In summary, these statistics variously suggest that young people leaving care are uneducated, unemployed, welfare-dependent, single parents, and/or criminals. It could be argued, and probably would be argued by some (Murray 1990), that these young people are, characteristically at least, members of Britain's emerging underclass.

These statistics undoubtedly represent a reality of deprivation, disadvantage and disenfranchisement. Yet behind these gloomy statistics lie complex biographies of young people leaving care. More importantly, the statistics give little indication of the contribution of policy and statutory decision-making to the after-care experiences of these young people. Young people are not admitted into care because they are uneducated, unemployed and welfare-dependent despite the high probability that many of them will leave care with these characteristics. The decision to admit children and young people into care is taken primarily because of serious concerns for their welfare or, in the words of the 1989 Children Act, they are seen to be 'at risk of significant harm'. Once again, behind this shared characteristic of being 'at risk of significant harm', lies a heterogeneous population.

Alongside differences of gender and race, young people in care are also differentiated by age at admission and reasons for admission into care. These two factors are important in that age at admission into care is strongly associated with reason for admission into care. Younger children are much more likely to be admitted into care for reasons of protection from abuse and neglect, whereas young people in their teenage years are more usually admitted for behavioural reasons, such as being beyond parental control or in moral danger. Until the implementation of the 1989 Children Act, they could also have been admitted for non-school attendance or incipient criminality, behaviour which itself may be a manifestation of earlier abuse and neglect. Packman (1986) categorises young people in care as including 'victims', 'villains' and 'the volunteered', whilst Farmer and Parker (1991) use the categories of 'the protected' and 'the disaffected'. Largely regardless of the reasons for admission into care, however, the public care system provides surrogate care and accommodation for the victims and the villains, the abused and the abusers, the innocent and the infamous, frequently in the same house, children's home, or secure unit (Coles 1995). In short, it provides an homogeneous service for an inherently heterogeneous population.

Once in care, young people can experience very different care careers. Young people over the age of 11 years are twice as likely to be in residential care than younger children, due mainly to the difficulties in finding foster families willing to care for teenage young people (Utting 1991). They are also more likely to experience a number of different placements in a shorter period of time resulting in geographic as well as domestic mobility (Rowe et al. 1989). For some young people, it is hardly worth them unpacking their belongings since they are moved on to new placements so quickly (Berridge 1985). This is evidenced by Garnett's study (1992) which noted that of those young people admitted into care during their teenage years, approximately half experienced more than three changes in placement during their final two years of being in care, and one in ten had experienced more than five changes in the same period.

The potential effects of extensive movement in care are the impact upon self-identity and feelings of belonging, although a much more apparent, and arguably fundamental, effect is the often commensurate extent of movement between schools and the impact this can have on the educational attainment of young people in care. The lack of priority given to the education of young people in care results in care becoming an educational hazard (Social Services Inspectorate 1991). The fact that one in five of the social workers participating in the study by Biehal et al. (1992) did not know whether the young people leaving care had any educational qualifications or not is perhaps indicative of the level of priority given to education. The high level of non-school attendance and, more importantly, permanent school exclusions among young people in care further explains their educational under-achievement. A joint study by the Office for Standards in Education (OFSTED) and the Social Services Inspectorate (1995) reported that 12 per cent of all children and young people in care of statutory school age either did not attend school on a regular basis or were excluded from school. This figure increased to 26 per cent of 14- to 16-year-olds who should have been studying for General Certificate of Secondary Education examinations. Small wonder, therefore, that all recent studies of young people leaving care report that the vast majority are unqualified. The majority of young people in care are excluded both from a stable living environment and from a stable educational environment, the effects of which have considerable implications for the transitions they make to adulthood.

The low levels of formal educational achievement help to explain, at least in part, what opportunities young people in care are afforded at the age of sixteen. Without any qualifications, they have little alternative but to leave school at sixteen. Yet, at this vital time in their lives, they are also being required by their local authorities to consider, if not begin, their housing transitions out of care and into independent accommodation. At the age of sixteen, therefore, many young people in care are expected to enter both the labour market and the housing market, both of which are notoriously inaccessible to young people. In the study by Stein and Carey (1986), 50 per cent of the young people were unemployed after one year of leaving care, and by the end of the second year of living out of care this figure had increased to 80 per cent. The researchers describe young people experiencing a cycle of unemployment, training, insecure jobs and further unemployment with increased dependency on state benefits.

Lack of participation in the labour market is only one dimension of the after-care transitions of young people. An equally important and interdependent factor to be considered is the often highly tenuous nature of young people's relationships with the housing market. Again, research shows that many young people experience a number of accommodation moves which in some cases can be explained by the inappropriate allocation of move-on accommodation provided by social services (Biehal et al. 1992, 1995; Garnett 1992). It is not unusual to find young people being placed in bed-and-breakfast accommodation, lodgings and hostels at the ages of 16/17 years. In Stein and Carey's study (1986), only 20 per cent of the young people had remained in the same accommodation for two years after leaving care and, perhaps more worryingly, over half of the young people had experienced more than three changes of independent accommodation within the same period. Young people's enforced departure from the care system results in accelerated and inherently unstable housing transitions with homelessness being a frequently experienced outcome.

In summary, young people in care, with the state acting as their corporate parents, characteristically grow up in an environment of frequently changing placements with numerous carers compounded by limited educational opportunities. Their transitions to adulthood are marked by a similarly unstable environment of unemployment and frequent housing movement. Even their dependence upon state benefits is becoming tenuous due to the stringent nature of assessment for severe hardship payments, whereby estrangement from families has to be proved, and the impending withdrawal of housing benefit for young people in care, either on a Care Order or accommodated under Section 20 of the 1989 Children Act. If some of these young people turn to crime, we should not be surprised. Indeed, far from leaving care for independence, many young people face a future of continued instability and dependence on the state.

Despite some success stories of young people leaving care (Baldwin 1996; Biehal et al. 1995; Garnett 1992), for a significant minority their futures are also likely to be played out in institutions with children's homes being replaced by Young Offender's Institutions.

CONCLUSION

This chapter has reviewed our understanding of the youth transitions of two groupings of 'vulnerable youth'. It has illustrated the ways in which these are framed not so much by decisions young people take about their own career development but upon social policies affecting the institutions which frame their lives. To be looked after in care or to be educated in a special school (and for some young people both), can frequently have a long-lasting impact upon youth transitions. The chapter has also illustrated that this is not only confined to the impact that forms of special education and/or care might have upon school qualifications or the school-to-work transition, but also patterns of family support, leaving home and preparation for independent living. Here, there are marked contrasts between the two groupings. For whilst policy trends in special education mean that disabled young people are likely to experience protracted or extended transitions, young people leaving care are likely to experience accelerated and unstable transitions.

The chapter has also argued that the two groupings are both heterogeneous and that they experience youth transitions in remarkably different ways. Although often differing in social background and educational circumstances, many young people with disabilities or from care find themselves amongst the long-term unemployed, the homeless and the socially isolated. Yet it is unfortunate that, by implication, the term 'underclass' has been applied to the young people described in this chapter. To be sure, young people leaving care have been shown to be highly over-represented amongst the homeless, the prison population, teenage single parents and, in recent media attention, those involved in prostitution (Barnardo's 1996b). Disabled young people are often unlikely to obtain open employment commanding a living wage and more likely to be dependent upon long-term welfare support. Tomlinson and Colquhoun infer that because disabled young people are both 'special' and '(un)employable' they, too, are part of the underclass (1995: 200). Yet, whilst in general term members of the groupings explored here may share some characteristics, the social processes through which these are ascribed are manifestly different. It is our central contention, therefore, that the use of the slogan 'underclass' hinders rather than helps accurate analysis. Proper and effective policy solutions must be based upon a correct diagnosis of the nature of the problems being addressed. To leap to policy conclusions couched in the language of welfare cuts might be music to the ears of New Right politicians. To do so, however, would heap further disadvantage upon the disadvantaged and, in the final analysis, infer blame upon 'vulnerable youth' for their enforced social exclusion.

Chapter 7

Youth homelessness and the 'underclass'

Gill Jones

The underclass is an issue with which the academic world is having to engage, but it is first and foremost a political issue, and therefore impossible to discuss without reference to current British politics and media concerns. While rhetoric from the Right on 'the underclass' is based on a series of deviant stereotypes and emphasises individual responsibility and choice, the response of many on the Left is to stress structural inequalities and constraints. This chapter considers this polarity, and discusses whether homeless young people are responsible for their own predicaments or whether they are new victims of an increasingly uncaring society and a diminishing welfare state. Issues of choice and constraint, agency and structure, are therefore addressed. It is also relevant to note the context in which a 'moral panic' (Cohen 1973) has developed about homelessness, and the implications for policy and practice of labelling and treating homeless young people as an underclass. The discussion draws on empirical evidence from a recent study of housed and homeless young people in Scotland (Jones 1995a).[1]

THE UNDERCLASS: EMERGENCE OF A CONCEPT

Approaches to the concept of underclass usually take two broad forms, individualist or structuralist, as indicated in Chapter 1. Table 7.1 indicates the polarisation of these two paradigms, referred to by Gallie (1994) as the 'conservative' view and the 'radical' view. According to the former, homeless people are responsible for their own misfortunes, while according to the latter they are the victims of circumstances such as the changing nature of the housing market, the welfare state and the economy. In sociological terms, the debate is over the relationship between agency and structure, and in policy terms, between negative and positive interventions.

The underclass thesis itself formed part of a response to structural determinism. Margaret Thatcher asserted in 1987: 'There is no such thing as society; there are only individual men and women and there are families.' Her politically inspired comment was paralleled in sociological debate as structuralist explanations of the social

Table 7.1 Individualist and structuralist models of the 'underclass'

Individualist	Structuralist
Basic principles	
Emphasis on agency	Emphasis on structure
Self-determination	Determinism
Individual choice	Social constraint
Based on monetarism	Based on social justice
Based on 'tradition'	Based on social intervention
Role of Individual/state	
Welfare state disempowers	Welfare state empowers
Stress on individual responsibilities	Stress on collective rights
Characteristics of 'underclass'	
Homogeneity	Heterogeneity
Stability	Impermanence
Culture of poverty	Class culture
Deviance as strategy	Deviance as survival strategy
Self-reproduction	Social reproduction
Solutions	
Punishment	Prevention
Less 'nanny state' intervention	Intervention to redress inequalities
Lower financial cost	Lower social cost

world were being challenged by post-modernist ideas; it was argued that the collapse of the structures of modernity resulted in the loss of social-class solidarity and family and community support, but also that individuals were less constrained by the structures of inequality and were able to exercise choice and develop their own biographies to a greater extent than before. The result was that more people faced risk (Beck 1992). In their way, these post-modernist ideas provided the intellectual forerunner to socio-political constructions of the underclass.

The concept of an underclass, as adopted within the New Right, suggests that the welfare state (the 'nanny state') has spawned a culture of dependency, within which an unruly, immoral and feck-less underclass is thriving at the expense of the respectable tax-paying citizen. By 'blaming the victim' (Walker 1990) – whether lone parents, or those without jobs or homes – the government has apparently found a rationale for failing to intervene to reduce poverty. The emphasis is on individual freedom and choice: thus, as observed in Chapter 1, Charles Murray argues (1990: 17) that many of the unemployed *choose* not to take jobs, and that this choice is possible because of the way welfare is structured. He suggests that state benefits act as disincentives to work and should thus be reduced if not withdrawn. He suggests that welfare benefits create a climate which fosters single parenthood. In making these comments, Murray is applying a model of *economic rationality* which assumes that people make rational choices based on economic criteria and might opt for unemployment, lone parenthood and even homeless-ness if welfare structures are in place to protect people in these situations. Though he does not specifically target homelessness he nevertheless asserts that the culture of the underclass is so powerful that even if people in Cardboard Cities were given work, they would 'revert' within two years (Murray 1990).

It has been interesting, if depressing, to follow the development of a moral panic about the homeless over the last few years. Thus, John Major, as Prime Minister, has suggested that homeless people sleep rough because they want to (BBC Radio 4 *Today* programme, prior to the general election in 1992, and again in April 1994); beggars are described as an eyesore which should be dealt with by the law (John Major again, in May 1994); and there has been a succession of denouncements by government ministers of teenage mothers 'who jump the housing queue' and jobless 'shirkers' who live at the taxpayer's expense. Homelessness is even reconstructed as a problem for those who have to witness it, rather than for those who have to experience it. And, indeed, the government's Minister for Housing described 'the homeless' as 'the sort of people one stepped over on the way out of the opera' (Sir George Young, in 1992).

The underclass hypothesis attempts to provide a moral rationale for the gradual withdrawal of the state safety net from young people, in particular. A whole raft of measures have eroded state support for young people making the transition to adulthood (see also Chapter 4). Government ministers have reduced or withdrawn benefits that they identify as financial 'incentives' for young people to leave their parental homes or care situations and set up new households of their own. Income Support, Housing Benefit, Board and Lodgings Payments and Exceptional Needs Payments have been cut and the distinction between householder and non-householder levels of allowance withdrawn in a vain attempt to reduce homelessness through regulating housing demand in youth. The idea is that, if incentives to leave home are withdrawn, young people will defer leaving home and thus not make demands on a housing market which is not geared to cater for their needs. In the meantime, parents are expected to fill the gaps left in the state safety net and to provide a home and financial support. The extension of the responsibilities of parents in this respect was cloaked in calls for a return to 'traditional family values'. Since many parents are unwilling or unable to extend their support for their children (Jones 1995a), and some young people, such as those who have been in care (see Chapter 6), cannot turn to their families for this support, there are many young people who are facing increased risk with no safety net to protect them.

POLARISED VIEWS

In all, therefore, we have an individualist underclass argument emanating from the Right, and a more structuralist response mainly from the Left. In seeking to combat the stereotyping of homelessness as deviancy, some on the Left try to redress the balance by applying positive stereotypes of their own. Organisations seeking more housing provision for young people may need to stress the 'ordinariness' of homeless young people in order to focus the debate on housing issues, and to combat the deviancy stereotyping. The result is a polarisation between those who seek to regulate housing demand (blaming the young) and those who seek to extend housing supply (blaming the government). The polarisation is not, however, clear-cut. Liddiard and Hutson (1991) suggest that hostel staff may emphasise to the outside world the 'normality' of homeless young people, yet still operate an internal gate-keeping system which distinguishes between deserving and undeserving cases. Countervailing sets of assumptions thus inform both policy makers and those working with homeless people. The polarisation of response to homelessness becomes a part of the phenomenon (ibid.). Both paradigms in their different ways over-simplify the problem and obstruct its solution.

What is needed is a theory that is adequate for understanding the extent to which youth transitions – including transitions into housing or homelessness – are shaped by choice and constraint. Some of the ideas developed under the umbrella of 'high modernity' can help to reconcile the structure–agency dichotomy. It is argued that individual life-courses are led along a 'reflexive biography' (Giddens 1991, 1994) in which there is a dynamic interaction between agency (self-determination and choice) and structure (affecting inequality and constraint). Individuals may thus hold some responsibility for their own actions within the structure of opportunity which is available to them, but this varies between individuals in an unequal way (see also Jones and Wallace 1992 on the relevance of these theories to the study of youth). This is, in a sense, the middle road. It allows a view of the world in which people are not simply regarded either as 'cultural dupes', as implied by over-deterministic approaches, or as free individuals, as implied by individualistic ones.

Beck (1992) describes the modern world as the 'risk society'. The notion of survival strategies, or ways of responding to and attempting to avoid perceived risk, helps us to understand the relation between individual action and unequal opportunity structure. Young people leaving home and facing inequalities of opportunity in the housing market adopt strategies for increasing their housing chances, those who have nowhere to live adopt strategies for survival in the open, and those without any money may beg, borrow or steal (see also Chapters 8 and 9). Often in such situations, as we shall see, the aim of the strategy adopted is short term, and it is not always a matter of rational and conscious choice.

However, we live in a complex world, and while some people might develop strategies which reduce risk (e.g. housing strategies which reduce the risk of homelessness – see Jones 1995a; Pickvance and Pickvance 1994), others may consciously take risks, as we shall see. Giddens (1994: 58) suggests that risk-taking can be seen as a means of bringing the future under control (a point also considered by Blackman in Chapter 8). In some circumstances, risk-taking itself can thus be employed as a strategy by young people who feel that they lack real power to control their futures.

A HOMELESS UNDERCLASS?

In the following pages, I focus on homeless young people and will address two questions which are crucial to the individualist explanation of the underclass. First, are the homeless a distinct group? Second, are their actions governed by economic rationality? The following analysis and its discussion will show that the answers to these questions are not straightforward. There are elements of the individualist position which cannot be abandoned in favour of a purely structuralist approach: a middle-road explanation seems necessary.

The study

The research on which the remainder of the paper is based was part of a two-year project, *Young people in and out of the housing market.*[2] The research was multi-methodological, using quantitative self-completion surveys and qualitative interview data from a number of sources (see Jones and Stevens 1993). This allowed us to examine homelessness from a number of angles and in a broader social context. Importantly, it gave us the rare opportunity to compare currently homeless young people with currently housed ones.

Data came broadly from three sources. First, national data provides a backcloth. The *Scottish Young People's Survey* (SYPS), conducted by the Centre for Educational Sociology at Edinburgh University over many years, was a biennial, 10 per cent, national postal survey of secondary school pupils in Scotland, sampled in their final compulsory year at school. Data come from two of the longitudinal cohort surveys in the SYPS series: young people were surveyed at average age 16¾ years and again at 19¼ years, in 1987/89 and 1989/91, producing samples of around 4,000 young people in each cohort by the age of 19 years (Brannen et al. 1991; Brannen and Middleton 1994). This provides a national comparison group. Second, two samples of homeless young people are also used in this analysis: the first of these is a subset of eighty-six young people in the SYPS 1989/91 who said they had experienced home-lessness since leaving their parental homes; and the second is a 1992 survey, conducted as part of the project, of 246 homeless young Scots aged 16–22 years (the Homeless Survey). Finally, the study also draws on qualitative data: this comes from follow-up interviews in 1992 with twenty-six SYPS 1987/89 respondents aged 22 years, deemed to have been at risk in the housing market on criteria which are discussed below (see also Jones and Stevens 1993; Jones 1995b for further information). Table 7.2 draws on all the quantitative survey data; Table 7.3 on the Homeless Survey alone; while the quotations below come from the SYPS follow-up interviews.

Are the homeless a distinct group?

Just as commentators on the Right tend to emphasise deviancy as a characteristic of homeless young people, so those on the Left emphasise their normality. The SYPS national survey contained eighty-six 19-year-olds who had experienced homelessness since leaving their parental homes – this is 6 per cent of all those who had left their parental homes by the age of 19 years. Table 7.2 compares the characteristics of this group and of respondents to the Homeless Survey with those of a nationally representative sample of 19-year-olds in the SYPS. In comparison with the national SYPS sample (shown in the centre column), both homeless samples appear to have experienced problems from an early age, in their family and school life, before leaving school and home. They were less likely to leave school with qualifications, and more likely to have truanted. They came from larger families, often where there had been family breakdown, and where their parents were more likely to be unemployed. Their experience of training schemes appears to have been negative, since a higher proportion did not finish their schemes and became unemployed afterwards. Many more were currently unemployed, and a higher proportion were currently pregnant or had children of their own. A higher propor-tion left home because of family conflict. Despite becoming homeless, only a small proportion of respondents to the Homeless Survey had returned home to live again, though a higher proportion of ex-homeless in the SYPS had done so. Both homeless samples were also less likely to have received financial help from their parents in the preceding twelve months.

Table 7.2 Comparing SYPS 1991 respondents who had experienced homelessness (3) with all SYPS respondents (2) and with respondents to the Homeless Survey (1)

	1 *Homeless Survey*	2 *SYPS 1989/91*	3 *Homeless in SYPS 1991*
No. of cases	183	4,019	86
Age range	16–22	19¼	19¼
General (% of total)			
Sex male	43	48	41
Living with partner	2	6	26
Has child (or pregnant)	13	6	34
Education			
Median age left school	16.00	16.92	16.17
No qualifications	22	2	6
Truanted (day or more)	63	15	40
Any post-school course	65	69	58
Jobs and training schemes			
Ever done YT	70	31	49
Finished scheme	20	51	18
Unemployed after YT	54	15	36
Currently employed f/t	8	50	26
Currently unemployed	56	9	30
Job opportunities seen as 'below average'	44	30	58
Family background			
Three or more sibs	63	24	42
Both parents at 16 years	29	82	61
Step-parent at 16 years	13	4	14
Mother in f/t employment now	26	36	34
Father in f/t employment now	43	66	49
Parental help with money	32	56	44
Leaving home			
Left home by 19 years	94	39	100
Left home because problems	70	12	56
Ever returned home for 6 months	12	29	37

It seems clear from the table that young people with these characteristics are more likely to become homeless than those without them,
and that risks (and perhaps also opportunities for risk avoidance,
which might include family support and returning home) are thus
not shared. There are structural inequalities affecting access to
housing and risk of homelessness, but this analysis also indicates
that the processes of social exclusion (or indeed underclass production) may have begun early in life, and may include factors to do
with family relationships (see also Kiernan 1992).

Among those in the Homeless Survey, 60 per cent had left home
because of family conflict, one-third had been in care since the age
of fourteen, and one-quarter had a step-parent at the time of interview. Other research has reported similar findings (Ainley 1991;
Hutson and Liddiard 1994; MORI 1991). There is clearly a relationship between earlier experience of difficult family life, and later
experience of homelessness. This is not surprising in a current
policy climate which shifts responsibility from the state on to the

Table 7.3 Housing and homelessness careers

Type of accommodation	Percentage of sample base									
	1st	2nd	3rd	4th	5th	6th	7th	8th	9th	10th
Parental – owned or rented	2	12	6	8	5	11	8	7	6	7
Other – owned or rented	37	26	22	22	16	23	17	23	12	7
Bedsitter, student or nurses' hostel	6	5	3	3	1	3	2	2	6	4
Institution – prison or hospital	2	1	2	3	–	2	2	7	6	7
Homeless (including hostels)	26	47	52	51	64	56	62	58	67	70
Other	9	8	14	13	14	5	9	2	3	4
ALL (=100%)	230	193	161	107	80	64	52	43	33	27

Source: Homeless Survey 1992

family, and thus highlights family dysfunction. Family relationships can affect the timing and manner of leaving home, the possibility of returning, and the availability of essential financial support (Jones 1995a and b). My argument is thus that family factors (current family structure reflecting both current and past family relationships) can both increase the risk of homelessness and decrease opportunities for risk avoidance. The family factors themselves, however, can also be outcomes of antecedent structural inequalities: family breakdown is associated with unemployment, and family conflict may be exacerbated by poor housing, for example. This argument thus runs counter to that of Murray and his followers who blame absent fathers or working mothers for family dysfunction without recognising the socio-structural context (Dennis and Erdos 1992; Murray 1990, 1994).

Table 7.3 draws on the Homeless Survey 1992, and shows how the processes continue into housing and homelessness careers. Respondents described their different housing situations over time, giving a maximum of ten addresses. The higher the number of addresses, the lower the sample base, since some people had only relatively recently become homeless and thus had few addresses. The more addresses someone who is currently homeless has had, the more likely they are to have been homeless for longer and to be in accommodation for homeless people or in institutions, and the less likely are their housing careers to involve returns to parental homes. Though returning home might be a means of preventing homelessness for some young people, for many it provides only a short-term strategy. Some homeless young people had returned home several times, only to become homeless again on each occasion.

The upshot, however, is that without successful intervention, long-term careers of homelessness can develop. It seems that there is greater homogeneity in this group of longer-term homeless. More research is needed on housing and homelessness careers to understand how some young homeless people gain a secure foothold on the housing ladder, and the processes which may lead to others remaining excluded.

Are their actions governed by economic rationality?

I suggested earlier that Murray's argument assumes a model of economic rationality: that people act in response to financial incentives and disincentives. Conservative government policy to combat homelessness in the late 1980s and early 1990s was based on this assumption, and indeed assumed that the restriction of opportunities for independent incomes in youth, and the withdrawal of most state support for setting up home would act as disincentives to leave the parental home. The aim was to reduce housing demand rather than increase housing supply. Thus, young people who leave home when they cannot afford to do so are acting in a deviant way, making unreasonable demands on the housing market, and are responsible for the consequences of their leaving home, including their housing problems. Young people are expected to support their own transition to adulthood, through their incomes. When these are not sufficient, they should defer their transition to independent housing, or obtain subsidies from their parents. State support should not be providing this subsidy. At least, this is the argument of the Right.

Support for the transition to adult independence would appear to depend on social recognition that a young person is deserving of support. A normative model of leaving home has developed, which attaches social legitimation to some types of behaviour but not to others (Jones 1995a; Burton et al. 1989). This is a social construction, of course, subject to historical and cultural variation. Before social support (including economic help) is going to be available to young people, they nevertheless have to show that their behaviour has the necessary social legitimation (i.e. that they are 'deserving' of support, either from their parents or from the state). By giving legitimation to some forms of behaviour and denying it to others, a normative model of leaving home is developed. Those not complying are seen as deviant and undeserving. This deviancy labelling thus has a practical outcome in terms of justifying the withdrawal of support. The only problem, intellectually, is that the concept of a normative pattern of leaving home is very suspect.

Patterns of leaving home respond to changes in education, the labour market, the housing market and the rest of the social world, and they vary between social groups. While the expectation may be that the extension of education or training will result in young people remaining in the parental home, there may be many reasons why it has the opposite effect, encouraging young people to leave home earlier, especially where no local courses are available. Nevertheless, the risk of homelessness among young people increases among those who leave home for 'problem' reasons, and at an age which appears to be regarded at 'premature'. Table 7.4

clearly shows that young people leaving home for 'traditional' reasons likely to gain social legitimation (to marry, to take up a job, or to study) run only a small risk of becoming homeless, while those leaving home for reasons associated with economic or social problems (to look for work or because of family rows) are far more likely to become homeless, especially if they leave home before the age of 18 years. In practice, 25 per cent of those who left home below the age of 18 years, and for 'problem' reasons, became homeless. I would suggest that this discrepancy is because of the lack of either formal or informal support structures, from the state or their families, for young people leaving home 'the wrong way' or at 'the wrong age'.

It was probably not economically rational for the under-18s shown in Table 7.4 to leave home when they did, but economic rationality may not have been their primary consideration. Let us consider several sets of circumstances. First, family breakdown and reconstitution can affect young people's behaviour and that of their parents or step-parents towards them: young people living with step-parents tend to leave home earlier than those with both natural parents or than those living with a lone parent; they are more likely to leave home because of family rows; they are less likely to receive economic support from their parents towards setting up a home of their own (Jones 1995b); and they are over-represented in the

Table 7.4 Experience of homelessness by reason for leaving home and age at leaving

	Proportion in each group who became homeless (%)		
Reason for leaving	Left at 16–17	Left at 18–19	ALL
'Traditional'	2	2	2
'Problem'	25	19	23
Independence	11	3	6
Other	10	5	7
ALL (N=86)	7	4	5

Source: Scottish Young People's Survey 1989/91

homeless population.[3] Second, young people leaving local authority care are unlikely to be able to choose the optimum timing for leaving their care situations, and in many cases may lack after-care support, and so it is no surprise that around one-third of homeless young people have been in care since the age of 14 years (Jones 1995a; see also Chapter 6). Finally, a less visible group are young people from rural areas who leave home because there are no jobs or courses in their home areas: young people from the remote rural areas of Scotland, for example, are twice as likely as those from the towns to have left their parental homes by the age of 19 years (Jones 1995a, and current work), but they are subject to the same housing and financial problems when they migrate to the towns as other young home-leavers. We do not know what proportion of urban homeless young people originate from rural areas, though rural homelessness is increasingly becoming recognised as a social problem. There are no doubt other examples, but, in these cases, economic rationality is unlikely to play a major part in their deci-sion-making – at least, not at the time.

Retrospective justification

The SYPS case study interviews with 22-year-olds who left home in their teens throw further light on the relationship between social legitimation, rationality and risk. The case studies were chosen on the basis that the respondents had left home by the age of 19 years for reasons other than to study, and thus had a housing need, but might also have had a problem accessing family support because they were leaving families where there had been unemployment or marital breakdown (the criteria are described in full in Jones and Stevens (1993)). These respondents were thus selected on the basis of potential risk in the housing market, and it transpired from the subsequent interviews that one-third had indeed experienced home-lessness, indicating that the selection criteria held some validity as indicators of risk. The aim of the interviews was to understand how some of those at risk of homelessness may have been able to employ strategies to prevent it.

The following analysis shows that young people appear to have internalised normative models of leaving home. It explores first how young people retrospectively apply models of normative behaviour, based on rationality, and seek to justify their own earlier actions in these terms. It then considers the value of risk-taking in youth, the importance of perceived choice in a world of constraints, and the willingness of young people to accept responsibility for their situations, however inappropriate it may be for them to do so.

It is striking from the case study accounts that young people have a sense of right and wrong ways of leaving home and have internalised what they perceive to be normative patterns of behaviour. Some volunteered the information that the first time they left home it had been in the wrong way, and that next time they would 'do it right'. This would involve having an income and a flat to go to, and planning one's departure. Leaving home on the spur of the moment was not seen as the appropriate way to leave, though many of them had done so first time round. Economic rationality was thus applied retrospectively. Terry and Patricia both returned to their parental homes. Terry says that if she left home again she 'would do it right', so she is going to wait a few years until she is ready. 'Doing it right', for Terry, means leaving home in order to 'better' oneself. 'Just moving out' is in her view 'stupid'. After returning home from her first attempt at leaving, Patricia thought: 'I'm going to get a nice job and save up money and get a flat myself and start it all again, and do it the way I should have done it.'

Like many other younger home-leavers and homeless young people, several of the SYPS case study interviewees left home following or during rows with their parents, and may have had nowhere planned to go to. Some had little choice about the way they left home, but were told to leave. Janice describes to the interviewer (LG) the rows with her mother which led her to leave home:

JANICE   When I say arguing, it just wasnae shouting and bawling, it was like battering each other and kicking lumps of each other – that sort of thing. And she just like told me to go and I just wasnae going to stay there wi' her going on like that.

LG   Did you pack your bags and go?

JANICE   I just put everything, all my clothes in like a big bin bag it wis, and I just took that frae place to place.

LG   So you didn't know where you were going when you left?

JANICE   No. I just went to a friend's and stayed there for a while, then just kept kind of moving on.

Giddens (1994) suggests that a distinction should be drawn between choice and decision-making: decision-making involves choice, but not necessarily that of the person making the decision.

Janice may thus have made a decision to leave home, but the choice was structured by her mother. The implication is that the housing demand from young people leaving home cannot be regulated simply by withdrawing the 'incentives' for them to leave, because leaving home is often not a simple matter of economic rationality, though this may be applied in retrospect.

Risk and responsibility

Young people who feel they have no control over their lives may however claim responsibility for their actions in a process of 'creative redefinition' (Breakwell 1986, quoted in Hutson and Liddiard 1994: 137). Giddens (1994) indicates that risk-taking can be seen as a means of bringing the future under control. This further confuses the issue of responsibility. Those who feel power-less may assert themselves through action – for instance, leaving home – even where this involves risk, and thus lay themselves open to criticism from those looking for scapegoats. For some young people, adult independence means emancipation from parental control as well as 'standing on your own two feet' in economic terms, and the two may go hand in hand.

Whatever the risk, young people may leave home as a means of testing, and hopefully proving, their ability to be independent indi-viduals. This is much more than just living independently: it is an assertion of their identity, if it works. By taking risks, some could prove to their parents that they could cope. Thus Terry says that when she left home, her parents were apprehensive, but now they have more faith in her ability to live independently. And asked by his parents if he was sure he was doing the right thing in leaving home when he did, Kevin replied: 'You don't know till you try . . . You just have tae wait and see if it works oot or not.'

It is part of a young person's lack of power and their need to be able to take increasing responsibility for their own lives – an impor-tant aspect of the transition to adult independence – that leads them to take risks. May says that people learn by their mistakes: 'It's just something you've just got to learn by yourself.' Jill says: 'There was no good anybody had sat me down and said, "You're no' ready to leave home", because I was convinced I was.' For Patricia, the opportunity to take risks was equally important:

I wanted just a bit of freedom so that I could make my own choice.

But my choices were getting made for me, so I wanted to say: 'Right. OK, I'll make that decision.' And most of the time it was the wrong decision, and I learned from my mistakes, but if I could make that mistake myself that was fine. *It was my mistake. I made it.*

In other words, their needs to feel responsible for themselves and become emancipated from external control make young people ideal fodder for those who prefer to deny the state's responsibilities and to consider the homeless and jobless as a self-perpetuating and deviant underclass.

CONCLUSION

When moral panics emerge, the focus tends to be on the problems a defined group of people appear to pose for society, rather than on the problems society creates for them. Young people are often so defined. They tend, at the best of times, to be presented in political and media rhetoric according to a series of stereotypes, almost entirely negative ones. This seems to occur whenever young people become publicly visible. Stan Cohen's (1973: 204) analysis of the Mods and Rockers phenomenon of the mid-1960s contained the prediction:

More moral panics will be generated and other, as yet nameless, folk devils will be created. This is not because such developments have an inexorable inner logic, but because our society as presently structured will continue to generate problems for some of its members – like working class adolescents – and then condemn whatever solution these groups find.

Moral panics are irrational but they serve a purpose. The rhetoric stressing the need for a return to 'traditional values' is difficult to debate. Cohen (1973) suggested that deviancy is defined and deviants scapegoated in order to 'clarify normative contours'. Walker (1990) suggests that the poor are perceived to be poor because they do not conform to prevailing social values. There seems currently to be a great deal of uncertainty about what the prevailing social values are, and calls on tradition appear to be a vain attempt to define them. As Giddens (1994) has indicated, in the modern world 'tradition' defies logic, requires no defence, discourages dialogue, and is invented for the purpose of power. This may be why the individualist model of the underclass is difficult to engage with intellectually either in general or with regard to homelessness.

I have concentrated here on the tension between individualist and structuralist explanations of the underclass in relation to youth homelessness. I have not engaged with the moral aspects of the underclass thesis as identified by Murray, and I have not discussed the possibility of a criminal underclass among the homeless. The analysis has suggested that in addition to structural factors causing systematic disadvantage, experience in the family is important, and the effects of family conflict and breakdown should not be ignored. Structural inequalities appear to increase the risk of homelessness, family factors exacerbate this risk, and in seeking to cope with these constraints, young people's own actions may compound the problem. This is not to suggest that they could have acted otherwise. It is a long way from saying that young people are homeless because they want to be, but it is also a long way from suggesting that the cause of homelessness lies solely in the lack of housing.

Young people may need state support, not only to live in their families of origin, but also to leave them. There still appears to be no political recognition of the fact that positive support for the transition to adulthood could benefit society as well as individuals. By emphasising negative stereotypes of young people, we are in danger of forgetting the positives. When asked what would make their lives better in the future, most of the homeless young people who were surveyed replied that they wanted not just a home, but a job and a family. This does not sound a very deviant response to me.

NOTES

1   The project was undertaken by the author at the Centre for Educational Sociology, University of Edinburgh, in conjunction with the Scottish Council for Single Homeless. All the interviews were conducted by Linda Gilliland (LG).
2   The Joseph Rowntree Foundation supported this project as part of its programme of research and innovative development projects, which it hopes will be of value to policy makers and practitioners. The facts presented and the views expressed in this report, however, are those of the author and not necessarily those of the Foundation.
3   Though Table 7.2 showed that 13 per cent of those in the Homeless Survey, ranging in age from 16 to 23 years, had a step-parent at the age of 16 years, 25 per cent had a step-parent at the time of the survey in 1992.

Chapter 8

'Destructing a giro'
A critical and ethnographic study of the youth 'underclass'

Shane J. Blackman

INTRODUCTION

The central aims of this chapter are to present an ethnographic and theoretical understanding of young people between 17 and 25 years of age who are homeless and unemployed. The study will put forward qualitative descriptions which I hope show that the homeless young do not represent an 'underclass'. The chapter places an insistence on lived meanings which demonstrate that those young people who have been branded as a deviant 'underclass' by the New Right, engage in rational cultural and economic activities which counter the idea of an emergent underclass. The account also details the self-destruction, violence and lack of opportunity which the young homeless encounter and assesses their strategies to bring about a resolution. The rationale behind their actions is similar to that of mainstream society although it needs to be understood as part of a socially and economically marginalised culture (Matza 1969).

In this chapter I am seeking to apply a qualitative interpretation which demonstrates empathy with respondents who have been dispossessed, and then project 'ethnographic authority' in their accounts to challenge the legitimacy of the notion of a deviant 'underclass' (Wellman 1994: 578). Thus the aim is to use ethnographic data and analysis to present a critique of the New Right theory of an 'underclass' as lacking both evidence and explanatory power (Murray 1990). I shall argue that the term 'underclass' for the New Right is used as a means to heighten social fears and promote the idea of an 'Other' with the aim of ensuring conformity among the working and middle classes.

The data derives from a research evaluation study of an advice and information service for young people called the '108 Project', which was open seven days a week from 4–7 p.m. throughout the summer. It was situated in a seafront arch on the Brighton side of West Pier. Brighton is a seaside town on the south coast of England, which has historical links with British royalty – in particular, Brighton Pavilion and the Prince Regent. It also has a significant gay community, a thriving artistic market – both mainstream and alternative – and a tough criminal reputation, as illustrated in the Graham Greene novel *Brighton Rock*. The research was funded by the Central Drug Prevention Unit, London, and facilitated locally in Brighton by the Youth Service. The majority of the young people at the drop-in centre were males who were single. In the period of my study from March to November in 1992, nearly 100 young people visited the seafront project – of whom 21 per cent were women and 79 per cent men (Blackman 1994). The fact that contact with the informants was made at the drop-in centre has implications in terms of those studied, in that these people were coming to an agency with problems for which they sought a solution.

In general, the young people who came to ask for advice had many problems, so the nature of their enquiries tended to be multiple – for example, relating to alcohol, benefits, drugs, housing, health, rights, mental health, pregnancy, relationships, and so on. These personal problems were intimately bound together with other social, economic and psychological problems. Also, the experience of being homeless brought a greater risk of these young people coming into contact with individuals who misuse drugs and alcohol, or being drawn into criminal subcultures.

From the data gathered on the origins of the young homeless, it is clear that the '108 Project' was visited by many people from further afield than Brighton itself. Overall, most of the homeless young people tended to come from the London region and south-east England, although some came from across the United Kingdom, including Scotland, the north of England and the Midlands. The total number of registered contacts at the '108 Project' was ninety-seven, not including return visits. Many informants visited the '108' only once or twice, but there also developed a regular group, who frequently used the service for advice, company and fun. The ethnographic data is largely focused on this core group of twenty-two individuals.

To carry out the research, I used a method of urban ethnography derived from the Chicago School (Palmer 1928). As the study proceeded, my research role expanded to also include that of action researcher, drinking partner, friend, colleague and football player. In terms of techniques, I found that the conventional social research interview was an impossibility with the individuals in the study due to their suspicion of such forms of enquiry. The main research instrument was the field diary – a method I had previously used in my ethnographic research on schools, youth training, equal opportunities, workplaces, youth cultures, illicit drugs and the police, as well as youth homelessness (Blackman 1995).

This qualitative case study of homeless young people seeks to document and assess their cultural and social lives while they were unemployed and without secure accommodation. The ethnographic material will be presented as a series of narratives described as a culture of survival. I will also give an account of homeless young people's struggle to achieve responsibility and a resolution to their condition. The final section will offer a theoretical elaboration of the potential of ethnography to construct a culture and offer authority. It is argued that the term 'underclass' is ambiguous and specifically operates as a set of ideological beliefs which promote hegemonic control of subordinate social classes.

NARRATIVES OF A CULTURE OF SURVIVAL

Here, I want to sketch out a few features of what could be described as a culture of survival through a series of narratives. These descriptions derive from immersion in the data through reading the field diaries in detail. On this basis, it was possible to use the explanations of experiences given by homeless young people and attempt to generate a series of first-order descriptions which could lead to a more analytical account of their situation. The young people were not a homogeneous group; there were significant differences between each person's story of their situation. The narratives are told in their terms and allow a view into a personal and subjective world where opportunity has been stripped bare. This intimate data gives an insight into the real experiences and daily lives of young people whom some would undoubtedly characterise as an 'underclass'.

'Fear of the fall'

A large number of young people who visited the drop-in centre shared a mental and physical condition which can be described as the 'fear of the fall'. The exact meaning of this idea of a 'fall'

risking more, when their own experience of being told they are a failure led them to conclude that the outcome would be defeat. These individuals have already fallen perhaps twice or three times before. They share a condition of having lost social attributes such as a role or identity. The 'fear of the fall' amongst homeless young people represents a socially shared decline in life.

All the young homeless had a personal story to tell. The narrative told was often dramatic, depressing and sometimes horrific (Beauchamp 1989). Stories often appeared to lack a defined time-frame. Stories related to the past, for example, childhood, or the present, such as last week. When Jon, Barry, Julie and others told me their personal story of decline, I knew it related to the past, although from the narrator's point of view the spoken story was told in the manner of its current impact upon thought and behaviour. The format to each narrative followed a general pattern, and in most cases the meaning of the story was that the young person declined into a state of non-action where the narrative itself could become a self-fulfilling prophecy. In the telling of the ritual narrative, the young people explained an experience (or series of experiences), as a consequence of which they came to their present situation. In very many cases, the person told of how they had been abused, raped, exploited, violently shocked, or experienced bereavement, betrayal or rejection. Sometimes, the story was a cumulative narrative where the incident that had a major effect on them was merely the 'tip of an iceberg' of previous injustices with which they had been struggling. In each case, the time or date of the specific experience was of less relevance than its influence and the way in which it had marked their consciousness and become part of a daily identity and self-questioning problem. However, it would be incorrect to assume that the projection of hopelessness often put forward by homeless young people is their only belief. The latter part of this chapter discusses a range of activities and resolutions informants undertook to change their situation.

The body as the last item of personal capital

Some homeless young people were presented with the opportunity of undertaking work in the informal economy, or work in the illegal economy including drug dealing and prostitution (female and male). Some of the younger homeless people had tried the option of so-called 'easy money' to be made from prostitution or drug dealing, but such actions were not generally part of an organised activity and seemed more related to an individual's immediate economic circumstances. Colin, a 23-year-old, said:

> When I lost my full time job I started doing some dealing. Well, I was making a good earning selling speed. There was a lot of mixing and fixing. But my problem was that I began snorting too much and using alcohol. Things got a bit confused, there were some bad deals and bad feelings. I had to stop. I'm still drinking though.

Perhaps one of the most contradictory elements of the young people's behaviour was their attitude towards their own bodies. In many cases, young people's options in life had been so severely reduced that the last resource left to them was the personal capital of the body. This did not mean that they immediately sold this item for cash when they could, although I found both females and males who had taken that option. Selling the body for sexual purposes meant that the body was merely a mechanism to obtain money. Some young people saw their relationship to the body as going beyond mere collateral, it became their last resource. This was shown through tattoos both professional and amateur, and forms of body piercing. Here, the body is seen as a haven where strength exists because it is the last thing over which they can exercise control or choice. In addition, young people were using their bodies as their final resource of pleasure, to be exploited as the last thing that is available to them which is free. Their situation of being homeless, however, had a severe impact on most activities which offered bodily pleasure because of their lack of control over their own environment. Carol, 22 years old, specifies the problems she encountered:

> At the place where I live, this woman died last week. The other night we had about fifteen people round all getting out of their trees. What am I supposed to do? I hate it there. But there's nowhere to go. Most people I know take drugs, some take a few, they're the ones I get on with. I don't see any problem in that. Others take a lot all the time. Everything becomes drug-related and I'm drowning. This drop-in is the only real bit of sanity round here, but it isn't enough because I'm surrounded by it all the time.

Bombarding the body with a variety of different substances frequently went beyond pleasure for a number of the people in the study. In some cases, they could be seen as gaining pleasure by extending the body to its limits; in other cases, such experiences were achieved at the cost of self-inflicted injury. In extreme cases, this led to self-abuse and is also related to the wider question of being abused as an infant, child or adolescent.

Another avenue for seeking pleasure was sexual activity. Again, the experience of homelessness, the absence of a private space, and the nature of the young people's interactions had negative implications with respect to their actual experience of sexual relationships. Many young males experienced sexual relations with considerable difficulty and expressed disgust towards themselves after having slept with a woman (Holland, Ramazanoglu and Sharpe 1993). Both Gary and Dave had 'girlfriends' but spent little time with them except for occasional sex, but even here they expressed problems about receiving and giving sexual pleasure. Gary, a 19-year-old, said:

> I don't know why I go with her, because people say everybody's shagged her. But I love her. And Dave keeps telling me he's been shagging her as well. I hate him but he's my best mate.

Many of the young men interviewed had hostile attitudes to women who were sexually available, conveyed through derogatory labels (such as 'slag'). In seeking pleasure through sex they wanted a private bodily experience which was within their control, but they often presented a very contradictory understanding of relationships derived from hostility towards, or fear of, women. In this context, the young people can be seen as experiencing homelessness as a constraint on their options and as having a negative impact on their attempts to gain pleasure from the one resource available to them – the body.

Dull days

A central preoccupation for all young people in this study was how to fill the day. Being unemployed and homeless constantly meant that they had, in the forefront of their minds, their personal feelings about who and what they were. As a consequence of this, they spent a considerable time at the start of each day questioning their failures, as these problems constituted their everyday reality. In this sense, individuals faced the daily routine of having to deal with their own identity in a very self-conscious, reflexive manner. The young people frequently commented that passing the time can become 'very boring when you know that there is nothing to do'. It was found that they generally had a geographical route around the town. This route had a number of small individual variations but began at the day centre for breakfast and then dinner, followed by wandering around, visiting the drop-in centre, followed by the soup run, then going to one of the hostels to watch some television, wandering around again, going to the pier (where some might sleep) or returning to the bed-and-breakfast. Their options were few without money.

At other times, young people had a full day which was composed of visiting a number of different agencies in order to deal with prescriptions, housing benefit, solicitors, the benefit office, hospital or the unemployed centre. Each of these visits cost money and took considerable time given their reliance upon public transport. Where the young people were unable to meet these formal arrangements because of delays, their inability to get to 'where you should be' further reduced their self-esteem, because for them it reinforced their unreliability in their own eyes.

In some cases, the difficulties of how to fill the day were compounded by low levels of concentration, where individuals were easily distracted from their purpose. One of the clearest causal indicators of this problem was a belief instilled into young people by teachers, social workers or other agents of socialisation that they were 'unintelligent'. Here, low self-esteem meets low expectation which brings about enduring self-labelling of personal under-achievement. Young people felt no joy in recognising that they were unable to meet people's expectations of them; it simply made them feel more empty, or as Gill, 18 years old, explains:

> You know your body is alive physically because you have got to walk from place to place, but as you do this it's almost as though you've died in the mind. There's nothing in there at all. This is the problem of being deprived and on the dole. You suffer from boredom.

The problem of boredom was theorised by Corrigan (1976) in terms of 'doing nothing', which was seen by him to be full of incident and constantly informed by 'weird ideas'. However, from the young people's perspective, doing nothing was not conceived of as 'the simple but absorbing activity of passing the time' (ibid.: 103): it meant only boredom. For Corrigan, the two main components of 'doing nothing' are vandalism and fighting, which he goes on to suggest 'don't carry too many risks' (ibid.: 104). Therefore, 'doing nothing' could lead to excitement on the street where something might happen, but for these young homeless 'something happening' usually meant that they were attacked and beaten-up. Attacking homeless young people was reportedly seen as a sport by sections of Brighton's night-club scene, who would play 'kick the beggar' or 'piss on the beggar'. This was not a rare occurrence, but was part of everyday existence for the homeless. As Martin, a 24-year-old, puts it:

> Nobody speaks to us except those who are like us or you lot who know us. We don't have contact with any others. It becomes lonely. We can't speak to others because they think we're the lowest of the low. If we do you've got to be real careful, it can easily get out of hand and you end up taking a beatin'.

Violence, whether symbolic or actual, is a common experience amongst the young people observed.

Living on the margin

In Brighton, a number of the young people sold the *Big Issue* maga-zine as their means of survival. It is a magazine which homeless people buy for 35 pence and then sell for 80 pence and keep the difference. For these young people, selling the paper had the effect of providing opportunity for brief conversation with those who bought it. It also served as a marker of status, giving them recogni-tion and frequently drawing statements of sympathy or support. On one occasion, Pete, 25 years old, said: 'This bloke who bought a copy of the *Big Issue* the other day said that I was a member of the underclass.' Although all young people accepted that they were living on the margins of society – asserting that 'nobody cares for us' – they did not like to be labelled as members of the 'underclass'. This topic was discussed by all the young people who thought it was derogatory; overall they preferred to be described as homeless or unemployed. The common identity of marginality, born out of elements of shared experience, brought them together. This relation also functioned to make young people highly sensitive to negative or critical attitudes towards them such as the labelling of them as members of an underclass; some of the young people said they felt they were persecuted.

Individuals had three differing strategies when dealing with their social marginalisation: first, *attention seeking* – they demanded that their problem should receive resolution by presenting themselves as a helpless case that still had to be solved; second, *passivity* – rather than demonstrate that they were experiencing discrimination, young people sometimes lapsed into inactivity or attempted to hand their problem over to others and resigned themselves from taking responsibility for their own situation; third, *exaggerated action* – this was attempted by individuals seeking to prevent further exploitation. This took the form of a series of uncoordinated or spontaneous actions, such as 'going out' in the day or evening – where an individual, without guidance, seeks resolution to their particular personal decline, which sometimes ended up reinforcing the young peoples' own problems, for example, through violence or abuse.

According to informants one basic feature of life when living on the margin of society is that 'you have nothing to lose'. Given this principle as the benchmark of personal social action, I found that in extreme cases this leads to a zero-option being seen as an opportunity. In other words, some young men viewed a prison sentence, for instance, not as something negative, but positively, as somewhere to be for the winter, with regular food, warmth and communication. At other times, resignation and defiance could be derived from the same individual within the same conversation when talking over these matters. However, this did not mean that such individuals were stupid or unintelligent, merely that differing contradictory pressures had affected them and this often resulted in them adopting different and sometimes contradictory strategies to deal with their social marginalisation.

'Destructing a giro'

A giro is the fortnightly state unemployment benefit cheque. The term 'destructing a giro' was used by informants to summarise their experience. For some, 'destructing a giro' was a moment of celebration. It was an action of joy where the main aim was to get 'wrecked'. The means by which a giro is 'destructed' is through the purchase of alcoholic drink and/or illegal drug substances. This usually meant that the young people were not seen on the streets for a day or more. There was a regular pattern of events leading up to, and on, giro day; during the former, it was a case of coping with being dry (having no access to alcohol) and how this influenced behaviour and, on the latter, it was a preoccupation with 'getting out of it'. Time was spent arranging, collecting and then using the drugs or, in the case of alcohol, a lot of time was spent either drinking in a public house/on the street or else more intensive drinking was undertaken 'at home'. Certain young people found it possible to 'destruct a giro' within hours and certainly within a day. Others were able to 'spread' the giro over a longer period; this meant that not quite so much frustration is experienced on the days leading up to the arrival of the next giro. Much sharing can take place at such times and the youths were never overly possessive about their money even though their financial resources were very small.

The act of 'destructing a giro' meant that informants became able to take part in more everyday aspects of social life through intentional consumption. This gave integrity and choice, where none existed before. It gave personal pride simply to buy a drink for a friend. In this sense, it gave a feeling of well-being in a situation where there was little hope. Drink was the major stimulant used by all the young people. It was also used in combination with drugs, mainly cannabis. Some had taken 'hard' drugs in the past, but in general they had not returned to this type of drug use.

What marks out the 'destruction of a giro' as something notable is the level of intensity with which pleasure is sought. On reflection, some thought that the end result did not often resemble the satisfaction normally associated with pleasure. Young people recounted experiences of waking up to find that they had been beaten-up, or were in hospital, their money all spent or stolen, that they had been raped or that the few possessions they owned had been taken. Therefore, it was recognised that a high degree of danger was also experienced in the 'destruction of a giro'. The main features of this danger were potential mental and physical health problems. This dilemma is accurately described by Richard, 24 years old:

When I see young people drinking on the street I say, 'That's me'. Looking a complete wreck, it's awful. The problem is I still do it now, but not so much, I tend to drink indoors. And the people you knock about with, they all do the same, nobody has an alternative. That's what we all do, so we all do it. You can't get a sensible word out of them because they all talk a lot of fucking shit, you know what I mean. And I should know because I've done it myself. I'm the same. Their minds have gone. When you're into all that that stuff.

It would not be an exaggeration to state that many young people felt shame and guilt about their anti-social drug- and alcohol-related behaviour, but due to their more public profile of being on the street, the young homeless thought that they were an easy target for social criticism. They were quick to condemn their own behaviour, but sometimes they seemed merely to repeat previous judgements that were made of them by professionals, even though young people claimed that these professionals 'knew little about them'. The irony here is that such views give an impression of the young people being unfamiliar with themselves. This could be a marker of personal estrangement. The continuous bombardment of the body and mind through activities allowed by the 'destruction of a giro' begins to influence the mind, causing young people to begin to lose track of time. Steve, 20 years old, remarked:

> I was down the day centre the other day, and what I thought was that I'd been down here for about five weeks but, in fact, I have been coming here for well over a year.

Andy, a 23-year-old, expressed a similar feeling:

> This bed-and-breakfast I'm in is really bad. Yesterday, I thought right, I've been trying to get a job and move out of this hole, and I thought it was about nine months I've lived here. But then I realised it's been over two years. It's been gradually grinding me down. Down, I've almost lost my soul.

During informal conversations some informants said that they were not receiving the help they needed from any of the services offered them. For some, this led them to believe that they were in the early stages of going mad. In some circumstances, this meant that intensifying the way they 'destructed the giro' was the only means they had of communicating to themselves that they were not mad, since this was one of the few self-directed actions over which they exercised control. However, at the same time, this brought with it the effect of making them doubt their mental stability due to the stressful consequences induced by their actions. I want to point out here that 'destructing a giro' is the only avenue for autonomy, control and expression which leads to behaviour being read as anti-social and violent by those who promote the notion of an 'underclass'.

The impact of 'destructing the giro' brought major time disorientation problems for individuals, and, more significantly, served to reinforce their feelings of social and economic dislocation, as they were cut free from the time discipline of the workplace or even their own more standard everyday routine. The effect of these different strategies of survival is that it causes greater problems for homeless people in moving back to a mainstream lifestyle, which is, at the same time, their primary ambition. A common phrase used among the young homeless was: 'I am thinking about putting down roots.' Such ideals suggest that these young people, although currently displaced, share an adherence to aspirations common to the wider public.

Independence and resolution

A central criticism often aimed at these young homeless people was their perceived inability to do things, because of their lack of motivation. Here, I will focus on the achievements of a number of individuals in the context of their struggle to become independent. For the young homeless, this process was not consistent or developmental because it was often punctuated by set-backs (the 'fear of the fall'). One of the most positive developments was their success in obtaining a home, or at least more secure housing. Such a move promoted further changes in attitude and, for instance, gave young people greater confidence to use the telephone to respond to job and housing advertisements or to arrange to visit available accommodation. Although it is difficult to prove in quantitative terms, for those young people who moved into more secure accommodation, this change seemed to be accompanied by a degree of improvement in their mental health. This could be shown by less aggressive interactions, and improvements in communication with and support for others.

A number of informants gained different types of employment, including retail shop work and labouring, or undertook voluntary work, or were accepted on to college courses. Labour market opportunities, however, were not straightforward for these young homeless. There was a wealth of employment experience amongst the informants: they had worked as painters, decorators, cleaners, bricklayers, shop assistants, skilled metal workers, taxi drivers, miners, labourers, nurses and nannies. It was certainly not the case, then, that these individuals avoided employment or lacked labour market experience. Nor was it the case that the young people were unwilling to work, but in each case the first decision that had to be made related to how work would affect their benefits, such as income support (Jordan et al. 1992). Work in the informal economy meant that an individual could retain benefit, and that this could be supplemented by real wages.

It is important to note that young people stated that the demand for 'off the cards' work came from employers who insisted that workers agree to be hired on that basis or not at all. It was not the case that they wanted or even had a preference for work in the informal economy, but that was all they were offered (MacDonald 1994). Young people argued they would have preferred to 'go legal', but stated that this was not an option. Most considered a 'proper job' as being worthwhile, even when this meant having to sign off benefits and the likelihood of the work being short term which would mean them having to renegotiate income support (with all the 'hassle') again later. Some expressed a sense of guilt about working and claiming because, as Bill (a 19-year-old) said: 'Although it was a real change to get the brass, and it's exciting doing the dodge, there's nothin' like having a proper job.' These feelings clearly related directly to personal pride and dignity. In other cases, where work was offered 'off the cards', it was declined because, as Ian (aged 20) said: 'it wasn't getting me any further, back to the real world of work'.

CONCLUSION

This chapter argues that there is a gap in our understanding of young people's experiences of being homeless and unemployed. What is most absent from accounts of youth homelessness is a qualitative analysis of individuals' personal experiences. Through this ethnographic case study of homeless youth, it was found that these young people experienced many social difficulties. They were experiencing multiple problems in bleak cultural locations; they experienced what I have called cultural immersion. They had become submerged in a localised subculture with specific strategies for coping with the difficulties of their everyday lives, which ethnography can reveal as understandable elements of a culture of survival.

The issue of cultural immersion relates to an individual's material economic existence. Many of the young people were surrounded by a culture of violence, both in terms of being victims and also being the perpetrators of violence. Due to their economic circumstances, individuals explained that the spaces they inhabit are also the places where there is likely to be more risk of violence. As a result, they found that they continually experienced aggression but this was far from their choosing. I also found that this cultural immersion was played out in terms of other aspects of young people's experiences such as drug taking and excessive alcohol

consumption. Options for young people were very limited. In the
setting in which they lived, alternative realistic and plausible role
models were practically extinct. Under these circumstances – where
individuals have very few chances left and are caught in an
economic and cultural trap – their behaviour was sometimes misin-
terpreted as being irrational. However, the evidence gained from
this study of young people's behaviour suggests that it is more accurate to describe their behaviour as erratic. Actions may be uncertain
and irregular but, with the close knowledge of a young person's
complex problems, the majority of behaviour patterns were understandable and far from irrational.

A central finding of this study was that drug taking and especially excessive alcohol consumption was not part of a pleasurable
lifestyle: drug use was endemic not epidemic (Blackman 1996).
These deviant patterns emerge out of a variety of individual
circumstances and social conditions such as the experience of hopelessness under economic and material poverty. All the young people
observed aspired to become part of the 'normal' society. The
evidence revealed that what they need most are employment and
housing (Hutson and Liddiard 1994). What united these individuals
was not that they rejected society's values, as some versions of the
underclass thesis would suggest, but that they had no stake in
society – they had been separated from participation in society and
shared the stigma of their position.

Using the ethnographic data as a foundation for interpretation, it
was possible to build a series of theoretical descriptions in a dialog-
ical relation between data and theory (Atkinson 1990; Clifford
1986). Thus, the experiences of the different homeless young people
played a dominant role in the elaboration of the theoretical descriptions, rather than the reverse. The manner in which individual
stories and group explanations evolve and are told is from a holistic
and theoretical understanding of that culture, that is, from an inside
view (Geertz 1973; Willis 1982). Where social research focuses on
individuals and groups who are on the margins of society, the
method through which data is collected is often in the form of
biographic details or life histories. This data is often of a highly intimate nature. The researcher is drawn into the lives of the researched
through their human narrative. As Warren (1988) states 'emotions
are evoked in the fieldworker while listening to respondents'
accounts of their own lives' (ibid.: 47). These accounts from fieldwork with homeless young people reflect the respondents' lives, and

the theoretical descriptions which emerge are also partly an identification with the pain they experienced. One strength of ethnographic descriptions is their ability to convey experience from within the subject's perspective and develop theory which is rooted in feeling as a legitimate category to inform writing and analysis. However, significant problems do remain due to the very nature of ethnography, as Stacey (1988: 24) states:

I now perceive that the ethnographic method exposes subjects to far greater danger and exploitation than do more positivist, abstract and 'masculinist' research methods. The greater the intimacy, the apparent mutuality of the researcher/researched relationship, the greater is the danger.

This ethnographic approach gave priority to individuals' experiences offering local memories which revealed knowledge of struggles and encounters with social violence. Sarup (1993) argues that genealogical analysis, as described by Foucault, seeks to examine the 'discredited, the neglected and a whole range of phenomena which have been denied a history' (ibid.: 59). The critical aim of the ethnographic method is to write a 'thick description' which creates the potential to record 'from below'; accounts derived from the disqualified. The political result of critically advancing Foucault's historiography is that although the homeless are denied legitimacy to speak, as they are seen to be a social problem, the qualitative method can project their feelings, honestly and plausibly, to critique the social order. For Foucault (1977), the state organises the social production of deviance as a means to remind the lower strata that they should maintain hostility towards so-called deviants because they embody illegality. Foucault also notes that the accompanying popular cultural discourses of newspapers and novels establish that 'delinquency appears both as very close and quite alien, a perpetual threat to everyday life, but extremely distant in its origins and motives' (ibid.: 286).

The purpose of the term 'underclass' for the New Right is that it serves as an easy means to heighten social fears (Wainwright 1994). The underclass thesis of Murray and associates has a dual role. In the first place, to highlight and explain deviant behaviour as being associated with a particular group of people, most notably a youth underclass, which rejects society's values. This 'underclass' is represented as being 'not like us'. The underclass is constructed in terms of an 'otherness'. They are defined as outside of society and, by definition, as a threat to society (Foucault 1977). The ideological purpose is to exaggerate an artificially constructed difference between an 'underclass' and ordinary working-class people so that the 'underclass' comes to be seen as being outside the boundaries of social responsibility and not meriting the concerns of legitimate society (Bagguley and Mann 1992). In the second place, the 'respectable' working classes are reminded that, unless they conform, they could end up in this same situation. The example of the 'underclass' is used as a weapon to ensure that people are constantly reminded of what they could face, for instance, if they lose their job or become pregnant outside of a stable relationship (Campbell 1993; Dean and Taylor-Gooby 1992). For the New Right, the underclass idea operates to establish a new social division by constructing a class of people as *without* society, so distancing those people from social concern and reinforcing the conformism of those *within* society.

ACKNOWLEDGEMENTS

The research was funded by the Home Office Central Drugs Prevention Unit, London, and this support is gratefully acknowledged. I would like to thank staff at the unit for their advice. In particular, I would like to thank the youth workers and, especially, the young homeless in Brighton who gave me their time. I should also like to thank the editor, Robert MacDonald, for his comments, and Debbie Cox for her critical comments and for reading this document.

Chapter 9

The 'Black Magic Roundabout'
Cyclical transitions, social exclusion and alternative careers

Steve Craine

Round and round and round we spin, there's something evil hems us in.

(Slumshine, *The Black Magic Roundabout*)

INTRODUCTION

This chapter argues that the New Right formulation of the underclass is both empirically deficient and politically malevolent. What follows is based on a review of the relevant research literature and data drawn from my own longitudinal ethnography of youth transitions in a high unemployment inner-city area. I will argue that the alleged formation of a youth underclass constitutes an ideological smokescreen which, to paraphrase C. Wright-Mills, diverts attention from government culpability, presenting 'public issues' of policy failure as 'personal issues' of degeneracy and moral turpitude (Craine and Coles 1995; Macnicol 1987; Walker 1990; Westergaard 1992).[1]

RESPECTABLE FEARS AND MORAL PANICS

They who have put out the people's eyes reproach them of their blindness.

(John Milton)

The New Right version of the youth underclass, caricatured as 'violently criminal bastards who refuse to work' (Mann 1992: 106), continues an Old Right, historical tradition of middle-class fears and moral panics circumscribing the workless youth of the 'dangerous class' (e.g. May 1973; Mungham 1982; Pearson 1983). In the 1970s, an emergent, moral, right-wing intelligentsia led by the so-called 'new realists' (Brewer and Lait 1980) and 'intellectuals for law and order' (Platt and Takagi 1981), contemporaneously extended this tradition to lead a sustained, ideological assault on what was described as the 'permissiveness' of 1960s ideas and institutions (Morgan 1978). The ensuing debates accompanied the repoliticisation of youth policy, public spending, state welfare and crime and punishment in the period leading up to, and beyond, Margaret Thatcher's 1979 General Election success (Davies 1986; Muncie 1984; Pitts 1988). Once again the recipients of state welfare, the 'undeserving poor', were targeted in an unprecedented round of 'scrounger bashing and scrounger phobia' (Golding and Middleton 1982), as were the offspring of the 'contaminating' class (Murray 1989: 27) who were said to constitute a syndrome of 'New Barbarianism': 'a conglomeration of behaviour, speech, appearance and attitudes, a frightening ugliness and hostility . . . a delight in crudity, cruelty and violence' (Morgan 1978: 13).

The mobilisation of moral panics and respectable fears over 'scroungers' and youthful 'barbarians' provided the Radical Right with a method for identifying the legacies of economic hardship and social disadvantage as phenomena produced by those forced to endure them. As a rhetorical smokescreen, such campaigns were linked to 'law and order' issues and served to obfuscate the social and economic consequences of what, in 1983, Dennis Healey described as 'Sado-Monetarism'.

The current manifestations of this theoretical and ideological legacy are allegations of a new underclass, found principally in the work of Charles Murray (see Chapter 1). His views may be understood as a contemporary manifestation of the history of respectable fears and moral panics which have periodically focused on the concept of a 'social problem group'. This concept has been periodically resurrected because of its 'symbolic importance' as part of conservative policy strategy and tends to be invoked and supported by those who wish to diminish collective responsibility for social welfare (Macnicol 1987).

YOUTH RESEARCH: THE SCREAMING SILENCE

Go get the seat of your pants dirty in real research.

(R. E. Park)

Populist theories of a pathologically criminogenic 'social problem group' have gained ground despite the avalanche of youth research produced during the past two decades. In part, the growth in popularity of allegations of a youth underclass may be viewed as a consequence of empirical gaps within the youth research literature.

With the onset of mass youth unemployment in the late 1970s, the predominant focus of youth studies became the transformation of post-16, post-school transitions (see Chapters 2 and 3). Youth research has been unambiguous in documenting the 'long' (Hollands 1990), 'uneasy' (Corbett 1990), 'broken' (Griffin 1986), 'fractured' (Wallace 1987), 'extended' (Furlong 1992), 'ragged' (Wallace 1987) and 'protracted' (Roberts 1987) post-school transitions into the labour market, into adulthood, and, for some, into long-term unemployment, 'non-citizenship' and social exclusion. Within youth research, there have been some preliminary attempts to explore and document the 'coping tactics' and 'survival strategies' of young adults in high unemployment areas (Banks et al. 1984; Macleod 1987; Seabrook 1987; Turner et al. 1985; Ullah 1987). Despite commentaries about a criminal youth underclass Roberts et al. (1982b: 5) identified just three individuals from a sample of 551 'who were not seeking work, having discovered more remunerative (illegal) activities'. On the Isle of Sheppey in the mid-1980s, Wallace (1987: 139) discovered that some of the long-term unemployed had access to the informal economy, but these were a statistical minority. The massive Economic and Social Research Council *16 to 19 Initiative* similarly made only passing reference to routine opportunistic theft associated with trans-generational unemployment (Banks et al. 1992: 85) and some unqualified YTS trainees (Riseborough 1993: 172).

Echoing the screaming silence within youth research, one ethnographic study of youth transitions in 'the recession black spots of the North East', found 'no one whose life was organised around crime as a career, or who had adopted a criminal identity' (Coffield et al. 1986: 149). Yet this study was conducted in the same part of the country where, more recently, youth riots laid waste large areas at Meadow Well (North Shields) and in the Elswick and Scotswood districts of Newcastle.[2] It is the same part of the country where young 'ram-raiders' conducted a protracted struggle for territorial supremacy with the police. In this campaign, the families of at least four policemen were forced to move house as a result of attacks and intimidation, police cars were destroyed in petrol bomb attacks, death-threatening graffiti was painted on police houses, and there were widespread reports of radio-scanners being used to monitor police activity, with lists of police radio frequencies being sold in Tyneside pubs (Bennetto 1991: 2). Moreover, Campbell (1993) has pointed to the irreducible poverty and trans-generational unemployment, sometimes running into three generations, as responsible for the 'big business black economy' and a youthful propensity towards crime on Tyneside. However, within Coffield et al.'s study, reference is made to one of the major reasons why recent ethnographic research has failed to address the issue of law-breaking amongst the young unemployed, namely concerns over the problem of confidentiality:

> Technically undeclared work is illegal too but . . . it was usually their only means of eking out their benefit and of keeping skills and self respect alive. The various jobs on the side which they worked have not been referred to in the main account for reasons of confidentiality, *but a majority had . . . undeclared earnings* [SC's emphasis].

(1986: 53–4)

Thus, although Coffield and his colleagues had access to a significant area of contemporary sociological interest, they chose not to confront this because of the ethical problems involved.

During the early stages of my own research, in a personal communication, David Morgan warned that the 'ethical/confidentiality/political implications and ramifications' involved in researching social and acquisitive criminality amongst the long-term unemployed would be 'formidable'. Similarly, Bob Coles (1986: 6) highlighted the negative ideological consequences of producing unrepresentative ethnographies of the 'glamorous fringe' with the possibility of creating a distorted image of the long-term unemployed, the majority of whom *do not* seek out anti-employment lifestyles and status-systems. Thus, because of the complex nature of the ethical and political issues surrounding ethnographic research with 'powerless groups', recent youth studies have told us virtually nothing about, for example, the burgeoning informal economy (MacDonald 1994; Mattera 1985). Yet, a decade ago, at least one study indicated 'working "on the side" when registered as unemployed is morally condoned to a greater degree than most other illegal economic activity . . . [and] . . . most people out of work will take any "side-jobs" available' (Turner et al. 1985: 487). Moreover, very little has been revealed about factors governing the development of localised illicit 'alternative opportunity structures' or neighbourhood 'alternative enterprise cultures' (Craine 1988; Hobbs 1989). Similarly youth research has added little to our understanding of the processes involved in post-school transitions to 'alternative careers' of petty and/or serious law-breaking (Craine

and Coles 1995; Foster 1990; Robins 1992). Despite the formidable
ethical dilemmas, the study of law-breaking activity in its 'natural
setting' may be justified precisely *because* of the empirical gaps in
the existing literature (Polsky, in Becker 1963: 171 n. 7). Some of the
main methodological difficulties concerned with research on criminality are: most crime remains undetected; only a third of crimes
are reported to the police and therefore recorded; only one in ten
crimes results in prosecution (Barclay 1992). However, by the age of
thirty, one in three young men will have been convicted from a
'standard list' of offences (Home Office 1989). Whilst young adults',
especially young men's, involvement in crime is widespread (Tarling
1993), much of the research that does exist is based on an inherently
'skewed sample studied in non-natural settings' (Polsky 1971: 120).
Whilst there is some interesting work on career-routes into crime,
much of this is based on data derived from 'failed' law-breakers;
those who get caught and incarcerated (Little 1990). In addition to
'sampling bias', such research is also 'too heavily retrospective'
(Polsky 1971: 121).

In the light of debates about the imputed pathology and moral
defectiveness of the so-called youth underclass, this empirical gap
reveals the necessity for detailed exploration of the informal
cultural and subcultural adaptations to the new 'broken' transitions.
In a situation where politicians, senior church and police representatives and media opinion-shapers are, almost daily, prepared to
offer public comment on the issues of unemployment and youth
crime, it seems inexcusable that youth researchers are reluctant to
enter this debate. Evidence suggests that researchers either do not
have access to the relevant data or, when they do, ignore or refuse to
engage with it (e.g. Wallace 1987: 8). Political ramifications are, of
course, difficult to gauge and there is always the danger of lending
academic credence to reactionary ideologies (e.g. Hirsch 1983: 16).
However, theories of an alleged youth underclass have been propagated irrespective of whether or not there are data to sustain them.[3]
Although youth research has clearly laid bare the homogeneous
impact of policy on post-school transitions, little has been revealed
about the heterogeneous *consequences* for the different categories of
'vulnerable youth' most acutely affected (see Chapter 6; Craine and
Coles 1995).

As such there has been only tentative exploration of the policy-
driven processes which underpin, for example, the development of
'alternative careers', or indeed, the 'critical choice points' through

which alternative careers are proactively constructed. It is partly as a consequence of such empirical deficiencies in the contemporary understanding of career transitions – or perhaps in spite of them – that stigmatising populist theories of a homogeneous, criminogenic youth underclass have flourished. The goals of future research should be both to develop a more nuanced understanding of the complex processes of social exclusion for 'vulnerable youth' and, on the basis of such understanding, to establish a more informed youth policy agenda (Coles 1995).

FIELDWORK IN BASILDEANE

What follows is based upon a ten-year research project located in a high unemployment inner-city ward of Manchester that I have called 'Basildeane'.[4] The study was based on a specific cohort of thirty-nine unqualified early leavers (nineteen young men and twenty young women) who left school in 1980. This group was part of a larger group of fifty young people who were originally contacted in the late 1970s as part of a youth and community project. The study group was researched throughout the decade of the 1980s, with five years of intensive fieldwork between 1985 and 1990. Data was collected ethnographically, with the original database, entrée into the field and 'insider-status' derived from my residence in the study area and former employment there as a detached youth worker.

Research methods were participatory and included various forms of interviews (some of which were taped), 'naturalistic' hanging about and observation, and involvement in participants' extended social networks. Accounts were collected about labour market, family and household experiences and involvement in the 'alternative economy' and crime. The study is, therefore, an examination of the main axes of youth careers and also the socio-subcultural response to the experiences of youth transitions, in a disadvantaged inner-city area, during the 'Thatcher decade'.

Throughout the 1980s, Basildeane was an area of chronic long-term unemployment and housing decay: an area blighted by the decline in local manufacturing employment; lack of investment in a poor and decaying stock of local authority housing; and heightened poverty amongst the working-class residents as a consequence of both the recession and the political programmes of the Thatcher period (Edgell and Duke 1991; Manchester City Council 1985, 1986; Peck and Emmerich 1992). Local authority housing predominated and one of the estates, Chicken Lane, became known locally as 'the Jungle'. This was the place in which the majority of long-term unemployed study participants grew up. The families living there were decanted from areas of slum clearance in the first wave of housing developments under the local authority's redevelopment programme. By the 1970s, the estate had developed a stigmatised reputation. Once ensconced, families from the Chicken Lane estate were refused council transfers elsewhere. In short, the estate became a 'dump' for so-called 'problem families'. A careers officer described it as 'full of defaulters, layabouts and thieves'.

TRANSITIONS AND CAREERS

My study sought to examine the three main axes of youth transition, labour market, domestic and housing 'careers' (see Chapter 6), and the ways in which the social and economic environment of inner-city Manchester interfaced with young peoples' 'career choices'. Utilising the concept of 'career' allowed for an examination of the interplay between institutional and structural features – such as the collapse of the local youth labour market and policy interventions in training, housing and welfare – and young adults as active social agents, often responding proactively to structural and institutional developments, rather than being 'propelled' or 'programmed' by them (Roberts 1993: 223).

These are important considerations in terms of the underclass debate. For whilst it is true that some young people in my study actively *chose* to avail themselves of 'alternative opportunity structures' to develop 'alternative careers' in crime, such choices should not, as Murray (1990) has implied, be interpreted as indicative of unconstrained patterns of motivation or 'free choice'. Although choices were made and individual biographies and careers constructed, these were frequently desperate survival adaptations within 'the canopy of structured inequality' (Bates and Riseborough 1993: 2). Structural and institutional constraints, as they impinged upon individual choices, were recognised by study participants – as JW put it: 'No jobs, no money, what fuckin' choice?', or as Jimmy Bee similarly declared: 'Beggars can't be choosers'. However, this is not to imply a crude cultural or materialist determinism; for participants were, indeed, active in the construction of their own history, but not as they pleased, nor under circumstances of their own choosing. As Willis has similarly argued: 'there are choices, but not choices over choices' (1990: 159). Therefore, we must address two important sides of the careers equation and the host of different actors influencing both the opportunity structures available to young people and their choices with regard to them (Craine and Coles 1995).

As well as the three main axes of youth careers, my research also identified three broad patterns of post-school progression. These were 'traditional', 'protracted' and 'cyclical' transitions (Roberts 1987). The first, which involved an atypical minority of three participants, was a *traditional* post-school transition directly to primary employment. These participants also followed complementary, almost stage-like, domestic and housing careers. By their mid-twenties, all three had effected residential independence, marriage and parenthood. A traditional transition to primary employment provided the economic foundation upon which stable, traditional adult roles and statuses were constructed. Fieldwork revealed various factors related to working-class 'respectability' to account for this minority transition. These included: secure housing status; prolonged familial and/or parental employment; parental commitment to employment; and the ability of parents, or family members, to confer labour market advantages through informal workplace contacts. These also translated into an existential 'getting on–getting out' frame of reference (Brown 1987: 105). The traditional transitionaries sought to 'get on' in the labour market and wider society, and to 'get out' of their working-class neighbourhood.

The second pattern involved a slightly larger group, and was a *protracted* transition via combinations of experiences which included: unemployment, underemployment, and a variety of schemes and special programmes. The protracted route served to extend the progression to 'proper jobs' for periods of between four to almost eight years. Domestic and housing careers were similarly elongated, characterised by economic instability and social insecurity. Relationship/family formation was typically extended and complex, delayed by lack of income, marred by residential dependence and, in some cases, characterised by psychological precariousness. Although the protracted transition included participation in various training schemes and special programmes, interspersed with extended bouts of unemployment, this did not result in labour market withdrawal or an erosion of work commitment. Parental influence, family background and residential location gave rise to an existential 'getting in' frame of reference

(Brown 1987: 131). Protracted transitions to typically low-skilled jobs provided the means to 'get in' to the adult working-class world. Most participants who effected a protracted transition came from families residentially situated at the mid-point of the locally defined 'rough–respectable' continuum. Such families contained at least one member who was in full-time employment; these provided role models of work commitment. Work was typically viewed instrumentally as a symbolic marker of adult status and work commitment sustained because of the realisation that the wage provided the means to 'get into' the adult world to enjoy leisure time and courtship patterns.

The third, and by far the most common, pattern involved a *'cyclical'* post-school transition. Cyclical transitions entailed early careers in which participants became trapped on a (not so) merry-go-round of unemployment, government schemes and special programmes, youth jobs, work in the informal economy, more unemployment, more schemes, and so on (MacDonald 1997; Roberts 1987: 17; Roberts and Jung 1995: 183). Described by study participants as the 'Black Magic Roundabout', cyclical transitions have prompted at least one sociologist to raise the question: 'Transition to What?' (Bynner 1987). It is a life-course which has 'cut a swathe through young peoples' landscapes, leaving an open wound filled with broken transitions, massive disillusionment and smouldering resentment' (Chisholm 1990: 42). Generally, this majority transition preceded the slide into long-term unemployment, scheme refusal and labour market withdrawal and rejection. The contexts, components and career consequences of the Black Magic Roundabout are examined in the following sections.

CYCLICAL TRANSITIONS AND GOVERNMENT SCHEMING

Participants who entered youth training schemes generally accessed 'sink schemes' which were completely 'detached' from the labour market (Raffe 1987; Roberts and Parsell 1989). Designed primarily for the unqualified and located at the bottom of the status–quality hierarchy, such schemes came to serve a 'warehousing' function. Participants were provided with various 'training opportunities' on community-based schemes which included: clearing local graveyards; clearing derelict land; renovating a Boy Scouts' hut; cleaning and decorating an old people's home; clearing debris from canals and rebuilding canal walls; demolishing and clearing away redundant boundary walls; tree planting and grass cutting. Generally these schemes were allocated to male study participants under the ironically titled 'Youth Opportunities Programme'. Girls were more likely to be allocated to 'feminised caring work' (Wallace 1987: 24), such as: placements in old persons' homes; pre-school nurseries; office skills and typing workshops; cleaning placements in regional department stores. Trainees complained of inadequate facilities, lack of 'proper' training, pointless 'boring' and repetitive tasks – and of being treated 'like shit', 'like some sort of moron', 'like dirt'. A local folklore developed about the schemes which were pejoratively perceived as being designed for 'space-cadets', 'mongs' (Down's syndrome), and 'fuck-ups'. The most derisory comments were reserved for the 'social and life skills' training components, which were viewed as irrelevant to the requirements of any particular job. For example, JW 'walked out' of one placement after spending three days being taught how to 'answer the bleedin' phone'. According to Bynner, 'inadequate facilities, largely untrained teachers, weak educational structures and low aims, produced an educational outcome that was worth little to most young people involved' (1991: 652). The most common complaint was that 'proper jobs' had failed to follow their participation in the training programmes. The cyclical movement into and out of sink schemes and special programmes produced reactions of outrage and betrayal – 'it was like a bloody circus except we were the clowns' (Tracy).

> So what's the fuckin' choice? . . . Oh yeah do YT fuckin' S [Youth Training Schemes] for buttons, don't be a cunt. Sign on with the sheep . . . 'ands an' knees job forra packet o' straights [cigarettes] . . . fuck it . . . I'd rather do bird [go to jail] . . . [hustling] . . . it's all I know an' it's all I want to know, the rest of it's for cunts.
>
> (Willie)

There was no evidence that multiple scheme participation provided access to employment or compensated for social and educational disadvantage. The thirty-nine young people between them had amassed a total of almost ninety training schemes of different varieties and styles. In terms of the aggregate amount of time, this represented a staggering total of almost sixty years of their lives. In only one case had scheme participation provided access to a proper

job. The disillusionment associated with cyclical transitions preceded
the slide into long-term unemployment and labour market withdrawal. As Maz put it: 'We knew there was nowt down for us. It's
what they were tellin' us right from the off, teachers, probation, my
old man . . . Fuck 'm all, no work, no money, *we knew it was up to us
to get it sorted*'.

THE 'BLACK MAGIC ROUNDABOUT'

Ethnographers of the urban young have noted the relevance of
graffiti and graffiti art in signifying the collective symbolic parameters of both psycho-social and geographical territory for (male)
working-class informal groups (e.g. Coffield 1991; Jenkins 1983).
During the early 1980s, when employed as a detached youth worker
and later, between 1985–1990, when my fieldwork was underway,
walks around my study area would be illuminated by the colour,
humour and vibrancy of the local graffiti artists. One significant
graffiti mural or 'piece' (from masterpiece) was strangely discon-
certing. Sited on a main wall outside the local careers office, it
displayed the familiar characters from the children's television
series, *The Magic Roundabout*, but the faces of the various characters Dylan, Dougal, Zebedee, etc., were grotesquely distorted with
sinister, demonic eyes and embittered scowls, or faces drawn in pain
or anguish. Underneath, in mock-gothic script was emblazoned the
phrase 'Black Magic Roundabout'. The meaning behind the piece
took some time to unravel, but it emerged that it was connected to a
cult amongst the young unemployed of watching day time repeats
of *The Magic Roundabout*. Coggs, one of the young men in my
study group, was not only a leading figure in the small group of
Magic Roundabout devotees, but, it transpired, had also constructed
the piece outside the local careers office. He explained that the
inspiration for the piece also related to a song of the same title by
the local band Slumshine. As Coggs explained:

> It's to do with yer life . . . runnin' round in circles an' gettin'
> nowhere . . . like YOPs an' all the other shit. Watchin' *Magic
> Roundabout* ain't bad . . . see you've stopped runnin' round. It's
> like the 'shine [Slumshine] say it . . . goin' nowhere when you
> think you should be goin' somewhere. That's where the fuckin'
> grief is man . . . goin' round on a fuckin' ride that's goin'
> nowhere . . . That's what the piece is about as well . . . It's in the

fuckin' song [by Slumshine] . . . about an evil spell that makes you blind, fucks you up . . . sends you chasin' yer own arse like the bastards down the careers place.

As a pictorial metaphor for futility and alienation, the Black Magic Roundabout concisely articulated the revolving door of cyclical post-school transitions. Located outside the careers office, here was the setting as far as Coggs was concerned, where illusions were peddled under the guise of careers guidance, or where (un)employment training schemes were offered on the back of youthful desires for 'proper jobs'. The locally generated music and artwork expressed the embittered cynicism of many study participants and reflected their unwillingness to be locked into the cyclical (non)transitions which were available:

> If the government stopped thinkin' we was so fuckin' 'divvy' [stupid], they'd stop tryin' to piss us about . . . I'd rather fuckin' die than go on another [scheme] . . . It gets me steamin' just talkin' about it . . . On my last 'un I was supposed to do carpentry . . . a trade like so I thought yeah, fuck it we'll 'ave a go like . . . within two days I was fuckin' washin' pots an' peelin' fuckin' spuds . . . 'cos they sez they was short . . . [in the canteen] . . . Fuck 'em I'd rather go 'graftin' [thieving] man, at least yer get to 'old yer fuckin' 'ead up . . . Well you can laff . . . would you do it, peelin' 'undreds o' fuckin' spuds, washin' pots? . . . Fuck off I told 'em, put me on t' carpentry or I'm off . . . He said I 'ad the 'wrong attitude' . . . snotty fuckin' git . . . I told 'im to stuff it an' walked out . . . That's it . . . never doin' another . . . end of story . . . nothin' else to say.
>
> (Poolie)

The resentment engendered by such experiences provided a partial explanation for the progressive abandonment of labour market commitment and the proactive development of alternative careers and status systems.

CYCLICAL TRANSITIONS AND LABOUR MARKET WITHDRAWAL

Despite the chimera of increased opportunity through training schemes, throughout the decade it was young people from socially and educationally disadvantaged backgrounds who were most vulnerable to prolonged unemployment (Banks et al. 1992; Furlong 1992). However, as White and McRae (1989) have argued, it would be mistaken to depict long-term unemployed youth as 'an unqualified residue in the labour market', as they have similar social and educational backgrounds to young workers employed in low-skilled occupations. Unemployment is caused by a lack of demand for labour rather than by inadequacies in the labour force: 'Those who are unemployed in a recession are perfectly acceptable to employers when labour demand is high' (Furlong 1992: 87).

Aside from their original residential locations on the estates characterised by persistently high unemployment and from within families at the 'rough' end of the locally defined 'rough–respectable' continuum, those who became long-term unemployed were also characterised by extensive familial unemployment. Of the twenty-five participants who by their mid-twenties had entered apparently permanent unemployment, twenty-two had other family members who were also unemployed. Redundancies during the early part of the recession had left many family income providers unemployed in their forties or fifties, at an age when the potential for acquiring other jobs, or retraining, was vastly diminished. In the case of eight of the long-term unemployed, parental figures were absent due to death, divorce and separation, or long-term imprisonment.

Most of the long-term unemployed abandoned their commitment to 'proper-jobs' and effectively withdrew from the labour market. Labour market withdrawal enabled participants to 'maintain some semblance of a positive identity' and to 'reject the official authorised interpretation of their social situation' (Macleod 1987: 150). As Mick Kent put it: 'D'ya wanna know what my motto is now? Fuck 'em all!'

Cyclical transitions, long-term unemployment and labour market withdrawal had significant consequences for participants' domestic and housing careers. Labour market withdrawal was articulated within distinctly gender-bound domains – the home and the street. Whereas young men typically fell back on an exaggerated version of working-class masculinity and the locally available alternative opportunity structures, women generally retreated into home-based domestic careers. The domestic careers of the eleven long-term unemployed women were circumscribed by a working-class cultural emphasis on a domestic apprenticeship of home-care and child-rearing. Aspirations and opportunities were additionally limited by patriarchal assumptions in the labour market and sexism in scheme allocation procedures. As one local careers officer confessed:

> To be honest there is discrimination in the system [of careers guidance]. We know most of them [unqualified girls] are going to end up pregnant . . . employers also recognise it . . . there's an in-built tendency not to take them quite so seriously.

There was some evidence of resistance within the home in terms of contest over the traditional assignment of domestic tasks and through the solidarity of the 'girls night out'. However, early domestic careers of pregnancy, childrearing and home-caring served, typically, to locate young women in situations of economic and often domestic, subordination. The four exceptions to this general picture were women who had created independent, alternative means of acquiring 'undeclared income' by, in one case, fraud and drug-dealing, in another prostitution, and in two cases by 'working on the side'. But these were the minority. By 1990, nine of the eleven long-term unemployed women were responsible for the care of at least two dependent children, and ten were either cohabiting or married. Four of these young women had originally undertaken lone parenthood in their teenage years. Although most young women did not 'plan' to have children, lone parenthood was less the product of irresponsibility than the result of a fatalistic ethos generated within a context of institutionalised economic and social insecurity. Wallace's research similarly notes that unemployed women 'drift into' parenthood 'for lack of positive alternatives' (1986: 28).

For the unemployed young women in my study, the 'mothering option' provided a socially acceptable alternative to cyclical transitions or long-term unemployment. Paradoxically, of all study participants, the eleven long-term unemployed women were those who had most successfully undertaken early movement towards sustained residential independence. In 1985–6, by which time they had reached their early twenties, ten of the eleven had left home (seven to live in public sector rented accommodation and three in private sector rented accommodation). In part, early residential independence reflected local authority accommodation allocation procedures which favoured couples with dependent children and lone parents: 'I thought 'bout 'n abortion . . . but I knew they'd gimme a [council] flat an' anyway there was nowt else . . . nowt else in me life' (Lynda).

For men, cyclical transitions and labour market withdrawal typically resulted in a retreat into the norms, values and alternative status systems of their peer group subcultures. Participants built on a collective sense of identity constructed out of an exaggerated version of working-class machismo. Group bonding and solidarity ensured that same-sex friendship patterns and affiliations formed the predominant focus for domestic progressions. For six of the long-term unemployed young men, commitment to the generating milieu of their localities and peer groups militated against early residential mobility. Eight of the group, however, sustained early residential independence as a consequence of income derived from 'fiddle' jobs or acquisitive crime. Of all study participants, the long-term unemployed young men displayed the most complex variation in domestic career transitions, but most were generally unsuccessful in sustaining ongoing childrearing relationships. The pressure, insecurity, lack of stable routine, and sometimes danger, associated with alternative careers, militated against commitment and emotional durability in relationships. Continuity in relationships was sometimes broken by conflict with the law and periods of absence spent on remand or in prison.

Although the majority had undertaken childrearing partnerships and fathered one or more children, only three successfully sustained ongoing relationships with their original partners. An exaggerated emphasis on 'hardness', emotional detachment and perceived machismo inhibited the development of a durable intimacy with women. There was a general pattern of absentee parenthood, of visiting their former partners periodically, ostensibly to 'see the kids'. Sometimes these 'visits' would last for several weeks until they were called away by a combination of financial necessity and the demands of 'the street'. Some lived semi-nomadic lives, moving between their own flats, the homes of their friends and current girl-friends, their parents' home and the homes of their former partners. Cyclical residential patterns were fuelled by drug taking and lack of routine associated with detachment from the disciplines of full-time jobs. Such instability was also reflected in the cyclical 'booms and slumps' of their alternative careers.

ALTERNATIVE CAREERS

You shut your mouth, how can you say, I go about things the wrong way.

(The Smiths)

By far the largest group were those who had endured cyclical transitions on the Black Magic Roundabout and who had moved into enduring unemployment. This group came to restrict their social contacts to others in a similar situation. They came to recognise and build on a shared sense of identity and progressively relinquished commitment to the 'orthodox' labour market (e.g. Banks et al. 1984; Macleod 1987). To those for whom employment was perceived as a distant, diminished possibility, alternative careers and status systems were subculturally evolved. Such alternative careers could be divided into three broad stage categories: early careers (including legal, but undeclared, work in the informal economy); intermediate careers; and anti-employment careers.

Early careers were frequently undertaken as 'coping strategies' for economic survival on the minimal provisions of welfare benefits. According to Turner et al.: 'Among the younger generation . . . the only way to cope on Social Security is to develop a new strategy of . . . "cheating" ' (1985: 487). Cheating amongst study participants involved such strategies as minor benefit fraud and various forms of 'off the books', 'fiddle jobs' (MacDonald 1994). Some of the available opportunities were controlled by two notorious 'hard families' (the Hattons and the Donoghues), who operated a range of both licit and illicit economic activities which, over time, came to constitute an 'alternative opportunity structure'. Participants would be recruited by the two families for various tasks, some of which included: market trading; 'barking' (unlicensed street trading known elsewhere as 'fly-pitching'), and 'touting' (selling 'black-market' tickets and ephemera at sporting events and pop concerts). Ten of the unemployed young men had been provided with early 'career apprenticeships' through operating as 'touts' on behalf of the Hatton family. One example of a 'successful' touting 'scam' involved selling unofficial programmes outside the G-Mex Conference and Exhibition Centre in Manchester during an appearance of the famous Olympic ice-skating duo Torvill and Dean. On this occasion, a 'crew' of participants were provided with white cotton 'ice-cream men's coats' and bundles of inferior, poorly printed (unofficial) programmes. The programmes were sold in large numbers for £2 each to unwitting fans by what appeared to be official programme sellers.

As with teams of 'barkers' recruited to conduct unlicensed street trading on behalf of the Donoghue family, the 'touts' would similarly operate as a team, or crew, for 'working the punters' (pop and sports fans outside major venues). Like the 'crews' involved in unlicensed street trading, the 'touts' employed similar methods of protective organisation to ensure a measure of safety in what were essentially illegal street transactions. Thus, when the focus was the retail selling of unofficial sports and pop ephemera, 'touts' would be serviced by 'runners' who supplied the 'touts' with goods held in a vehicle nearby. Like the unlicensed street traders the 'touts' would operate on a commission basis and purchase their next supply of goods, via the 'runner', with the income generated from the initial supply of goods, and so on. Through lifestyles organised around movement into and out of the informal economy, participants were able to derive income, autonomy and status from living off their wits. However such early apprenticeships produced a 'drift' into a semi-legal, marginalised existence: 'This shady world blends imperceptibly into the fully criminal existence' (Gofton and Gofton 1984: 282).

What I have described elsewhere as the 'intermediate range of alternative careers' (Craine 1988) can be grouped under the local terms *totting* and *hustling*. These involved a wide range of non-legitimate enterprise activities including: 'totting from the social' (systematic benefit fraud); buying and selling stolen property; unorganised shoplifting; opportunistic theft; and unorganised drug dealing at street level. For participants who had crossed the boundaries of illegality by 'working on the side' without declaring the income to 'the social', status roles such as 'hustling' represented the increased coalescence of an anti-employment ethos: 'rather than tolerating regular hours for low pay, there can be more status in proving one's ability to get by without surrendering to the system' (Roberts et al. 1982a: 174).

The final stage in the evolving alternative career structure was the development of anti-employment careers, represented in such activities as: *dealing* (the systematic retail of prescribed drugs, often in 'wholesale' quantities); *hoisting* (organised shoplifting); *grafting* (systematic property theft, usually burglary); and *blagging* (robbery and armed robbery). The anti-employment subculture which sustained such activities was characterised by 'an angry and apocalyptic' separation from mainstream norms and values (Willis 1984: 14). Those concerned were generally informed by an ethos which involved not merely the rejection of conformist values, such as work commitment, but an inversion of such values, so that the ability to prosper without recourse to waged employment became a virtue in itself. As Maz put it: 'You're never gonna make big quids if you're out at work all day.' The ability to reap high rewards for the minimum of effort provided status and self-worth within the subcultural milieu: 'A job?! Fuck that! . . . I can make more in a coupla 'ours than my ol' man used to make in a week . . . Fuck workin' (Tex).

Anti-employment careers were not necessarily discrete areas of economic activity and some participants undertook movement between categories as opportunities arose. Thus JW, for example, though primarily involved in a career of semi-legal economic activity with the Donoghue family, on one occasion made extra income through joining Davvo and Summers for a burglary. A cheque book and cheque card obtained from this exercise in 'grafting' provided for a brief flirtation with 'kiting' (forging) the stolen cheques for money and goods. The income obtained from the stolen cheques was invested in the purchase of a quantity of 'draw' (cannabis), which was passed on to the local hustlers for distribution through the informal street networks. The income derived from 'dealing' was then utilised to 'go-halves' in an enterprise with Davvo that involved a stolen vehicle. The income generated from the sale of the 'ringer' (stolen vehicle) was, in turn, invested in the purchase of a quantity of 'snide' (counterfeit) designer-label sports shirts, which were sold, via JW, through genuine retail market outlets, and so on. In contrast to Murray's (1990) notion that benefit payments discourage initiative and encourage welfare dependency, my research indicates that long-term benefit dependence, paradoxically, *promotes* a distorted 'parody' of dominant values (Seabrook 1987: 21) and encourages 'the penny capitalism of the poor' (Cohen 1982: 45). To argue that welfare payments engender passivity is to ignore the fact that benefits are set at a level too low to live on (HMSO 1992; Piachaud 1991). Economic initiative is required simply in order to survive (Edin 1991). However, once embarked upon 'alternative careers' within, for example, the local informal economy, a series of incremental choices were made to access other, progressively more illicit, rungs on the ladder of alternative opportunity.

In part, alternative careers were sponsored, or influenced, by the alternative entrepreneurial activities of the Donoghue and Hatton families. Alternative careers were evolved within a cultural and subcultural landscape of alternative enterprise that was, to some degree, tolerant of acquisitive law-breaking as a domain for economic activity and resistance (Hobbs 1989). Evidence similarly suggests that, despite its illegality, acquisitive 'social crime' has been 'tolerated' for generations and even 'condoned as legitimate' within certain lower working-class communities (Humphries 1981: 151; Lucas 1973). Utilising the skills, organisation and networks that were already in place provided for the 'successful' development of certain careers. Even the drugs trade should not be viewed as a sinister creation set up from outside, but was rather, 'an adaption of long-established trading mechanisms which were already central to the irregular economy' (Parker et al. 1988: 107).

The development of alternative careers occurred within an interconnected and cumulative ecology of disadvantage, which included: stigmatised residential location; (for some) absentee fathers; enduring poverty; trans-generational unemployment; negative policy interventions in housing, benefits and training; plus the cynicism and alienation engendered by post-school labour market experiences. Such factors cannot be overstated. In a social context, where adult 'success' is defined in terms of income and occupation, the young long-term unemployed of Basildeane were faced with considerable handicaps. In attempting the traditional transition to adulthood they were, in objective terms, 'triple failures'. They had 'failed' educationally, 'failed' to secure post-school employment, 'failed' to 'get into' working-class adulthood through employment, even after participation in a succession of government schemes and special programmes. They were frequently viewed as 'failures', or potential failures, by prospective employers and the Careers Service. Some even viewed themselves as having 'failed' (Sennett and Cobb 1977); as Jimmy Bee revealed, a cyclical transition, protracted unemployment and the consequent inability to provide a 'decent start' to married life for his partner and child had left him feeling 'a blown-out nobody'.

The retreat of unemployed young women into home-based domestic careers, via the 'mothering option', and the proactive development of alternative careers and anti-employment subcultures by unemployed young men, together with the erosion of work commitment that these strategies entailed, must be partially understood as attempts to avoid negative, stigmatised social judgements. Such strategies provided contexts within which participants could limit and off set threats to their socio-psychological well-being posed by poverty and their objective labour market positions. Affiliation to the subculture which sustained anti-employment careers for example, not only provided alternative routes to income, but also substitute criteria for defining status, identity and social meaning (Fryer 1986; Jahoda 1981; Kaplan 1980). Research has similarly indicated that low self-esteem is not an inevitable outcome of 'deviant' social labelling (Stager et al. 1983). On the contrary, once a group has evolved substitute criteria for defining 'success', those most committed to 'deviant' identities have high self-esteem (Kaplan 1980; Rosenberg and Rosenberg 1978). Within an 'overarching canopy' of diminished legitimate opportunity for asserting adult status and success, participants fostered subcultural status systems which accorded a sliding scale of prestige to law-breaking behaviours, demeanours and endeavours. This provided the final, psychological dimension in the coalescence of an alternative career.

CONCLUSIONS

The overarching context for study participants' labour market withdrawal and the proactive development of semi-licit and illicit sub cultural alternatives was the institutionalised economic and social insecurity of endemic unemployment. Professional crime is now the fourth largest 'industry' in Britain with an estimated annual turnover of £14 billion, 'employing' an estimated 420,000 people (Campbell 1992). Recent estimates of youth crime suggest it may be worth as much as £7 billion a year, much of it borne by private households as well as large corporations (*Independent* 22 September 1994). Although there are numerous well-known problems in interpreting aggregate crime figures, evidence suggests that recorded crime rose twice as fast under Conservative governments in power since 1979 (Young 1992). During the same period, there was a significant increase in the numbers of economically marginalised, socially excluded young people. The 'invisible hand' of policy-driven pauperisation and social segregation accompanied an inexorable increase in the rate of crime. Given the extra burdens on police forces and a dramatic reduction in 'clear-up' rates, senior representatives of the police hierarchy were increasingly compelled to implicate government policy. In Manchester, for example, the connection between long-term youth unemployment and increased crime rates in the inner city was explicitly acknowledged by former Chief Constable, James Anderton:

Burdens on police in Greater Manchester have grown against a background of alarming unemployment . . . with a much larger problem in the inner city. Perhaps of more telling significance . . . is the fact that the figure for long-term unemployment among the younger age groups in the worst affected parts of the conurbation ranges from 50 per cent to a staggering 80 per cent or more.

(Anderton 1985: 3)

Throughout the decade, numerous studies repeatedly asserted the unemployment/crime link (e.g. Box 1987; Chiricos 1987; Crow 1982; Crow et al. 1989; Farrington et al. 1986). Nevertheless, government ministers made recurrent attempts to locate the genesis of youth criminality elsewhere – for instance, in the decline of religious moral authority (*Guardian* 4 July 1992), or 'in greed and the excitement of violence' (Pyle 1987: 17). These responses echo the traditional conservative view of a social problem group characterised by moral turpitude, and a partial reading of my study could be cited as evidence of a congenitally deviant, workless underclass culture. However, my study sought to ethnographically explore the links between long-term unemployment and the development of alternative career transitions. During the decade of the 1980s, for at least one group of disadvantaged inner-city youth, the predisposition towards 'alternative careers' *must* be understood as rooted in the complexity of fractured post-school transitions; in material circumstances, social exclusion, cultural ecology, moral indignation and 'choices' circumscribed by government policy in employment, training, housing and benefits. The policy-bounded contexts which generated social exclusion and 'status frustration' linked institutional–structural *and* biographical dimensions in the career choice equation:

When pressures from unfulfilled aspirations and blocked opportunity become sufficiently intense many lower class youth turn away from legitimate channels adopting other means beyond conventional mores which might offer a possible route to success goals.

(Cloward and Ohlin 1961: 105)

For example, the overall unemployment rate for young women is broadly similar to that of young men. My study suggests, however, that whilst young men may turn to alternative careers of crime, the traditional roles for young working-class women have *intensified*. But, for the women of my study, like the men, the notion of 'choice' would only have relevance if there were a range of options to choose from: options such as free, adequate childcare; quality training; reasonable job prospects; and the opportunity for an independent style of life. Such demands should be at the core of policy development – but they are not, and, until they are, policy makers should not be surprised by the continued interest of working-class young women in gender-specific escape attempts to mitigate the meaninglessness of long-term unemployment or the Black Magic Roundabout of cyclical transitions. Whether lone parenthood is 'chosen', and whether or not it creates an alternative career-route towards a definition of adult identity, for most it results in poverty and social isolation with the dubious eventual 'escape' into often oppressive relationships with unemployed young men. The recent targeting of lone parents under a spurious Victorian morality indicates they, too, are to be shunted into the ideological category of the undeserving poor as a precursor for reductions in welfare support. Again, government culpability has been smokescreened behind Victorian moral rhetoric, and the policies of those who have precipitated the social conditions which foster such escape attempts remain concealed.

Of course, not all those whose lives are impoverished by long-term unemployment or the cynicism and alienation of the Black Magic Roundabout turn to alternative careers of lone parenthood or acquisitive crime. Indeed, elsewhere, I have provided hints at forms of social support and policy intervention which helped to promote and sustain positive outcomes for disadvantaged young people (Craine and Coles 1995). In some cases, it proved to be the intervention of housing professionals, those involved in the administration of criminal justice, or family members, who provided the opportunities to divert disaffected young adults into more mainstream housing, domestic and employment careers (see also Chapter 6). To develop an informed youth policy we must consider fully the failure of past policies and the political culpability of policy makers, in exacerbating the processes of fractured transitions and social exclusion (Audit Commission 1996; Williamson 1993). Without such consideration, it is virtually impossible to ascertain how the motivational elements of alternative career choices are generated. Unless, of course, we follow the New Right apologists of the underclass thesis and rest our analyses and future policy agenda on empirically deficient notions of social pathology and individual moral defectiveness. In the meantime, socially excluded youth will continue to construct their own solutions and make their own

history – no doubt fuelling further reactionary myths and stereotypes as they do.

NOTES

1 This chapter is dedicated to Joulo, Ila, Leon, Kieron and Liam.
2 See, for instance, 'Riot puts despair on the agenda' (*Guardian* 11
   September 1991) and 'No hope in No-Go Land' (*Observer* 15 September
   1991).
3 Ethical and confidentiality issues are much easier to address and there
   are numerous remedial strategies available to ethnographers to ensure
   protection both of research participants and themselves. These include:
   anonymising the text (Platt 1976: 7); the secure management and storage
   of sensitive materials (Sieber 1982: 112–15); delaying writing up and
   publication (Craine 1994; Patrick 1973); and securing a moratorium on
   access to unpublished work (Craine 1994).
4 Whilst based in the Manchester area, in writing up my research, place
   names and the names of study participants have been fictionalised in
   order to protect their anonymity.

Chapter 10

Changing their ways
Youth work and 'underclass' theory

Tony Jeffs

INTRODUCTION

This chapter concentrates on how changes in youth policy impact upon youth work. It charts the competing philosophies which have underpinned youth work since its initial development in the nineteenth century and shows how social fears about 'dangerous youth' have consistently fed into the practices of youth workers. The chapter argues that, across a range of policy areas which impact upon young people, we can discern emerging and wide-ranging, government-led attempts to control 'underclass' youth. Within youth work, underclass ideologies have helped shape a new authoritarianism which now jeopardises its long-standing democratic and educational principles and threatens to become the principle philosophy directing work with all young people.

YOUTH POLICY AND THE 'UNDERCLASS'

When the pre-eminent exponent of the underclass thesis, Charles Murray, is invited to give a private briefing to the Home Secretary, government ministers and senior officials, and he proceeds to inform them that the underclass is becoming unmanageable and that the key indicators of growth are the rising number of young single mothers and incidents of youth crime, some impact on government is predictable (James 1990). When, subsequently, a new Home Secretary declares that the same underclass in decaying inner cities is now 'the most formidable challenge facing western democracies' (Stephens 1992), modifications in youth policy are probably inevitable.

As no British government has ever openly assembled a coherent youth policy, or submitted one for parliamentary or public scrutiny, however, it is difficult to ascertain whether an overall strategy exists, let alone if fears regarding the growth of a youth underclass have changed its direction. As writers who previously sought to overview youth policy in Britain have found (Coles 1995; Davies 1986; Williamson 1993), all the outside observer can do is monitor individual policy areas for signs of cohesion and direction.

Outwardly, youth policy comprises a pot-pourri of inputs from central and local government and myriad voluntary and state sponsored agencies, such as Training and Enterprise Councils, the Rural Development Commission and the National Youth Agency. Individually and collectively, these deliver and construct policy in areas as divergent as employment, schools, housing, training, policing, further and higher education, income maintenance and youth justice. The range of agencies involved, allied to the apparent autonomy of local government and voluntary organisations, initially communicates an impression that the capacity of central government to manufacture something approximating to an intelligible package is severely circumscribed.

This may have been the case in the past, but recent Conservative legislation designed to create a highly 'unitary and centralised state' (Kingdom 1991: 258) – largely by removing autonomy from local government and extending central government control over whole swathes of funding – means this is no longer the case. Replacement of grants by competitive bidding procedures, imposition of predetermined outputs, increased monitoring and inspection, plus the ever-looming threat of centrally imposed curricula and guidelines, combine to curtail the independence of providers such as the schools and the voluntary and statutory youth work agencies. Although central government may not have publicly sketched a 'youth strategy', the resulting absence of documentation should not be taken as proof that one does not exist. Indeed, an analysis of both Conservative government policy, and how it has sought to mould public debate regarding the 'youth question', suggests a clear agenda has been constructed (Stenson and Factor 1995). In areas as diverse as juvenile justice and household income maintenance, schools and policing, youth work and housing, higher education and pre-school provision, policy configurations are distinguishable. These signify that the Conservative government has indeed assembled a youth policy and agenda, within which the control, management and eventual elimination of the 'underclass' is a major priority (for an extended discussion see Jeffs and Smith 1994).

YOUTH WORK AND DANGEROUS YOUTH: AN HISTORICAL OVERVIEW

Since the onset of industrialisation young people have been the object of 'respectable fears' relating to their criminal activity, sexuality, affiliation to the work ethic and overall behaviour (see Chapters 1 and 4; Pearson 1983, 1994). Their values, demeanour and attitudes have been unremittingly scrutinised by social commentators and analysts, who hope to secure some insight into the current condition and future prospects of the nation. Like contemporary champions of the underclass thesis, what they have traditionally seen has rarely reassured them. Then, as now, it seems youth is 'present only when its presence is a problem' (Hebdige 1988: 17).

Consequently, the overwhelmingly negative messages and images which dominated the debate two hundred years ago have held sway for the bulk of the intervening period (Gillis 1974; Griffin 1993). The prevailing public discourse has consistently served to furnish a subtle yet authoritative and enduring message to the effect that 'young people require a mode of regulation in which they are subject to constant if varying degrees of care and control' (Loader 1996: 25). It is thus possible to chart a ceaseless search for new and ever more effective means to discipline and control young people, each one of which has in turn encountered both resistance and accommodation. Within this discourse of control, young people have never existed as an undifferentiated whole – for class, gender and race always contribute complexity and subtlety to the debates. Therefore, to ask questions about what curriculum, what type of youth club, what sort of employment training, what kind of family life or what forms of leisure are desirable, has always invited a supplementary question: what sort of young person are we discussing? Schools and youth organisations have consequently always been structured, often in subtle but sometimes in crude ways, to cater for specific types of young people. Such differentiation has been a consistent feature of youth work, as much as it has of any other area of welfare and social policy (Williams 1989).

Youth work in its modern guise emerged as a discrete activity during the early years of industrialisation. Separation of work and schooling from the home was seen by many industrialists and Christian reformers as creating a new and dangerous void – unsupervised leisure. Here was the space in which youth unfettered 'got into trouble', 'acquired bad habits' and 'risked contamination'. It was in this context that youth work emerged to proffer a promise of control via the provision of acceptable leisure and, where appropriate, supplementary education.

These new youth organisations never sought to be generic, but each specialised by seeking to engage with discrete client groups: Raikes's Sunday schools for young men in industrial employment; Hannah More's clubs for young women working at home and on farms (Hopkins 1947; Jones 1952); the YMCA and YWCA for 'respectable' young men and women in the trades and professions (Williams 1906); Pound's ragged schools and clubs for the 'dangerous and perishing classes' (Carpenter 1857; Montague 1904: 30); Smith's Boys' Brigade for active working-class boys with parents unaffiliated to a Christian church (Springhall, Fraser and Hoare 1983); and the Boys' and Girls' Clubs for those from 'rough backgrounds' (Eager 1953; Russell and Russell 1932).

Specialisation enabled each to offer radically different programmes to young men and women whilst carefully calibrating the degree of autonomy and choice extended to members on the basis of social background, training and age (Jephcott 1943; Pethick 1898; Stanley 1890). In particular, clubs serving the 'dangerous' or 'submerged classes of the community' (Bosanquet 1896) were expected to impose, at least during the initial period of membership, a firm discipline upon their charges. It was unquestionably assumed that only amongst those from a 'prosperous home' would one encounter 'any significant degree of discipline' (Bray 1911; Paterson 1911: 125) or *'esprit de corps'* (Pelham 1890: 40). Success or failure of a unit therefore came predominately to be measured in relation to the extent workers managed to inculcate 'responsibility, duty, sympathy and self-expression' (Gillis 1974: 143).

The number of young people affiliated to clubs and uniformed organisations increased enormously in the years prior to the First World War. Leading organisations counted their memberships in tens of thousands, with every town and city of any size possessing an array of uniformed organisations – a YMCA and YWCA, numerous clubs and Sunday schools linked to churches of every denomination, a Girls' Friendly Society, and a Boys' and Girls' club (Jeffs 1979). However, despite this apparent success, even supporters of the youth organisations were convinced they were not reaching more than a small percentage of working-class boys, particularly those 'who ran wild, became hooligans and street-corner loafers' (quoted in Springhall 1977: 24; see also Paton 1908; Urwick 1904).

An influential government report by the Committee on Physical Deterioration (1904), which called for greater physical and mental education for adolescents, agreed. It concluded that existing youth organisations largely provided amusement, offered little in the way of education and failed dismally to reach the mass of boys. This was a view shared by the government, which opted to address the 'youth problem' by expanding the role of schools, and via legislation – in particular, the 1908 Children Act, which enabled it to supervise to an unprecedented degree the home lives and public behaviour of working-class youth (Hendricks 1990, 1994).

The youth organisations continued to grow until they peaked in terms of membership during the Second World War. However, they no longer had a serious welfare function and became predominately providers of leisure and social facilities, offering young people the chance to develop friendships, engage in group activities and, within strict limits, play a part in the management of the small community that was the club (Barnes 1945; Reed 1950).

Hendricks suggests that, by 1914, the generalised transfer of the residual welfare role to other agencies left youth workers with little to play with apart from 'philanthropy and religion' (1990: 179). This somewhat despondent reading of the situation ignores the ways in which this reallocation created an opportunity for workers to develop from an alternative tradition. This is what Butters and Newell (1978) dub the Social Education Repertoire: it set in train a piecemeal migration from social control and character building towards an emphasis on 'community development' and 'self emancipation' (Smith 1988).

Although all the available evidence points towards youth work predominately taking place with 'respectable' and 'safe young people', this was never exclusively the case (Paneth 1944). Because so little was expected or demanded by the state from youth work – and what eventually became known post-1945 as the Youth Service – it was largely left to plough its own furrow. Denied lavish funding it gained, by way of compensation, the freedom to develop small pockets of radical practice and, above all, the space and privacy in which to address sensitive issues. It employed informal education and group work techniques to enable young people to discuss and learn about those issues and topics excluded from the school curriculum and which few schoolteachers would dare to broach, even outside the classroom. For all the gaps and weaknesses in provision, youth clubs, projects and organisations consistently allowed young people to form, on a voluntary basis, relationships with adults with whom it was 'safe to talk'.

Alongside mainstream provision, it is possible to identify a tradition of youth work which has tenaciously sought to find ways of engaging with the 'tough young gangsters' (Hall 1952: 232), 'unattached' (Morse 1965) and 'disorganised youth' (Goetschius and Tash 1967). As a result, innovative ventures designed specifically to engage in informal education with 'dangerous and threatening youth' emerged. Attention needs to paid in particular to three of these.

First, *detached youth work*: youth workers have always engaged with young people on their own territory, on the street, and in other places where they congregate. This has been a well-tried and trusted way of working (Secretan 1931). What is new is the extent to which detached work has emerged as an identifiable mode of practice sustained by its own literature and history (Biven 1992; Goetschuis and Tash 1967). Over time, it has become perceived as possibly the key method by which workers are able to target 'marginal' and 'underclass' youth.

Second, *school-based youth work*: this approach also has a long history with many early clubs emerging from school-based settings (Montague 1904; Russell and Russell 1932). However, it began to acquire a separate identity in the 1950s with the appointment of teacher–youth workers in rural community schools. Subsequently, it spread, like the community school itself, to inner-city localities. The school was perceived as the only welfare agency which had both a physical presence and contact, however tenuous, with young people in a given neighbourhood. Like detached youth work, it is viewed as one of the few ways an informal educator can reach the 'unattached'. Even though school attendance might be compulsory, youth workers traditionally operated partly as detached workers making contact in corridors, canteens and anywhere the young people gathered, but also, in a more traditional way, setting up and running clubs and activities (Jeffs 1987).

Third, *Intermediate Treatment*: first launched in the late 1960s, Intermediate Treatment is unique in that contact between the worker and the young people is enforced by a court. Catering for those already convicted of a serious offence, it is designed to divert young people from further offending. The content of programmes has changed dramatically in recent years with the emphasis moving from social and informal educational approaches towards formal inputs, individual case work and group work designed to encourage the young people to 'confront their offending behaviour' (Pitts 1990).

Youth work has always embraced alternative and competing modes of practice (Butters and Newell 1978; Jeffs 1979; Popple 1995; Smith 1988; Taylor 1987), which have revolved around such issues as whether it should be centre-based or detached or whether it should be social issue-based or open access provision. However, differences between youth work approaches have often been exaggerated whilst key commonalities have been overlooked. In particular, insufficient attention has been paid to the core activity of creating educational dialogue through the medium of conversation within the setting of a voluntary relationship (Brew 1946; Jeffs and Smith 1990b, 1996b).

Thus, informal education lies at the heart of all youth work, but how it is structured has always been profoundly influenced by the assumed status of the young people upon whom attention is focused. As a consequence, every shift in the locus of youth work from mass towards selective provision, for those judged members of the 'dangerous class' or 'underclass', has had an impact on the methods used to foster opportunities for dialogue. In particular, those strands such as detached work, school-based practice and work with offenders (both in Juvenile Justice Centres and elsewhere) have been prioritised. Policy has judged it far better to dispatch the workers to find the 'unclubbables' and the 'underclass' than waste valuable resources trying to force them to affiliate to existing clubs or projects. Thus, detached and school-based work came to be reborn in new guises and Intermediate Treatment invented the distinction, which became accepted in the minds of many youth workers, between 'young people youth work does things for' and 'young people youth work does things to'.

UNDERCLASS THEORY AND NEW AUTHORITARIANISM

Central to all accounts of the underclass thesis is a belief that it is growing. It is claimed to be growing, first, because of irresponsible and promiscuous sexual behaviour amongst young women and, second, via the recruitment of young people who, owing to inadequate and negligent parenting (or genes), 'get into trouble', truant, reject training opportunities and 'real work' prior to eventually opting for the more attractive option of dependency upon state benefits and criminal activity (see Chapter 1; Dennis 1993; Dennis and Erdos 1992; Field 1989, 1993; Mead 1986). All solutions there-fore – apart from isolation via the creation of a *cordon sanitaire* around their ghettos – point to measures which involve dramatically altering the attitudes and behaviour of those young people seen as potential or actual members of the underclass.

As Macnicol (1987), Gans (1995), Kamin (1995) and Jones (1992) have demonstrated, the underclass thesis is a recycled version of long-discredited theories which encourage us to believe that the poor revel in their misery, spurn stable relationships, evade responsi-bility for their offspring and snub steady employment when it is offered. Like its predecessors, the underclass thesis encourages a view that the poor inhabit a different country enjoying a lifestyle 'as incomprehensible as it is self-destructive' (Jones 1992: 219). The all-embracing nature of the concept relegates a diverse agglomeration of individuals into a single, condemned, frequently despised class – assumed by the 'cognitive elite' (Herrnstein and Murray 1994) who sit in judgement on them to be intellectually, morally and ethically inferior. Irrespective of the validity of the thesis, it has served a larger political purpose in Britain and elsewhere by justifying reduc-tions in welfare expenditure and ever more vigorous intrusions into the daily lives of the poor (as discussed in Chapters 1 and 4).

Within the last decade, a plethora of policy initiatives have ma-terialised confirming the resolve on the part of the government to control those identified as the underclass. In particular, they have exhibited a willingness to adopt increasingly authoritarian policies to control and manage the young poor (Jeffs and Smith 1994, 1996a; Williamson 1993).

Within the *education sector*, a range of policies designed to enforce greater discipline in schools have been initiated. These include: a National Pupil Behaviour Strategy; legally enforceable parental contracts which require, as a condition of attendance, such things as endorsement of school rules, completion of homework and the wearing of a specified uniform; giving schools greater powers to select and exclude students; curriculum guidelines compelling schools to formally teach citizenship, awareness of community and morality; and wide-ranging policies to 'tackle' truancy, including attendance league tables and moves to introduce financial penalties which adjust the income of schools and colleges to take account of absences (Jeffs 1994).

For *young offenders*, policies include: the promise of mandatory sentences for serious and drug-related offences; secure training orders for 12- to 15-year-olds convicted of three imprisonable offences; creation of harsher and more rigorous 'Boot Camp' regimes for young offenders; courts being directed to enforce measures designed to impose parental liability by binding over parents to control their children or face fines and/or imprisonment; the 'naming and shaming' of young offenders by taking away anonymity from those aged 16 and over; and the proposed 'tagging' of offenders as young as 10 years old (Cavadino 1995; Gibson 1995).

In the area of *housing and income maintenance*, we have seen: legislation relating to the homeless adjusted to discriminate against young mothers by withdrawing their automatic rights of support; the decision to fund Foyer programmes – which make accommodation conditional on acceptance of full-time work or a place on an employment scheme – in preference to alternative independent housing; draconian measures to prevent squatting; reduction and curtailment of benefits for those aged under 25 (for example, the Job Seekers Allowance, introduced in 1996, specifically discriminates against anyone aged 18 to 24 and automatically pays them at a lower rate, and allows Benefit Officers to withdraw benefit from those judged to have inappropriate dress); Severe Hardship Payments made less accessible for young people because Benefit Agency officers now seek evidence from parents or a third party to confirm a young person's claim that they are unable to live at home; overall benefits for the young unemployed, for over a decade, continuously adjusted in order to drive those not in full-time education or employment into training schemes of an often dubious quality and to prevent them from leaving the parental home (see Jones in Chapter 7 and Dean, Chapter 4; Children's Society 1996; Gilchrist and Jeffs 1995; Mizen 1995; Pollock 1996).

All the above have been augmented by the use of the *law and programme funding* to manage the presence of young people in 'public space'. Such policies have included: the harsh legal restrictions imposed on 'New Age travellers' with the clear intention of preventing young people from adopting a nomadic lifestyle as an alternative to unemployment; new controls on the right to assemble (enabling the police to break up and harass groups of young people in public settings); legislation which makes it virtually impossible for young people to organise raves, festivals or 'unregulated' entertainment; and truancy patrols – comprising police, youth workers and Education Welfare Officers – which already operate in some localities to 'pick up' young people judged to be of school age. At an informal level, it is becoming commonplace in some localities to see shops displaying signs banning young people under sixteen unless accompanied by an adult. In the United States, the implementation of such restrictions has gone much further. Shopping malls and entertainment complexes have opened which specifically exclude young people under 17. Even more disturbing are the growing number of youth curfew ordinances and laws requiring young people (usually defined as aged 17 and below), not in the company of an acceptable adult, to be off the streets from 11 p.m. to 6 a.m. from Sunday through to Thursday, and from midnight to 6 a.m. on Friday and Saturday nights. First introduced in smaller towns (Plotkin and Elias 1977), these curfews have now been adopted by as many as 1,000 cities (Ruefle and Reynolds 1995). In 1994, the Supreme Court rejected a challenge to the Dallas curfew on the basis that young people do not have 'a generalized right of social association', upholding an earlier ruling that the city had a 'compelling interest' in reducing juvenile crime and 'promoting juvenile safety and well-being'. Subsequently, in a number of areas, these have been augmented by daytime curfews which make it illegal for young people to be outside during school hours. The first attempt at the implementation of a partial curfew has already occurred in England but, lacking the support of legislation, it was abandoned as unworkable. Support for youth curfews has, however, been forthcoming from leading politicians (Blair 1996), and, given the claims for their success made by American politicians and police officers, it seems likely they will feature in future political debates relating to the youth question (see Jeffs and Smith 1996a).

Youth work itself has not remained untouched by the ideology which propagated these policy changes. This has happened for two reasons. First, it is because many of the agencies in the 'front line' of the struggle being waged against the 'underclass' have come to believe the techniques of youth work offer an effective way of influencing the behaviour of young people, especially those perceived as being untouched by their schooling. City Challenge programmes, Urban Development corporations, the police, health authorities and even fire brigades have all employed youth workers and funded youth organisations in the hope that they will assist them in achieving their targets (Jeffs and Smith 1990a). Few of these agencies have any grasp of the traditions or concepts and ideas which have historically informed and shaped the youth work practice described earlier.

What they require is a solution to a problem – vandalism, hooliganism, petty crime, teenage pregnancy – and they are willing to try youth work as an alternative to CCTV or to employing a private security firm. The educational content of youth work is seen as secondary to that control, and voluntary affiliation is no longer an option for the predetermined client group (Tucker 1994).

Second, youth work units and agencies have found that the government has encouraged the construction of new funding mechanisms. These tie cash to short-term outputs whilst dramatically reallocating funding towards localities of high urban stress and work with young males. One result has been to seriously denude the resources available for work with 'non-threatening groups' such as young women (Benetell 1996) and rural young people (Kendrick and Rioch 1995; Paylore and Smith 1995).

These changes have had a profound but little discussed impact on youth work practice. Workers have been denied the capacity to create long-term relationships and build projects with at least an aura of permanence. This has meant that workers are forced to target specific groups and impose themselves on them in order to secure 'quick returns'. Consequently, youth workers are increasingly unable to adopt community development models of practice, or to build on success, or work in ways which over time allow young people to influence and develop future programmes (Popple 1995; Schorr 1988; Smith and Paylore 1996). In addition, funding conditions increasingly oblige youth workers to operate according to preordained definitions of need. Criteria are established and neither the young people nor the community are given the wherewithal to determine needs or negotiate priorities. As Barry (1996) observes, the participation and empowerment of young people, in and through youth work, does not figure high on this new agenda.

A mounting obsession with controlling 'underclass' youth has created a minor upsurge in the demand for youth workers. New, albeit short-term, projects have blossomed, ensuring that the youth workers being produced by the burgeoning number of training programmes have, against all the odds, secured employment (Jeffs and Smith 1993). A price has been extracted, however. In particular, workers have had to abandon many of the gains achieved in recent years relating to their professional autonomy. Traditions of practice developed over previous decades which sought to foster participation and democracy have increasingly been jettisoned. Instead, much youth work has embraced – either for self-serving reasons or because of an unquestioning belief in the inherent rightness of authority – modes of practice which are both authoritarian and oppressive. The educational *raison d'être*, which underpinned previous modes of practice, has been sidelined as intervention has increasingly been justified on the basis of crime prevention (Coopers and Lybrand 1994; Perfect and Renshaw 1996). The provision of quantifiable output measures for youth work is impossible; for who can measure the worth of a conversation, the value of an experience or the depth of an insight, on a scale of one to ten? Attempts to do so have, therefore, invariably retreated into counting contact numbers for detached workers, attendance levels for clubs and accumulating satisfaction ratings from young people (Hendry et al. 1994). In the absence of accurate outputs capable of satisfying funders anxious to control 'dangerous' and 'underclass' youth, the inevitable has taken place and data has been produced which purports to show youth workers to be cost-effective crime prevention and management agents (Coopers and Lybrand 1994; Perfect and Renshaw 1996).

The dangers of such an approach for youth work are manifest. First, it encourages a narrowing of both the focus of the relationship with young people and the client group to a small percentage of the cohort. In repudiating a broader social education role, it cuts adrift work with other key groups, in particular young women and 'respectable' youth. Second, it pits youth work against other means of crime management – such as private security firms, CCTV and additional police officers – all of which may be cheaper, have a higher and more acceptable public profile and be more capable of 'proving' their effectiveness. Given its voluntary and part-time base, youth work which is not orientated towards 'underclass' youth will survive much as alternatives did in the past. Sadly, such work will, however, be ever more under-funded and under-valued than it is at present and, if current trends continue, it will have to learn to coexist with a full-time, professional Youth Service which has neither sympathy for nor understanding of the role youth work plays in the lives of young people living beyond the 'underclass'.

BEYOND THE 'UNDERCLASS'?

Concerns about 'underclass' youth have thus encouraged and possibly created a 'new authoritarianism' within youth policy. In the main, these policies have centred upon young males and single mothers, the unemployed and homeless. Now there are strong indications both in the United States and United Kingdom that we are moving beyond a focus on the 'underclass'. Within political and academic circles, the debate appears to be shifting from an emphasis upon the minority 'underclass' towards youth in totality; in other words, a shift is taking place from a perceived crisis of 'underclass' youth towards an all-encompassing youth crisis.

Within the American media, as Giroux notes, coverage of youth issues begin to read more like 'dispatches from a combat zone' (1996: 27). The images conveyed are of a nation at war with its young. Young people are portrayed as turning feral, with more and more becoming involved in serious and petty crime, and other assorted anti-social activities (Smith 1995). Their indiscipline, it is claimed, is making it impossible for schools to deliver the curriculum and turning public spaces into no-go areas for 'respectable' people (Lerner 1995; Wooden 1994). In America, there has been a growing tendency to talk in highly alarmist terms of the threat posed to social stability by young people. The Attorney General has warned the nation that: 'unless we act now to stop young people from choosing a life of violence and crime, the beginning of the 21st century could bring levels of violent crime to our community that far exceed what we have experienced' (quoted in Thomas 1995). Academics such as Lerner (see also Hamburg 1992; Lipsitz 1994; Prothrow-Stith 1991) have endorsed this view:

> America is hanging over a precipice. Unless dramatic and innovative action is taken soon, millions of our nation's children and adolescents – the human capital on which America must build its future – will fall into an abyss of crime and violence, drug and alcohol use and abuse, unsafe sex, school failure, lack of job preparedness, and feelings of despair and hopelessness . . . I believe that the breadth and depth of the problems besetting our nation's youth, families and communities exist at historically unprecedented level.
>
> (Lerner 1995: xiii–xiv)

Gang membership, we are informed, is growing and membership is now encompassing more young women (Chesney-Lind et al. 1996) and young people beyond the ghetto (Short 1996). According to Wooden, the 'renegade kids' who are beyond control are not only the youth of the ghetto and inner city but now 'primarily males, of more affluent, suburban, middle-class neighbourhoods' (1994: 3). It is these as much as underclass youth, we are told by a senior academic at the United States Army War College, who are defeating the government's 'War on Drugs' (Rosenberger 1996).

This perception of a much wider crisis of youth has already been translated into policy initiatives at federal and local levels in the United States. Besides the widespread introduction of curfews applying to all young people, federal and local legislation has been implemented banning consumption and possession of tobacco and alcohol, and discriminatory drink driving laws have been introduced. In addition, compulsory community service has been incorporated into the school curriculum (see Jeffs and Smith 1996a). The latter policy has already been advocated in Britain by a working party set up by the Schools Curriculum and Assessment Authority. Such policies – in particular those which are designed to curtail the movement of young people – will, if introduced in Britain, pose a new challenge for youth work. In the United States, workers displayed little reluctance in collaborating with programmes designed to enhance the effectiveness of curfews and 'compulsory' volunteering. In Britain, the enthusiasm so many workers and organisations currently display for initiatives designed to manage 'underclass' youth suggests both will encounter few qualms about embracing policies and practices designed to similarly manage and control young people as a whole. It is not inevitable that the sort of discriminatory policies currently directed at young people who are seen as members of the underclass will be extended, but unless democratic and non-authoritarian alternatives are defended and given new life, a real danger exists that they will.

Chapter 11

Youth, social exclusion and the millennium

Robert MacDonald

What can we learn from these chapters about young people and their relationship to an alleged underclass? In answering this question the chapter is divided into three parts.

First, the key conclusions of these chapters in respect of some of the main problems of underclass theories are reviewed. The critique examines: social and economic change and the exclusion of youth; the complexity of processes of exclusion and the diversity of groups who become excluded; the extent of an underclass culture amongst excluded youth; and methodological issues in youth 'underclass' research.

The second part asks whether the underclass thesis should be revised or rejected and it explores the continuing popularity of underclass discourses given their weaknesses. Attention is given here to the part played by social science in neglecting some of the social problems and developments claimed to be underclass phenomena.

The third and final part suggests a potentially more productive way in which sociologists might begin to theorise and investigate the social exclusion of youth in relationship to the changing economic world young men and women encounter in their transitions to adulthood.

REVIEWING THE EVIDENCE: A CRITIQUE OF THE YOUTH UNDERCLASS THESIS

The following discussion highlights the main conclusions of the preceding chapters in respect of some of the key criticisms they make of underclass theories.

Social and economic change and excluded youth

I suggested in Chapter 1 that the majority of the contributions to this volume shared a broad view that underclass theses were not proven but also not as yet disproved. Contrary to Bagguley and Mann (1992), most felt that there was analytical and political value – necessity even – in subjecting the idea to conceptual and empirical scrutiny (Westergaard 1992). None were keen to ally themselves with the narrow, culturalist perspective of the Radical Right, and contributions were written from a broadly structuralist perspective stressing the importance of social inequalities and institutions in shaping youth transitions.

Early chapters highlighted the changing national economic situation of youth, and how their weakened labour market position has thrown up new patterns of social inclusion and exclusion in the 1980s and 1990s. Dean argues that this economic exclusion has been compounded by 'reforms' of the welfare system which potentially undermine social citizenship for young people. Maguire and Maguire draw attention to a host of labour market factors which have served to transform paths of youthful progression. There would appear to be some new opportunities for youth inclusion as well. The widening of access to further and higher education has opened up opportunities for educational advancement for young people disadvantaged in compulsory education (Ainley 1994). Now those previously excluded from colleges and universities can experience the personal, academic and vocational advantages of continued education; such developments are to be welcomed and may be indicative of a putative 'learning society' (although doubts remain over the quality of the 'student experience' in the 1990s: Jeffs and Smith 1995). Whether these extended transitions are able to provide non-traditional students with the sorts of higher level occupation normally brought by advanced qualifications will, however, depend on the contingencies of the national labour market for graduate level jobs. Graduate unemployment in the early 1990s sometimes came close to 50 per cent, and there were particular problems for students from the 'new' universities and/or with non-vocational qualifications (Teesside TEC 1995a). Many such new students, particularly women, will be constrained by domestic commitments to searching for jobs in their *local* labour markets; if these are economically depressed they may find themselves returning to the same low-level jobs they hoped to leave behind a few years earlier. In the 1980s, it was argued that training schemes for school-leavers had delayed the problem of youth unemployment until the late teenage years. High levels of graduate unemployment and underemployment (Scott-Clark and Byrne 1995) suggest that mass further and higher education may now be serving to postpone such problems until even later stages of youth transitions (MacDonald 1996c).

A significant minority of young people are left out of this process of increased educational participation. Their early 'career trajectories' – now largely absent of employment – lead them progressively towards the edges of their local labour markets. Maguire and Maguire hint that this *may* signal the development of a group of people who become more permanently excluded in the future *if* current structures of opportunity continue to prevail. They remain agnostic about the possibility of a youth underclass: the structural conditions necessary for its growth would appear to be in place, but it is too early to conclude positively that this will come about.

Williamson focuses on excluded, 'Status Zer0' youth in one area of Britain. This sharper focus – together with the insights of qualitative interviews with young people – again raise doubts about pessimistic underclass predictions. Yet Williamson is not wholly dismissive of the underclass idea. Like Maguire and Maguire, he accepts the theoretical possibility of such a thing developing for some who experience Status Zer0 in the long term *if* current institutional arrangements for out-of-school youth are not overhauled. Williamson calls for a rethinking of policy on youth training – now the major vehicle for moving unskilled working-class school leavers through their early careers – as part of a programme of social inclusion for such youth. If we do not, he suggests, then the 'underclass' may become a social reality rather than an ideological device.

Craine's study reaches similar conclusions regarding the way that young adults respond to the institutions and programmes they encounter in their early careers. The majority of his informants also rejected Youth Training as worthless (in terms of its immediate financial remuneration and labour market usefulness). Craine, though, was able to follow his sample through the 1980s to see where the 'Black Magic Roundabout' of poor-quality schemes and jobs led young people in their early and late twenties. This confirms the importance of studying youth transitions beyond the teenage years if we are to properly appreciate the new patterns of youthful inclusion and exclusion suggested by these chapters.

To sum up, although there is debate about the usefulness of the underclass concept to describe these outcomes, the authors tend to agree that social structural changes have generated serious economic exclusion amongst sections of the young population.

However, a number of the authors document how labour market marginalisation and unemployment is not the only aspect of exclusion. According to Baldwin et al. and Jones, young people's biographies are understandable in terms of family and housing transitions, as well as school-to-work transitions. It could be argued that successful economic transitions (i.e. the getting of decent jobs) underpins success in these other transitions, but a *broader* focus upon the movement from families of origin to families of destination and through risky housing careers can at least show how these three processes of transition interact in the *longer term*. This more holistic approach can also reveal diversity in youth exclusion.

Different problems and different processes: diversity and complexity in the exclusion of youth

Baldwin, Coles and Mitchell take two groups of young people (first, care leavers and, second, those with special needs and disabilities) who experience many of the 'social pathologies' and who are destined for the sorts of future usually taken to be indicative of a youth underclass. Their teenage years are marked by severe disadvantage and repeated failures. Compared with other young people, they lack qualifications and experience more unemployment, homelessness and, for the first group, involvement in crime. The family histories of care leavers are, by definition, not happy ones. In critiquing the underclass idea, however, the authors provide the empirical detail necessary for a more coherent appreciation of the way that social exclusion is determined for these groups.

Their critique has three elements. First, they argue that underclass theories ignore heterogeneity within and between the groups of young people lumped together under this label (see Jeffs, Chapter 10, and Dean in Chapter 4 makes a similar point about the social diversity of those who engage in 'fiddly work'). This is a common criticism of the underclass concept (Mann 1994). It attempts to incorporate such a wide variety of 'problem groups' (from the rioters of England's outer estates to the elderly poor), and the claimed membership is so heterogeneous, that it is difficult to see how it might be useful in describing one new social class formation with shared social characteristics and economic relationships (Gallie 1988).

Second, Baldwin, Coles and Mitchell suggest that the diversity of young people's routes *into* social exclusion – and their experiences of it – are not captured by one catch-all concept. Moreover, routes *out of* these situations will require quite different sorts of policy intervention dependent upon the groups involved (Mann 1994; Robinson and Gregson 1992; Roberts, this volume). Jeffs warns (in Chapter 10), however, that youth policy is becoming ever more geared to the control of young people (within and without the 'underclass') and that within youth work, for instance, policy towards marginal youth is now informed by a new authoritarianism which jeopardises more progressive and differentiated responses to particular groups of young people.

Third, the conservative underclass theory – and some more structuralist approaches within the study of youth transitions – fail to appreciate how the later labour market statuses and activities of young people are the outcome not simply of *either*, on the one hand, individual choice, *or*, on the other, social determination. Rather, they result from the interplay of earlier personal 'choices' (however limited), the decision-making of powerful others, the vagaries of institutional support and 'care' for young people and the inequalities and limitations of the adult world to which they head.

This is similar to the conclusion reached by Jones from her examination of youth homelessness. She, too, is critical of right-wing explanations but also argues that sociological responses typically do not capture the complexity of young people's housing transitions. Drawing upon the work of Giddens and Beck, she argues that young people 'reflexively' respond to the housing and labour markets they encounter. Young people are active agents, not 'cultural dopes' propelled helplessly along pre-set career trajectories. The structures with which young people culturally engage do not afford equality of opportunity and the varying and resultant transitions can be very risky. Accordingly, youth homelessness cannot be understood simply as an outcome of the lack of affordable housing (the crude Left position), nor as the outcome of the supposedly perverse actions of young people (the crude Right view), but as a product of the way that structure and agency combine in the creation of youth exclusion.[1]

I would suggest that these chapters – in tracing the interaction of macro-economic forces, institutional changes and policy interventions (in the spheres of education, training, housing, welfare and youth work), local labour market conditions, and localised, subcultural responses and individual strategies – provide a useful framework for understanding how different groups of young people become socially and economically excluded in different ways. In comparison, the underclass theory of Murray and his followers is simplistic. It cannot properly grasp the complexities of these processes, nor comprehend how the allegedly anti-social behaviour of 'underclass' youth might be the product, not of individual or subcultural pathology, but of the complicated interplay of structural forces with individual biographies.

Nevertheless, it still might be the case, as Dahrendorf has suggested (1987), that an outcome of the changing structural position of youth might be the evolvement of later (sub)cultural adaptations which serve to consolidate youth exclusion; that even if structural impediments were miraculously removed 'underclass' youth would remain marginalised by their own values, behaviours and outlooks.

An underclass culture amongst excluded youth?

Roberts suggests that, despite the political repugnance they may feel for conservative underclass theories, youth sociologists cannot easily reject them by reference to extant youth research. From his reading of youth research, he concludes, controversially, that the cultures of some marginal youth already point to the emergence of a youth underclass as a probability. He says that a minority of excluded youth in high unemployment areas express attitudes and develop coping strategies which are understandable within the terms of the underclass thesis.

Interestingly, several of those who suggest something similar quote a study conducted by Full Employment UK for the Conservative government in 1990. Roberts also uses this study as evidence that some of the long-term unemployed are 'not interested in the jobs that they are likely to be offered' and that this putative underclass outlook is 'fully documented'. The report, *Britain's New Underclass*, reviewed the difficulties the Employment Service had in encouraging the long-term unemployed off benefit and on to Restart and Employment Training schemes. It claimed to find an anti-work ethos amongst the unemployed:

[A] substantial number of unemployed people have developed attitudes and patterns of behaviour that reinforce their exclusion from the labour market ... most notably [this underclass includes] able-bodied young men and women who have spent their years since leaving school moving from one government scheme to another.

(Full Employment UK 1990: 1).

What is unusual about this small report (it extends to twenty-six pages) is the speed and vigour with which its conclusions were publicised by advocates of the underclass idea. Green (1992) uses it as the basis for his castigation of the feckless unemployed. Field (1990: 40) uses this 'pioneering work' to defend his proposal for more rigorous testing of the unemployed's availability for work. Clearly, it is worth a closer look. The main criticism involves sample construction. In all, fifty-nine people were interviewed in group 'consultations' in eight different localities (i.e. on average, eight people from each locality). Their average time without a job was three years and four months and they were selected because they refused to join, or had dropped out of, training programmes. It seems extraordinary that the authors can reach their sweeping conclusions about the growth of a disreputable underclass of work-shy fraudsters from such a small, unrepresentative sample. For instance, they talked to only twenty-five under-25-year-olds (across eight different localities) and yet describe unemployed young people as the most notable members of this underclass. They take the comments of these very long-term unemployed people as evidence of anti-employment sentiment amongst the unemployed population as a whole, yet the sample was purposefully selected to include only persistent scheme 'refuseniks'. The currency which this report gained – especially given that its findings run contrary to the vast majority of sociological studies of the unemployed (of which Field seems to be unaware) – demonstrates the eagerness of underclass theorists for research to buttress their theories (no matter how unscholarly or thin on the ground this may be). Dennis and Erdos's *Families Without Fatherhood* (1992) received even greater publicity, for the same reason.

These chapters regard long-term youth unemployment as an outcome of social structural change. Of course, Roberts does argues as well that the context to youth unemployment is one of extensive economic restructuring. This is not unemployment through choice, as Murray would have it. To suggest so, is victim-blaming (Bagguley and Mann 1992; Robinson and Gregson 1992; Walker 1990). Nor is it necessarily a result of lack of work experience (e.g. Blackman's homeless and unemployed youths had extensive and diverse labour market experiences) or lack of involvement in training programmes: Craine's interviewees collectively experienced sixty years of training with only one person securing a job subsequently. It is also hard to see their unemployment as a product of unrealistic or unusual expectations (as Williamson's Status Zer0 youth attest). Young people who were sometimes surviving in bleak and severely circum-scribed social environments *desired* no more than would be *expected* as a minimum by the majority of middle-aged, middle-class society. Jones's sample hoped for jobs and houses and families of their own. These are hardly perverse expectations.

A Joseph Rowntree Foundation study (1995a) of another group of supposed underclass youth – young single mothers – also found that they expressed quite conventional attitudes towards family life (and labour market participation). Like the young mothers in Craine's research, they had not strategically planned their 'deviant' family situations (in order to maximise welfare support) and retained aspirations for 'traditional' families. Kempson et al. (1994) report that the poor families in their study retained a strong commitment to work, that they could not be characterised as part of a dependency culture, and that it was normally the mothers who bore the brunt of poverty and 'went without' in order to alleviate the hardships faced by their children. A similar point is made by Campbell in her study of depressed and disorderly localities in Britain (1993): it is typically the women and mothers in such places who most strive to sustain family and community life. Kinsey (1992) adds that the attitudes of children from single parent, benefit-dependent families are not at all consistent with the picture of deviant, underclass families painted by Murray.

In addition, Alcock makes the argument (against Murray):

> that most lone mothers remain those separated or divorced (not the young mothers of illegitimate children), that most lone parents subsequently (re)marry, and that most illegitimate chil-dren are registered as living with both parents.
>
> (1994: 43)

Alcock regards all this as evidence of changing societal patterns of parenting rather than evidence of the failure of the family. Similarly,

Philips (1994) insists that these changes in family form are not restricted to Murray's 'New Rabble' but are also evident amongst the middle classes. And of course Murray, and the 'ethical socialists' who have joined him in attacking single motherhood, pay rather less attention to the problems (for instance, of violence, abuse and neglect) which seem to be apparent in more 'traditional' family forms.

Macnicol's telling point (1994a: 36) that the proportion of single mothers on welfare actually *decreased* in the 1980s in America heaps further doubt upon Murray's central claims for the growth of a welfare-dependent underclass during this period. In Britain, there is evidence that illegitimacy rates have stabilised in the mid-1990s, which also counters Murray's predictions (HMSO 1996). From the evidence presented here and in other studies, it is again difficult to find support for Murray's view that these changes in family form are the source of the social problems he associates with the underclass.

The studies in this volume of excluded youth confirm that the majority of young people do not cling on to political values or social expectations which are particularly different from those of their parent generation (Banks et al. 1992). They 'demonstrate how mistaken crude assumptions regarding the "differentness" of the young poor are' (Jeffs and Smith 1995: 69). Youth sociologists informed by their own particular theoretical and political agendas, who seek out the culturally spectacular and resistant, have a tendency to be quietly disappointed by the conservatism of youth. Perhaps it should be no surprise then that studies of 'underclass' youth uncover similarly mainstream attitudes.

These studies (perhaps with the exception of Craine's) show that even long-term unemployment is unlikely to generate alternative value systems which deplete work commitment. This finding confirms those of general surveys of the unemployed population (e.g. Heath 1992; Morris and Irwin 1992) which is of special value given that some of these have not included young people (e.g. Morris 1993: 407). Gallie concludes that:

> The response of the unemployed to the aggravation of labour market disadvantage lies not in the development of some highly distinctive subculture, but in the reinforcement of more conventional working-class beliefs.
>
> (1994: 756)

Indeed, he found that the long-term unemployed had levels of work commitment in excess of those of the employed! Payne and Payne, drawing upon longitudinal, large-scale survey data on the labour market positions of the unemployed during the 1980s, claim that 'the economic changes of the 1980s are unlikely to have produced an underclass as a general phenomenon amongst the unemployed' (1994: 18). Deindustrialisation not demoralisation is the key to understanding unemployment. The virtual unanimity of agreement on this in the British research literature might explain why Murray shies away from a detailed discussion of 'voluntary unemployment' in his 1994 treatise.

Even when we focus on some of the shadier ways of making a living (such as benefit fraud and 'fiddly work') thrown under the spotlight by Murray, it is not easy to interpret these as evidence of 'a something for nothing society' (Lilley 1992). Although it is notoriously difficult to measure the prevalence of 'fiddly work' in an economy (Harding and Jenkins 1989), Full Employment UK assert from their limited evidence that 'the growth of the hidden "black economy" continues apace and provides a substantial source of fraudulent earnings for large numbers of unemployed people' (1990: 25). Studies by Pahl (1984), McLaughlin et al. (1989) and Bradshaw and Holmes (1989) have been more circumspect and questioned the popular perception that this sort of activity is widespread. Nevertheless, Jordan et al. (1992) uncovered an apparently higher degree of benefit fraud and some of the people studied by Blackman, by Craine and by Dean had done undeclared, illicit work.

Even here, it is not wholly clear that these activities are driven by deviant, subterranean values. Dean shows that 'social security claimants who fiddle are not exercising a life-style choice' but that strong work motivation and economic hardship enforced this risky activity (Jordan et al. 1992; see Morris 1994: 103–4, for a review of other studies). Blackman argues that attitudes and behaviours which might on the surface appear to be evidence of a deviant, strange underclass culture can be revealed, through more in-depth ethnographic research, to be quite coherent, rational responses to the socio-economic conditions constraining the lives of the young homeless and unemployed.

Dean's research also suggests that the curtailment of welfare support for young people may have served to erode some of the social obligations attached to a sense of citizenship. In his sample, it was the young people who grew up in the 1980s – 'Thatcher's

Children' – who expressed the most amoral attitudes towards the welfare state and its provisions. This was the group that also had most experience of serious criminal activity such as burglary. Whilst Dean's discussion is tentative, his ideas seem to mesh with the conclusions of Craine's study of 1980s youth. Craine argues that early career involvement in 'fiddly work' work can lead to more criminal activities later. Benefit fraud shaded into drug dealing, shop-lifting, burglary and robbery. For some, crime replaced or, to be more exact, became work (see Hobbs 1989, 1994). Although Craine is at pains to argue that 'criminal careers' are understandable in the context of failing institutions and policy interventions, it is not difficult to see why some, like Murray, might take such deviancy as evidence of a youth underclass.

To sum up, the weight of evidence presented here suggests that the underclass thesis cannot as yet be proven by youth research. Certainly sections of the youthful population are experiencing new patterns of exclusion as a consequence of social structural change. The processes leading to exclusion are, however, too multifarious and complex to be understood within the framework of the underclass theory, and the social groups of youth so excluded are too diverse and heterogeneous to be classified together as one new social class formation (Mann 1994; Robinson and Gregson 1992). Perhaps, most importantly, there is little evidence that underclass cultures are emerging amongst the marginal and excluded youth discussed in these studies.

However, before we dispense with the youth underclass idea, it is necessary to reflect critically upon the *sorts* of evidence offered against it. Part of the thinking behind Roberts's more tolerant attitude to the underclass theory rests upon an awareness of some of the limitations of the studies which purport to reject it. In the next section some methodological issues in youth 'underclass' research are considered.

Hunting the underclass: methodological issues

Craine's study comes closest to locating Murray's underclass of prolonged and inter-generational unemployment, benefit dependency and fraud, crime, illegitimacy and single motherhood. And the way his study was designed methodologically made it arguably the most sensitive to uncovering an underclass if such a thing existed. Maybe other studies which argue against the existence of an underclass have missed something as a consequence of their methodological preferences?

Murray himself makes a methodological point about underclass debates:

> those who say that there is no underclass tend to rely on studies in which scholars go into poor neighbourhoods for a few hours at a time with clipboards and multiple choice questionnaires. Those who say there is an underclass tend to rely on studies in which scholars live in poor communities, and get their information from long conversations conducted over weeks and months with the people who live there.
>
> (1990: 70)

Of course, Murray's own methodology is hardly a model of good practice: it represents a hotchpotch of unsubstantiated assertion, local anecdote taken as general fact, statistical correlations presented as causal relationships, and ignorance of research countering his own position (David 1994; Deakin 1990; Walker 1990). Setting Murray's own work aside, he may still have a point about the appropriateness of methods used to hunt out the underclass and their cultures.

Roberts argues that the sampling frames of many studies – drawn as they are from official but partial records such as census returns and electoral registers – will exclude exactly the sorts of people categorised as an underclass. Wilkinson and Mulgan report that under-25s are four times less likely than other age groups to be on the electoral register (1995). Dedicated social surveys will also miss out the sorts of people likely to be in an 'underclass' (i.e. the sorts of people not likely to respond to questionnaire surveys). Heath acknowledges that 'members of the underclass may be disproportionately likely not to respond' to the surveys he uses as evidence against the underclass thesis (1992: 33). A telling caveat to Payne and Payne's rejection of the unemployed–underclass relationship suggests the same:

> This is not to deny that in some parts of the country there may already exist minority underclass cultures . . . Indeed, if such minority cultures do exist, they are not likely to be identified by large surveys . . . which rely on conventional methods of sampling and data collection.
>
> (Payne and Payne 1994: 18)

They say that the underclass is unlikely to be a 'general phenomenon amongst the unemployed' (ibid.) and this would seem to be true. But it must be remembered, as Roberts again points out, that Murray does not perceive the underclass to be a general phenomena: 'there is an ecology to poverty. Cross-sectional surveys of poor people or of the unemployed . . . are useless in either confirming or disconfirming this hypothesis' (Murray 1990: 69). To paraphrase Roberts, proving that the unemployed in general (and particularly the unemployed who are included in questionnaire surveys) do not share an underclass culture does not mean that the unemployed in some places at some time might not evolve cultures like those described by underclass theorists.

If we are to properly engage with Murray's thesis, what is needed, then, are studies which are able to explore in-depth and over time the values, activities and outlooks of people in places and during periods where underclass phenomena are most likely to show themselves. Only ethnographic, longitudinal studies of particular localities (down to neighbourhood level) and key social groups resident in them are likely to provide the evidence necessary to support or reject underclass theories (or to develop alternative theories of social exclusion). This sort of ethnography, as Blackman argues, also has a political purpose in that it allows the voices of the dispossessed to be heard in the debates about an underclass which go on above them. Recently, these sorts of study have been few in number within British sociology. Craine's is an example and, as I have noted, it comes closest to documenting a subculture at least *similar* to that described by Murray.

The design of the studies reported here was such that they have been unable to cast much light upon processes of *inter-generational* transmission of 'underclass' cultures. This is generally taken to be one of the most crucial elements of underclass theories (see Chapter 1). The focus of these studies upon young people only has meant that we have been unable to explore the potential connections between the social inequalities experienced by the parent generation and resultant patterns of cultural adaptation, and the way that youth may inherit similar behaviours and outlooks. Certainly, it would *seem* from this evidence that 'cultures of poverty' are not being passed down the generations. However, if we *were* to have discovered something reminiscent of an underclass culture, in the absence of this sort of inter-generational perspective it would have been possible to explain this (away) as an age effect (i.e. as evidence of the 'normal' misdemeanours of youth).

In future research, it would be useful to devise more panoramic perspectives which attend to the household situations and family relationships of excluded youth, in order to grasp more comprehensively the interconnections between the situations of youth and those of their parents.[2] A broader frame to youth studies would allow fuller investigation of the *earlier* processes of disadvantage which are set in place before the age of sixteen (e.g. how young people, like those studied by Baldwin et al. and by Jones, become 'vulnerable'), and of the ways that youth transitions feed into the *later* and longer-term processes and patterns of exclusion experienced by people in their twenties and beyond (MacDonald 1996c).

Finally, some research which challenges the underclass thesis is now a little dated. This is partly an outcome of the dawdling pace of social scientific publication. Claims of a contemporary underclass are countered with evidence from the 1980s or before. For example, Rutter and Madge's *Cycles of Disadvantage* (1976) is often cited (e.g. Walker 1990: 52) against the view that disadvantage is being transmitted culturally down the generations, yet its research data is now over twenty years old. In the intervening years, it is not impossible, for instance, that the youths of poor areas may have evolved new patterns of response in the face of near permanent, high unemployment.

To summarise, this section has drawn attention to some methodological issues in studies of youth and the underclass. It questions whether the certainty felt by some in rejecting underclass theories is warranted given the nature of many of the studies used as part of that task. To properly dispense with the arguments of Murray and others, approaches more sensitive to uncovering the alleged phenomena are needed. Existing research of the sort proposed *has* described youth subcultural careers which are similar to those described by Murray as indicative of an underclass, even if the researcher (Craine) might be deemed to have offered a more persuasive theoretical explanation of their causation.

THE YOUTH UNDERCLASS THESIS: REVISION OR REJECTION?

Despite some methodological reservations, we can conclude that conservative, culturalist underclass theories are – overall – flawed in too many respects to be useful in describing and explaining the contemporary social exclusion of youth. Structural variants do highlight socio-economic changes affecting the situation of British youth, but again it is doubtful that their outcome so far has been the formation of a youth underclass. Processes of exclusion and the groups excluded are too diverse to be described in terms of one new social class category (Morris 1994: 108). There is little evidence of the emergence alongside this socio-economic exclusion of a deviant culture favouring criminality and benefit dependency over more conventional family and work values (Walker 1990). Subcultures can develop which *appear* to match Murray's underclass but, on closer inspection, it becomes clear that their causation and their meaning are not captured by the explanatory framework Murray and others propose.

We can thus begin to see the strength of Bagguley and Mann's (1992) argument that the underclass theory is rhetorical, ideological and, in the main, untainted by empirical facts. It serves to 'blame the victims' of poverty for their own impoverishment and the unemployed for their own worklessness, thus negating the need for costly policy interventions (see Jeffs, Chapter 10). It seeks easy scapegoats for complex problems and feeds the bourgeois appetite for panics about the morality of social Others and the respectable fears of society's powerful, whilst obfuscating the *real* problems and causes of poverty (Pearson 1983; Jones in Chapter 7). The current underclass clamour may be a particularly clear example of a more general, rumbling, millennial angst about the moral health of the nation as we approach the new century (Slipman 1994).[3] Long-running discourses of 'troublesome youth' and 'the undeserving poor' come together in debates about an underclass (see Dean, Chapter 4, and Jeffs, Chapter 10) which claim to capture the 'state we're in'. 'Underclass youth' becomes a metaphor, a shorthand, for the coming, the new, the dangerous, the disordered (Griffin 1993). It is perhaps a further example of social science's romantic preoccupation with putative underworlds, underdogs and 'low-lifes'; another instance of sociologists gazing downwards to the misdemeanours of the powerless, rather than looking upwards to the arenas in which social inclusion and exclusion are determined, and where research agendas and funding are decided – to the delinquency, dependency cultures and crime of the powerful 'overclass' (Foucault 1977; Mann 1992, 1994; Nicolaus 1968).

Given all these doubts, should we now avoid underclass terminology and banish discussion of the underclass? W. J. Wilson now prefers the term 'ghetto poor' (see Chapter 1), Gans (1993) substitutes 'undercaste' and Byrne (1995) employs the phrase 'dispossessed working class' rather than 'underclass'. Robinson and Gregson (1992) come to a different conclusion: that the underclass term can be reclaimed from the Right to usefully describe new, structurally determined forms of poverty and economically driven changes in the class structure. More pragmatically, underclass terminology has become so widespread in journalistic and other accounts generated outside of academia that attempts by sociologists to curb discussion are likely to prove pointless (see Roberts, Chapter 3). Social scientists are unlikely to have much of an impact on wider political debates if we refuse even to use the very terms of these debates. To date, repeated insistences that 'there is no such thing as an underclass' have not staunched the flow of influential, non-sociological accounts which assume or assert that there is.

This is a difficult question to resolve. It may be the case that a pragmatic response is required which, at the same time as seeking to lift discussions of poverty and social exclusion out of the mire of underclass debates, also finds ways of challenging more popular, journalistic and political uses of the term.[4] Whatever the answer, it is crucial that we do not, in Britain, witness the 'mass intellectual surrender' Macnicol says typified liberal academic responses to the underclass debate in 1980s America (1994b: 103). Critical engagement with these powerful ideas within and without the discipline is vital.

But how can we explain the continuing popularity of underclass theories in the face of evidence which contradicts them? Reference to their ideological function provides part of the answer, as argued above, but we also need to consider the role social science has played in allowing room for these misconceived accounts.

Clearly, youth sociologists have a good opportunity to contend with underclass theories and the policy prescriptions which flow from them. Craine notes, however, that for too long youth research has tended to dismiss the possibility – elevated to the status of indisputable fact by the Radical Right – that some young people may evolve underclass-like cultures. Murray says that youths who, for instance, 'get in trouble with the law . . . will find no shortage of social workers and academics prepared to make excuses [for them]' (1990: 720). He agrees with John Major's assertion that 'we need to condemn a little more and understand a little less' (*Guardian* 22 February 1993). Such calls for a more punitive approach to the young receive popular support. Political parties in the US and Britain present themselves as 'tough on crime' to win votes. Echoing the Republican Mayor of New York, the then Labour Shadow

Home Secretary, Jack Straw, called for 'addicts and winos' (i.e. the homeless and destitute) to be cleared from the streets (*Guardian* 5 September 1995).

But what *is* needed is neither demonisations of youth as devils in red nor approbation of them as the saintly but wronged, but more balanced, empirically warranted and realistic representations of young people and their lives.

The 'screaming silence', as Craine calls it, in youth research regarding the potential for young people to become involved in deviant activities which *might* be understood through the underclass thesis has provided the intellectual space for the Radical Right to make the political running on these issues. In the 1980s and 1990s, the dearth of cogent, critical and comprehensive sociological investigations of illicit and licit youth cultural forms (and the 'social problems' associated with the underclass idea) has allowed this domain to be colonised by accounts which are partial, misleading and dangerous.

Thus, social scientists themselves are partly responsible for the currency now enjoyed by underclass theses; not, as Bagguley and Mann would have it, because we have been too quick to confer academic authority on them, but because we have been too slow to offer convincing alternative explanations. When the liberal Left and those who favour more structuralist explanations have been drawn into the underclass battle, they have tended to offer unrealistic, partial models of youth which juxtapose the Right's view of underclass youth as villains with a vision of youth as the hopeless, helpless victims of extraneous social forces (as explained by Jones in Chapter 7). Criminological theories of youth crime have been similarly blighted by 'a chronic tendency towards partiality' (Young 1994: 70).

For instance, because social scientists (and social work and youth work discourses) have too frequently explained (away) problems of youth disorder and wrong doing by recourse to the standard social constructionist battle-cry of 'moral panic' (e.g. Brown 1995), such explanations too frequently fail to find support beyond academia. This is what Jock Young calls criminology's 'great denial': a refusal to accept that there has been 'a real increase in crime or criminality' (1994: 78). Notions of 'moral panic' *can* help us understand how respectable fears emerge and are marshalled by the powerful and their interests at particular historical moments (see Blackman, Craine and Dean in this volume). But Roberts also reminds us that concepts like the underclass can serve an ideological function for ruling groups and can, at the same time, have foundations in empirical reality. Ideas which become hegemonic do so because they are, at least in part, rooted in the realities lived by oppressed groups. The chequered history and dubious political pedigree of underclass ideas do not disallow the fact that they may contain some 'fundamental truth' (Morris 1994: 9) or *describe* – partially – pressing social developments inadequately *explained* by the theories of the Right.

Assessing whether or not youth crime is increasing, and whether or not young people are correctly taken to be the main perpetrators of crime, is, of course, the subject of much complex debate (Young 1994). Young (1995) suggests that there has been a 120 per cent increase in crime as a whole since 1979, and Craine (in Chapter 9) argues that the link between rising levels of unemployment and rising levels of acquisitive crime over the same period is becoming clearer and clearer (see also Benyon 1993). James documents the alarming rises over the past decade in inter-personal violence, particularly that caused by young, low-income males (1995). Others are more sceptical and draw attention to the problems of interpreting criminal statistics as evidence of the reality of crime (see Jeffs and Smith 1995, for a concise review).

Putting the debate about the quantity of crime to one side, of at least equal importance is the qualitative impact of crime (by young people) on their communities. For those living in the poorest neighbourhoods of Britain, everyday life is now marked by fear of crime if not by crime itself (see Brown 1995; Joseph Rowntree Foundation 1995b). Such fears *are* fed by media discourses of the underclass young, but they cannot simply be written off as misplaced, 'false' consciousness.[5] The social and financial costs of acquisitive and more random and violent criminality (whether rising, falling or static) cannot be dismissed. The government's Audit Commission (1996) estimates that young people commit seven million offences per year at a combined cost to police, public services and victims of £8 billion. In Britain's 'dangerous places', crime, disorder and violence – particularly that perpetrated by young, working-class men – gnaw away at the social fabric (Campbell 1993; Hall 1995). Suggesting to those who are victims or fearful of crime that 'troublesome youth' have forever been with us, or are always the target for moral panics and disciplinarian programmes (Jeffs, Chapter 10; Pearson 1983), or that youth crime rates *may* in fact be falling, does not diminish the deleterious impact they have upon local community life (Pain 1995).

Similarly, debating the existence of a youth underclass – or the name which might better be given these phenomena – is understandably regarded as an academic luxury, reserved for those who do not face the immediacy of such social problems.

Robinson and Gregson note, correctly, that the underclass concept is 'now widely used . . . often not unthinkingly by people such as social workers, teachers and others repeatedly confronted by the realities of poverty and alienation' (1992: 48). This is, in fact, rather similar to Murray's point that:

> the people who deal most intimately with poor communities in their daily lives use the same distinction among poor people that I use. The managers of council estates, policemen in poor neighbourhoods, social workers, nurses, and physicians, may or may not bridle at the term 'underclass' but if the topic of conversation is . . . what life is like in the communities where they work, the distinction between the good folks and the underclass shines through after the first five minutes.
>
> (1990: 70)

We have shown underclass theories to be riddled with problems of a diverse nature. Yet the underclass idea retains potency and popularity partly because it grasps the fact, however tenuously, that *something* has changed in the worlds of the young, poor and unemployed. Macnicol, one of the most thorough critics of the underclass idea, puts it like this:

> Is there an underclass? No thoughtful visitor to the now-blighted inner city areas of Britain or America, whether Meadowell or Chicago's South Side, could deny that *something* new and frightening has happened: that there seem to have emerged groups of people who are suffering high levels of long-term unemployment and who may be permanently excluded from the labour process, and that this has had pronounced effect on social life in such communities.
>
> (1994a: 30, original emphasis)

Westergaard comments that although underclass theories may be shown to be a 'powerful myth which social science has a responsibility to explode' they may *also* suggest 'new paradigms of productive insight, which social science has a responsibility to explore' (1992: 581). In the following section, a perspective on youth and social exclusion which confronts the lived experiences and empirical realities of life in Britain's economically devastated locales and dangerous places is sketched out.

WORKING AT THE MARGINS: NEW PATTERNS OF YOUTH EXCLUSION

Deindustrialisation and surplus populations

This book documents how the institutions, arrangements and policies which have previously structured youth transitions – in employment, training, welfare, education, housing, the family, the criminal justice system – have themselves undergone dramatic restructuring in recent decades. The combined effect of these changes has been to make youth transitions riskier, more insecure and, for already disadvantaged youth, more prone to social exclusion. Prime amongst these processes has been the economic restructuring of youth.[6] Deindustrialisation and subsequent structural unemployment have hit young people disproportionately hard, obstructing paths to adult statuses, identities and activities. Sub-careers of 'poor work' (Brown and Scase 1991) at the margins of declining labour markets characterise the economic exclusion of an apparently surplus population; a population in which young people figure large.

Marginalisation and exclusion have generated new forms of urban poverty which afflict those exiled from the labour market mainstream in the US and Europe (Mingione 1993). Brown and Crompton (1994) consider exclusionary practices operating at (inter)national levels and see the possibility of a new pan-European underclass, comprised particularly of immigrant workers. US commentaries have been more certain that these developments have created a dangerous underclass (see Chapter 1). Gans suggests that social divisions may become so hardened that they create an 'under-caste' (1993). Some extend the underclass debate to offer visions of a dystopian future of social conflict, disorganisation and complete social collapse (e.g. see Macnicol 1994a). Fukuyama (1992) perceives this dangerous class as offering the only remaining threat to the dominance of the capitalist system. Others have talked of the anarchy coming as a consequence of the growing chasm, at international and national levels, between the rich elite and the poor underclass. Therborn (1986), for instance, talks of the 'Brasilianisation' of western societies with a rich middle class living (sometimes literally) above a growing mass of urban poor with the luxuries and wealth of the former guarded against the bubbling threat of the latter by increasingly authoritarian systems of security and punishment (see Galbraith 1992; and Davis 1990, on contemporary Los Angeles).

These are evocative scenarios of what might happen if current conditions and inequalities persist, and a powerful warning for Britain of the potential consequences of 'disastrous social and economic underdevelopment' (Robinson and Gregson 1992: 50). We *are* witnessing epochal social and economic transformations at global and national levels. Capitalism, in this 'post-industrial' period, has jettisoned its surplus population on an historically unprecedented scale. The International Labour Organisation estimates the world's unemployed to now total over one billion (reported in the *Guardian* 26 November 1996). And Macnicol is probably correct that the consequences for society will 'turn out to be the major item on the social agenda of the 21st century' (1994a: 38). Thus, some in this volume *do* hint at the emergence of a future underclass in Britain like that of the US (see also Smith 1992b; Dahrendorf 1987) and Silver (1993) reminds us that the creation of classes is an historical process likely to take several decades.

Britain certainly provides a good example of the way that the 'have nots' have become further distanced from the 'haves' during the 1980s and 1990s (Robinson and Gregson 1992; Westergaard 1992). But Britain is not America, and borrowing underclass scenarios from the American situation to describe futures here is misconceived (see Chapter 10; David 1994; Lash 1994).[7] Overall, British sociologists have been more restrained, less speculative, more closely tied to the empirical realities and *current* conditions of poverty, exclusion and *intra*-class division (Mann 1992). As Westergaard observes, these economic transformations and new forms of poverty have not in Britain *as yet* 'made for a new and distinctive divide between outcast "underclass" and incorporated "middle mass". There is no such sharp, single line towards the bottom of the pile' (1992: 580).

The labour market, social polarisation and new cultures of work

A number of commentators have – correctly, in my view – stressed the importance of keeping the labour market, and the opportunities it provides for people to work, at the heart of debates about social exclusion and the possibility of underclass formation (e.g. Maguire and Maguire in Chapter 2; Buck 1992; Morris 1994). The contingencies of British labour markets in the 1990s suggest that what we are witnessing – even in areas of seemingly intractable high unemployment – is not an underclass in the making.

Buck regards the long-term unemployed as 'not so much stable members of the underclass as unstable members of the working-class' (1992: 19). Westergaard notes that 'the turnover of people into and out of these [underclass] conditions is too high to fit the postulate of a distinct underclass' (1992: 577). Payne and Payne (1994) argue that the young unemployed of the early 1980s were able to rejoin the labour market later in the decade. A recent Department of Employment report (quoted by Wintour 1996) demonstrates that half of Britain's unemployed find jobs, lose them again within a year and return to claiming benefit (the figure for the north of England was 66 per cent reclaiming within a year). Similarly Daniel (1990) has drawn attention to the flows in and out of the stock of unemployed. Quoting Daniel's work, Cornford argues that there are 'almost as many poor people trapped in low paid work as on benefits . . . but what low income figures do not reveal are the *movements* between these groups' (1992: 61, my emphasis). Morris's research has been useful in exploring social polarisation in economically declining local labour markets (Morris 1992, 1993, 1994; Morris and Irwin 1992). She, too, questions the fastness of the divide between the economically inactive *unemployed* (the putative 'underclass') and those *underemployed* in 'new' types of casualised, non-standard work (Hakim 1987, 1989, 1990):

> [B]oth groups are clearly disadvantaged . . . and there is probably some movement . . . between them. The existence of an underemployed group, which seems likely to have grown given the changing patterns of employment throughout the 1980s, calls attention away from non-employment and towards the structure and operations of the labour market. The 'underclass' of the non-employed and state dependent then appears as an extreme position in the broader context.
>
> (Morris 1994: 162)

Thus, a focus upon these new forms of work, and how they have become organised and experienced in local labour markets in the 1990s, can give a picture of social polarisation and exclusion better than can underclass theories which focus only upon those perceived to be permanently deprived of work. Referring back to the definitions of the underclass given in Chapter 1 (by Runciman, Roberts and myself), it would seem that in poor areas of Britain there is *not* a class of people *beneath* the lowest class of the gainfully employed population almost *permanently* kept there by separate cultural outlooks and activities or by the structures of the labour market, but a restructuring of work typified by cyclical *movements* around peripheral work and unemployment. Unemployment, job insecurity and underemployment have become common *working-class* experiences, rather than the preserve of an underclass separated from and beneath them.

We know a lot about the numbing isolation and inactivity that many of the long-term unemployed will experience (e.g. Hayes and Nutman 1981; Jahoda 1982; Kelvin and Jarrett 1985). The sociology of employment has also told us much about the work that is done by the diminishing group who are able to get and keep standard jobs (e.g. Allen 1992; Salaman 1992). There is, however, now much more to the world of work than standard employment and complete unemployment. Between these labour market poles, as Morris says, lies a realm of casualised underemployment, made up of low paid, temporary and part-time work, self-employment and other types of informal economic activity (which employment or 'underclass' studies have said rather less about).

Global economic pressures, macro-economic restructuring, employers' strategies for 'flexibility' (Atkinson 1984) and government policies to deregulate labour markets have generated a growing culture of chronically insecure, risky and pluralised underemployment (Beck 1992; Hudson 1989; McLaughlin 1994; Morris 1994) in which women tend to outnumber men, and which adds to the 'feminisation of poverty' (Bruegel and Hegewisch 1994). Will Hutton (1996) reports a new study by Jarvis and Jenkins which estimates that over half the British workforce will be employed as part-timers, self-employed or temporary by the year 2000. It highlights the 'churning' of the poor and sometimes unemployed around these different, destandardised forms of work.

This transformation of work throws up a host of policy issues which should be of concern to sociologists (e.g. of low pay, as Cornford notes above, and the desirability of a Basic Income, of unequal access to segmented labour markets, of cumbersome benefit regulations based on a long-gone model of what work looked like). Cornford points out that 'we could greatly alleviate poverty, and reduce the nightmare of an underclass, directly and immediately by reversing many of the policies adopted over the last decade' (1992: 66). These chapters have suggested policy developments in respect of revamped youth training provision and allowances, less authoritarian youth work practice, more suitable housing provision for young people leaving home, more inclusive approaches to welfare and citizenship rights, more extensive childcare provision for young parents, and so on. None of this will come about, however, if the Conservative's lack of political will to grapple with issues of youth exclusion across a range of policy areas continues (Coles 1995; Jeffs, Chapter 10).

The most glaring gap in the agendas of all the main political parties is an honest discussion of structural unemployment and the future of work for young people. Politicians who recite the mantra of 'high quality training for a high skill economy' ignore the crushing facts of the new labour market conditions of the 1990s. For instance, in Teesside, according to official figures, only one in three youth trainees find employment afterwards (Teesside TEC 1995b). We need to ask again: training for what? The answer, given by these chapters, is probably some combination of unemployment and casualised work in the growing low-skill, low-wage sectors of the economy (see Chapter 2; McLaughlin 1994).[8]

Cultures of survival

This transformation in work, as well as demanding a new policy agenda, also demands that we progress theories of social exclusion beyond unrewarding hunts for a separate underclass to focus upon the range, forms and experience of underemployment and informal economic activity (MacDonald 1996c; Morris 1994). Attention shifts to the underexplored ways that those at the margins of the labour market engage with this rapidly changing world of work. Jordan and Redley propose a 'new orientation in research on social exclusion' which would investigate 'the survival strategies and cultures of resistance' of the poor and economically marginal (1994: 156). Coupled with this, a focus on the included, and how they come to be so, would be required. As Sibley reminds us: 'a study of exclusion . . . is necessarily concerned with inclusion, with the "normal" as much as the "deviant", the "same" as well as the "other", and with the credentials required to gain entry to the dominant groups in society' (1995: xv).

This perspective on the social exclusion and inclusion of young people would call for explorations of the *variety* of ways that young people respond to the changing structures of economic opportunity afforded them in labour markets undergoing rapid change (see Chapter 2). As Williamson in Chapter 5 implies, some older ideas from the sociology of deviance are pertinent (Cohen 1955; Matza 1964; Merton 1938). Cloward and Ohlin (1961) highlighted the way that subcultures formed in response to 'differential opportunities', prevailing in particular places and times, to achieve the dominant goals of a society. Young people in the 1990s tend to share quite conventional aspirations, but the paths of transition to mainstream, adult society have for some become blocked and for others more circuitous. As these chapters describe, the swift collapse of the economic certainties and stable welfare systems of Fordism (Crompton and Brown 1994) have generated new cultures of survival and new strategies of accommodation, negotiation and resistance amongst working-class young people.[9]

Murray implies that for working-class youth (particularly young men) there is one overriding response to growing up in poor, high unemployment locales (i.e. the rejection of work and all the other associated symptoms of the underclass). It is this 'deplorable behaviour in response' to these conditions which defines the underclass for him (1990: 68). What emerges in this volume, however, is that there is not simply *one* cultural response, even amongst youth who, on the face it, would be archetypal underclass members. Murray's advocates might respond that this does not preclude that one of these responses (amongst the others ignored) is the emergence of just such a criminogenic, anti-social underclass culture.

It is true that some young men turn to alternative careers of acquisitive crime. The impact upon the victims of their crimes, usually themselves poor people from the same class and locality (Anderson et al. 1992), *can* be 'deplorable'. Craine has shown, though, that these 'careers' emerge out of the context of severely circumscribed legitimate opportunities and that they are not understandable as a manifestation of a pathological underclass culture. Similarly, Hobbs has unearthed the various forms of illegal enterprise and innovative ways of 'doing the business' that surface as cultural responses to localised opportunity structures (Hobbs 1989, 1994).[10]

These *acquisitive* criminal careers are clearly gendered ones and a number of authors have now explored the way that masculinities can be related to more *violent* criminality (Newborn and Stanko

1994), particularly when young men have been cut loose from the incorporating structures of the economy. Campbell, for instance, describes how parts of Britain have been experiencing an extended 'economic emergency' since the mid-1970s, in which traditional forms of working-class, masculine identity have been dismantled together with the economies which supported them (1995). 'Marauding' working-class young men have become detached from useful, productive engagement with work and now prefer 'butch and brutal solutions to life's problems' (Campbell 1993: 23; see also Hobbs 1994; Slipman 1994). Hall (1995) also describes how the contemporary economic and cultural redundancy of particular forms of working-class masculinity finds expression in the nihilism and sometimes barbaric violence that dispossessed 'hard lads' inflict upon those around them.

This more realist approach to the delinquency of young men is a useful antidote to the excessive social constructionism which has pervaded liberal criminology (as discussed earlier).[11] It also reiterates the importance of appreciating the way that socially structured aspects of identity – particularly those informed by gender, class and race – help shape the cultural survival strategies of young people. Future research on social exclusion would need, for instance, to investigate more fully the way that some young men, sharing apparently similar social attributes, do not attempt the sorts of delinquent solutions described by Craine and others. Craine also notes that young women from the same locale again develop quite different responses. They tend to escape the dreary dead ends of the labour market by recourse to legitimate, traditional female activities and statuses: the 'mothering option'.

These gender-bounded responses may themselves be undergoing change. One recent survey has warned of a coming epidemic of violence amongst alienated teenage girls (Wilkinson and Mulgan 1995) and another has found evidence of young mothers turning to crime in order to provide for their families (Kempson et al. 1994). And although issues of race and racism have not been at the forefront of British discussions of the underclass (as explained in Chapter 1), writers such as Glasgow (1981), Pryce (1979) and Ullah (1987) have drawn attention to the diverse and changing cultural responses developed by black youth to the racial discrimination and class disadvantage they experience. As we approach the end of the century, the cultures of survival evolved by black youth and white youth, and by young men and young women, will continue to be multifarious, diverse, licit and illicit; and they will continue to demand more serious exploration from sociologists interested in the social exclusion of young people.

Getting by in the home of the 'New Rabble'

To conclude the book, and provide support for this perspective on social exclusion, I will take the liberty of drawing briefly upon my own research on Teesside in the north-east of England. This is a place which has undergone catastrophic economic collapse (Beynon et al. 1989). On the face of it, and using Murray's three indicators, it would seem to be a prime underclass locale. It is the sort of place social scientists might explore if they are to dispute seriously the underclass thesis. During the 1980s and 1990s, it has usually had the highest rates of unemployment in mainland Britain. It has exhibited the second highest illegitimacy rates in the country (Cleveland County Council 1992). Between 1971 and 1991, the area recorded the highest per cent increase in crime in Britain (up by 186 per cent) (ibid.). In 1995, Teesside residents faced a one in seven chance of being burgled, compared with a one in twenty-three chance in 1979. The incidence of violent crime has also risen dramatically (Home Office figures quoted in the Middlesbrough *Evening Gazette* 30 June 1995). Newspaper headlines pronounce Teesside to be the 'Car Crime Capital of Europe'. Nine out of ten offenders are not in full-time work (Cleveland County Council 1994). If we are going to find an underclass in Britain, it is going to be in a place like Teesside. Indeed, Murray singles it out as a home of the underclass 'New Rabble' (1994).

The methodology was, as well, the sort supported by Murray – not 'clipboards and multiple choice questionnaires' but 'long conversations conducted over weeks and months [years in fact] with the people who live there' (1990: 70) – and the sort that might uncover the localised 'minority underclass cultures' (Payne and Payne 1994), which might be hidden from conventional survey research. Qualitative interviews and discussion groups were held with over 300 working-class young people and adults between 1989 and 1994 (see MacDonald 1996b for a full discussion). None of them were in formal, standard employment or had been of late. All their work histories included lengthy bouts of unemployment. All but a few were, or had been recently, engaged in some form of informal economic activity or casualised work.

The studies documented changing cultures of work and the generally licit attempts at (re)establishing working lives. Some young people started their own small businesses or co-operatives and were lauded by Prince Charles, government ministers and enterprise agencies as budding 'young entrepreneurs' (MacDonald and Coffield 1991) albeit, though, with very limited commercial success in the long term (MacDonald 1996b). This was survival self-employment. Business failure led the vast majority back to the unemployment and benefit dependence which first motivated their enterprises. Their self-exploitative 'enterprise culture' was as wasteful – of individual hopes and energies, of working lives and state grants – as the alleged dependency culture which government intended it to replace.

Others volunteered, preferring work without pay to the idleness of unemployment (MacDonald 1996a). Indeed, a few risked losing their unemployment benefits because of their volunteering; hardly the 'economic rationality' Murray says characterises the unemployed's approach to welfare payments. Although we might classify these 'unemployed' volunteers as part of the economically surplus population, their care work was vital to agencies trying to fill the gaps left by cut-backs in social service provision. They were not 'unemployable', but became long-term unemployed because of the inability of their local labour market to provide these and other sorts of work as employment.

Some engaged in 'fiddly work' (MacDonald 1994). They did these risky – especially so since the government introduced the 'Benefit Cheats Hotline' – sometimes dangerous, always poorly remunerated, irregular scraps of work because of 'need not greed', as one Department of Social Security fraud manager candidly put it. 'Fiddly work' was needed in order to: maintain personal self-respect and identity; remain tied to the neighbourhood subcultures which distributed illicit *and* licit work; retain work disciplines; and to alleviate the poverty faced by benefit-dependent households. 'Fiddly work' was thus informed by quite conservative and moral considerations. Even those who had never done it largely understood and condoned those who had. A few interviewees had embarked upon quasi-criminal careers (e.g. in petty drug dealing) which intermingled with the search for more legitimate work. A small number moved away to seek their fortunes in more prosperous parts of the country or overseas in semi-nomadic careers, hunting temporary, casual jobs in the service and agricultural sectors of European economies. Other local people will have developed responses unrecorded by these studies.

Overall, the majority continued to carve out marginal 'careers' through permutations of: poor-quality government schemes (for under-18s then for adults); petty, doomed private enterprises; low-paid, low-skill, service sector 'McJobs'; irregular 'fiddly work'; occasional volunteering; and so on – all punctuated by lengthy periods of unemployed inactivity (despite increasingly stringent tests by the authorities of their availability for and willingness to work). They were experiencing first hand the cyclical movements between peripheral, non-standard work and unemployment typical of British labour markets in the 1990s.

There was one, inescapable conclusion which cut across all these studies. Both young people and adults wanted work. They would fail with flying colours the test Murray sets to prove the underclass's existence: 'offer them jobs at a generous wage for unskilled labour and see what happens' (1990: 21–2). They were extraordinarily dogged and enterprising in their search for work amidst the economic wreckage of their local labour market. They remained attached to remarkably durable, mainstream attitudes which valued work as the key source of self-respect, as the principal definer of personal identity, as a social (and in many cases moral) duty, as the foundation upon which to build sustainable family lives and respectable futures. Indeed, the way that they stubbornly clung on to orientations to work which are now possibly obsolescent, might be considered depressing given the limited supply of decent work – of 'proper jobs' as they called them – around. Their resourcefulness and energy was deserving of a more sustained and imaginative response from policy makers who seemed, then, to be content to further restrict access to diminishing state welfare support in the misconceived belief that the long-term unemployed 'underclass' need coercing into the labour market (Joseph Rowntree Foundation 1995b).

The interviewees were not necessarily representative of the local non-employed. They were selected *in order* to explore this sort of informal economic activity. But it is also true that there was no shortage of similarly inclined people to interview in such a prime 'underclass' location. Moreover, if underclass values are really 'contaminating the life of entire neighbourhoods' (Murray 1990: 4), it is strange to find no evidence of them infecting *this* group of precariously positioned poor people.

Howard Williamson, in Chapter 5, says that 'the jury is still out' on the question of the underclass. I suggest, however, that research which unearths the lived experiences and cultures of survival of the young, poor, unemployed and otherwise disadvantaged of 'under-class' localities will generate further evidence to prove them 'not guilty'. I would suggest also that such a perspective provides for a more productive recasting of research on contemporary youth, their transitions and social exclusion.

NOTES

1   It is difficult, however, to interpret this diversity in youth exclusion as evidence for the post-modernist claim that the structuring force of class is in decline, freeing social agents to follow individualised paths of transition (see Chapter 7 and Jones and Wallace 1992 for a critical discussion). What descriptions of the decision making of young people demonstrate most of all is the continuing role of class inequali-ties (and those attached to gender, ethnicity, disability and locality) in severely circumscribing room for social agency (Allen and Macey 1994). The 'deepening of social divisions in the context of disap-pearing solutions' (Bates and Riseborough 1993: 1) would seem to make post-modern rhetorics of individual liberty and choice, to borrow Robinson and Gregson's phrase, 'nothing more than a cruel joke' (1992: 46).

2   This sort of approach would assist in the complicated project of exploring the general relationships between precariously positioned young people and their past, present and future class locations (MacDonald 1991; Morris 1994: 109).

3   In autumn 1996, as this was being written, Britain was in the grip of a similar 'moral panic' sparked by the murder of headteacher Philip Lawrence, with Frances Lawrence's call for a new moral agenda, the earlier Dunblane tragedy and subsequent debate on gun control, and a series of exclusions of children from school (see the *Guardian* October 22, 26, 27 1996 for some of this). Again underclass terminology was used to link the debate about declining moral and civic values with anxieties about increasing violence, failing parents and, of course, delinquent youth.

4   For instance, by producing accounts within the discipline which move away from underclass theories compared to accounts in more public spheres (e.g. television and radio documentaries, newspaper features) which (reluctantly) retain underclass terminology but stress the struc-tural antecedents to the 'social problems' exciting media attention.

5   At a conference on youth crime – 'A Clockwork Orange: Deprived or Depraved?' – held in Newcastle in June 1995, it was noticeable how unreceptive the audience (primarily composed of local youth work practitioners, social workers, solicitors, teachers and others with everyday experience of youth offending) were to the idea that youth crime might be exaggerated in popular, media discourses on the subject. Contributions from the floor questioned Home Office statis-tics about the number of persistent young offenders, suggesting that in the experience of those present youth crime was far more widespread

than acknowledged either by official statistics or by liberally inclined criminologists. A recent report by Northumbria police also stated that they may have seriously underestimated the problem of persistent young offenders in the past (*Guardian* 12 November 1996).

6   I do not doubt the significance of other aspects of transition. For instance, housing transitions are vital in the creation of youth exclusion (e.g. homelessness). Patterns of, especially local authority, housing tenure can harden social polarisation for adult populations (Buck 1992; Byrne 1995; Smith 1992b). My contention is that such social processes are in the last instance, as they say, underwritten by processes of economic (dis)engagement with the labour market.

7   America and Britain have quite different economic, social and cultural histories, and, so far, dissimilar welfare systems. Exclusion, poverty and ghettoisation in the US cannot be understood without reference to the black American experience and histories of racial discrimination. Employment, the labour market and social class exclusion and reformation, not race, are the chief concerns of underclass debates in Britain (Morris 1994).

8   The training 'solution' is perhaps the most 'magical' and 'illusory' of all.

9   That these can be understood in the same way that, for instance, Hall and Jefferson (1976) theorise working-class subcultures is very much open to debate (and we still know very little about more middle-class youth cultural forms). I am arguing that young people's cultural articulation with work and the labour market, rather than consumption and leisure, is paramount. Yet one of the few sociological expositions of youth culture in the 1990s (Hollands 1995) suggests that, in places denuded of traditional forms of gendered employment, 'ordinary' young people instead begin to evolve cultural identities and feelings of belonging and community in relation to the new night-time club-cultures of British cities (see also Thornton 1995). Maybe it is through the detritus of debates about a youth underclass *culture* that we will see the welcome return of an invigorated sociology of youth culture in Britain.

10   The trading of illicit drugs will be of increasing importance in these illegitimate opportunity structures and will reflect rising levels of demand. Illicit drug use by young people has increased remarkably and become widespread and normalised *across* social class (and gender) categories in the late 1980s and 1990s (Measham et al. 1994; Parker et al. 1995). Illicit drug use is no longer, if it ever was, the preserve of a deviant (under)class. Rather than underclass theories which condemn drug use as just another indicator of immorality (Murray 1990), we desperately need more sociologically informed explorations of British drug cultures and the meanings ascribed by young people to different sorts of drug use (see Blackman in Chapter 8).

11   This new attention to changing forms of working-class masculinity has, admittedly, produced some uneasy theoretical bedfellows including: the right-wing neo-liberalism of Murray (1994), the socialist feminism of Campbell (1993), the ethical socialism of Dennis and Erdos (1992) and the historical materialism of Hall (1995).

Bibliography

Abberley, P. (1991) 'Counting us out: a discussion of the OPCS disability surveys', *Disability, Handicap and Society* 7(2): 139–55.

Ainley, P. (1991) *Young People Leaving Home*, London: Cassell.

—— (1993) 'The legacy of the Manpower Services Commission: training in the 1980s', in P. Taylor-Gooby and R. Lawson (eds) *Markets and Managers: New issues in the delivery of welfare*, Buckingham: Open University Press.

—— (1994) *Degrees of Difference: Higher Education in the 1990s*, London: Lawrence and Wishart.

Alcock, P. (1994) 'Back to the future: Victorian values for the 21st century', in C. Murray *Underclass: The Crisis Deepens*, London: Institute of Economic Affairs.

Allatt, P. and Yeandle, S. M. (1991) *Youth Unemployment and the Family: Voices of Disordered Times*, London: Routledge.

Allbeson, J. (1985) 'Seen but not heard: young people', in S. Ward (ed.) *DHSS in Crisis: Social security under pressure and under review*, London: Child Poverty Action Group.

Allen, J. (1992) 'Fordism and modern industry', in J. Allen, P. Braham and P. Lewis (eds) *Political and Economic Forms of Modernity*, Cambridge: Open University Press.

Allen, S. and Macey, M. (1994) 'Some issues of race, ethnicity and nationalism in the "New Europe": rethinking sociological paradigms', in P. Brown and R. Crompton (eds) *A New Europe? Economic Restructuring and Social Exclusion*, London: University College London Press.

Anderson, S., Kinsey, R., Loader, I. and Smith C. (1992) *Cautionary Tales: A Study of Young People and Crime in Edinburgh*, Aldershot: Avebury.

Anderton, J. (1985) *The Chief Constable's Report*, Manchester: Greater Manchester Police.

Andrews, K. and Jacobs, J. (1990) *Punishing the Poor: Poverty under Thatcher*, Basingstoke: Macmillan.

Armstrong, D. and Davies, P. (1995) 'The transition from school to adulthood: aspiration and careers advice for young adults with learning and adjustment difficulties', *British Journal of Special Education* 22(2): 70–5.

Ashton, D. (1992) 'The concept of the Youth Labour Market in the 1990s', paper given to International Youth Conference 'Youth and Social Change in Europe: Integration or Polarisation?', Moscow.

Ashton, D., Maguire, M. and Garland, V. (1982) *Youth in the Labour Market*, Research Paper No. 34, London: Department of Employment.

Ashton, D., Maguire, M. and Spilsbury, M. (1990) *Restructuring the Labour Market: The Implications for Youth*, London: Macmillan.

Aspire Consultants (1996) *Disaffection and Non-participation in Education, Training and Employment by Individuals Aged 18–20*, London: Department for Education and Employment.

Atkinson, J. (1984) 'Manpower strategies for flexible organisations', *Personnel Management* 28–31 August.

Atkinson, P. (1990) *The Ethnographic Imagination*, London: Routledge.

Atkinson, P., Rees, T., Shone, D. and Williamson, H. (1982) 'Social and life skills: the latest case of compensatory education', in T. Rees and P. Atkinson (eds) *Youth Unemployment and State Intervention*, London: Routledge and Kegan Paul.

Audit Commission (1996) *Young People and Crime*, London: Audit Commission.

Audit Commission/OFSTED (1993) *Unfinished Business: Full-time Education Courses for 16–19 Year Olds*, London: HMSO.

Auletta, K. (1982) *The Underclass*, New York: Random House.

Bagguley, P. and Mann, K. (1992) 'Idle thieving bastards? Scholarly representations of the "underclass" ', *Work, Employment and Society* 6(1): 113–26.

Baldwin, D. (1996) *Leaving School – Processes and Routes taken by Disabled Young People in Two Local Authorities*, DPhil thesis, unpublished draft chapters, Department of Social Policy and Social Work, University of York.

Banks, M., Breakwell, G., Bynner, J., Emler, N., Jamieson, L. and Roberts, K. (1984) 'Unemployment and less qualified urban young people', *Employment Gazette* 92(8): 343–6.

—— (1992) *Careers and Identities*, Milton Keynes: Open University Press.

Baran, B. (1988) 'Office automation and women's work: the technological transformation of the insurance industry', in R. E. Pahl (ed.) *On Work*, Oxford: Blackwell.

Barclay, G. C. (1992) *Digest 2: Information on the Criminal Justice System of England and Wales*, London: Home Office.

Barnardo's (1996a) *The Failure of Social Policy to Meet the Needs of Young People Leaving Care*, Ilford: Barnardo's.

—— (1996b) 'Children are being sold for sex in Great Britain', press release, 20 August 1996, Ilford: Barnardo's.

Barnes, C. (1991) *Disabled People in Britain and Discrimination: A case for anti-discrimination legislation*, London: Hirt.

Barnes, L. (1945) *Youth Service in an English County*, London: King George's Jubilee Trust.

Barnett, C. (1987) *The Audit of War: The Illusion and Reality of Britain as a Great Nation*, Basingstoke: Macmillan.

Barry, M. (1996) 'The Empowering Process: Leading from behind?', *Youth and Policy* 54: 1–12.

Bates, I. and Riseborough, G. (eds) (1993) *Youth and Inequality*, Buckingham: Open University Press.

Baxter, J. L. (1975) 'The chronic job-changer: a study of youth unemployment', *Social and Economic Administration* 9: 184–206.

Beauchamp, M. (1989) *On the Streets*, London: Harrap.

Beck, U. (1992) *Risk Society: Towards a new modernity* (trans. M. Ritter), London: Sage.

Becker, H. S. (1963) *Outsiders: Studies in the Sociology of Deviance*, New York: Free Press of Glencoe.

Benetell, D. (1996) *Invisible Women: Detached Youth Work with Girls and Young Women*, Leicester: Youth Work Press.

Bennetto, J. (1991) 'Police families terrorised in war with ram raiders', *Independent on Sunday*, 22 December 1991.

Benyon, J. (1994) *Law and Order Review 1993: An Audit of Crime, Policing and Criminal Justice Issues*, Leicester: Centre for the Study of Public Order.

Berridge, D. (1985) *Children's Homes*, London: Blackwell.

Beynon, H., Hudson, R., Lewis, J., Sadler, D. and Townsend, A. (1989) '"It's all falling apart here": Coming to terms with the Future in Teesside', in P. Cooke (ed.) *Localities: The Changing Face of Urban Britain*, London: Routledge.

Biehal, N., Clayton, J., Stein, M. C. and Wade, J. (1992) *Prepared for living*, London: National Children's Bureau.

—— (1995) *Moving On: Young people and leaving care schemes*, London: HMSO.

Biven, B. M. (1992) *The Finality of Youth: Tramps, Beats and Runaways*, Lima OH: Fairway Press.

Blackman, S. J. (1994) *Youth at Risk*, report submitted to the Home Office Central Drugs Prevention Unit, London.

—— (1995) *Youth: Positions and Opposition – Style, Sexuality and Schooling*, Aldershot: Avebury.

—— (1996) 'Has drug culture become an inevitable part of youth culture? A critical assessment of drug education', *Educational Review* Spring: 131–42.

Blair, A. C. L. (1996) Speech given at CPU Conference, Cape Town, South Africa, 14 October 1996.

Bone, M. and Meltzer, H. (1989) *The Prevalence of Disability among Children*, OPCS Surveys of Disability in Great Britain, Report 3, London: HMSO.

Bosanquet, H. (1896) *Rich and Poor*, London: Macmillan.

Bosman, R. and Louwes, W. (1988) 'School careers of children from one-parent and two-parent families', *Netherlands Journal of Sociology* 24: 117–31.

Bottomley, V. (1994) 'The government and family policy: background note', in *Report of the All Party Parliamentary Group on Parenting and International Year of the Family UK*, Parliamentary Hearings, London: HMSO.

Box, S. (1987) *Recession, Crime and Punishment*, London: Macmillan.

Bradshaw, J. and Holmes, H. (1989) *Living on the Edge*, Tyneside: Tyneside Child Poverty Action Group.

Brannen, K. and Middleton, L. (1994) *Scottish Young People's Survey 1991 (Autumn): Technical Report*, Centre for Educational Sociology: University of Edinburgh.

Brannen, K., Jones, G., Middleton, L. and Robertson, L. (1991) *Scottish Young People's Survey 1989 (Autumn): Technical Report*, Centre for Educational Sociology: University of Edinburgh.

Bray, R. (1911) *Boy Labour and Apprenticeships*, London: Fisher Unwin.

Breakwell, G. (1986) *Coping with Threatened Identities*, London: Methuen.

Brew, J. (1946) *Informal Education. Adventures and Reflections*, London: Faber.

Brewer, C. and Lait, J. (1980) *Can Social Work Survive?*, London: Temple Smith.

Brisenden, S. (1989) 'Young, gifted and disabled: entering the employment market', *Disability Handicap and Society* 4(3): 217–20.

British Youth Council (1992) *The Time of Your Life? The truth about being young in '90s Britain*, London: British Youth Council.

Brown, P. (1987) *Schooling Ordinary Kids*, London: Tavistock.

Brown, P. and Crompton, R. (eds) (1994) *A New Europe? Economic Restructuring and Social Exclusion*, London: University College London Press.

Brown, P. and Scase, R. (eds) (1991) *Poor Work: Disadvantage and the Division of Labour*, Buckingham: Open University Press.

—— (1994) *Higher Education and Corporate Realities: Class, culture and the decline of graduate careers*, London: UCL Press.

Brown, S. (1995) 'Crime and safety in whose community? Age, everyday life and problems for youth policy', *Youth and Policy* 48: 27–49.

Bruegel, I. and Hegewisch, A. (1994) 'Flexibilisation and part-time work in Europe', in P. Brown and R. Crompton (eds) *A New Europe? Economic Restructuring and Social Exclusion*, London: University College London Press.

Buck, N. (1992) 'Labour market inactivity and polarisation: a household perspective on the idea of the underclass', in D. Smith (ed.) *Understanding the Underclass*, London: Policy Studies Institute.

Burghes, L. (1994) *Lone Parenthood and Family Disruption: The Outcomes for Children*, London: Family Policy Studies Centre.

Burton, P., Forrest, R. and Stewart, M. (1989) *Growing Up and Leaving Home*, Luxembourg: Office for Official Publications of the European Communities.

Butler, T. and Savage, M. (eds) (1995) *Social Change and the Middle Classes*, London: UCL Press.

Butters, S. and Newell, S. (1978) *Realities of Training*, Leicester: National Youth Bureau.

Bynner, J. (1987) 'Transition to what? ESRC's new 16–19 initiative', *ESRC Newsletter 61*, November, Swindon: ESRC.

—— (1991) 'Controlling transition', *Work, Employment and Society* 5(4): 645–58.

Byrne, D. (1995) 'Deindustrialisation and dispossession: an examination of social division in the industrial city', *Sociology* 29: 95–115.

Campbell, B. (1993) *Goliath: Britain's Dangerous Places*, London: Methuen.

—— (1995) 'Masculinity, crime and community crisis', paper given at conference entitled 'A Clockwork Orange: Deprived or Depraved?', held at Newcastle-upon-Tyne, June 1995.

Campbell, D. (1992) 'Making crime pay, to the tune of £14 billion', *Guardian*, 17 August 1992.

Carpenter, M. (1857) 'Juvenile delinquency in its relation to the educational movement', in A. Hill (ed.) *Essays upon Educational Subjects*, London: Longman, Brown, Green, Longmans and Roberts.

Cavadino, P. (1995) 'The Criminal Justice and Public Order Act 1994 and young offenders', *Youth and Policy* 48: 71–83.

CBI (1989) *Towards a Skills Revolution*, Report of the Vocational Education and Training Task Force, London.

Chatrik, B. (1996) 'Severe Hardship claims reach an all-time high', *Working Brief* 73: 14–15.

Cherry, N. (1976) 'Persistent job-changing – is it a problem?', *Occupational Psychology* 49(4): 203–21.

Chesney-Lind, M., Shelden, R. G. and Joe, K. (1996) 'Girls, delinquency and gang membership', in C. R. Huff (ed.) *Gangs In America*, Thousand Oaks CA: Sage.

Children's Society (1996) *Severe Hardship Payments: a matter of discretion*, London: Children's Society.

Chiricos, T. G. (1987) 'Rates of crime and unemployment: an analysis of aggregate research evidence', *Social Problems* 34(2): 182–203.

Chisholm, L. (1990) 'A sharper lens or a new camera? Young people and social change in Britain', in L. Chisholm, P. Büchner, H. Krüger and P. Brown (eds) (1990) *Childhood, Youth and Social Change*, Lewes: Falmer Press.

Cieslik, M. (1996) 'Underclass youth and the family: the problem of single mothers', paper presented to conference on 'British Youth Research: The New Agenda', Glasgow.

Clarke, J. and Willis, P. (1984) 'Introduction', in I. Bates, J. Clarke, P. Cohen, D. Finn, R. Moore and P. Willis *Schooling for the Dole: The New Vocationalism*, London: Macmillan.

Cleveland County Council (1992) *Review of the Assisted Areas of Great Britain: A Response to the DTI Consultation Paper from the Local Authorities in Cleveland County*, Middlesbrough.

—— (1994) *Unemployment in Cleveland*, (March) Middlesbrough: Department of Environment, Development and Transport.

Clifford, J. (1986) 'Introduction: partial truths', in J. Clifford and G. Marcus (eds) *Writing Cultures: The Poetics and Politics of Ethnography*, Berkeley CA: University of California Press.

Cloward, R. and Ohlin, L. (1961) *Delinquency and Opportunity: A Theory of Delinquent Gangs*, New York: Free Press.

Coffield, F. (1991) *Vandalism and Graffiti: The State of the Art*, London: Calouste Gulbenkian Foundation.

Coffield, F., Borrill, C. and Marshall, S. (1986) *Growing Up at the Margins*, Milton Keynes: Open University Press.

Cohen, A. (1955) *Delinquent Boys: the Culture of the Gang*, New York: Free Press.

Cohen, P. (1982) 'School for Dole', *New Socialist* 3 (January/February): 43–7.

Cohen, S. (1973) *Folk Devils and Moral Panics*, St Albans: Paladin.

Coles, B. (1986) 'Gonna tear your playhouse down: towards reconstructing a sociology of youth', paper given at 'Conference of Social Science Teachers', University of York, June 1986.

—— (1995) *Youth and Social Policy: Youth Citizenship and Young Careers*, London: UCL Press.

—— (ed.) (1988) *Young Careers*, Milton Keynes: Open University Press.

Commission on Social Justice (1993) *The Justice Gap*, London: Institute for Public Policy Research.

Connolly, M., Roberts, K., Ben-Tovim, G. and Torkington, P. (1991) *Black Youth in Liverpool*, Culemborg: Giordano Bruno.

Convery, P. and Chatrik, B. (1994) '120,000 unemployed 16 and 17 year olds: 3/4 have no income', *Working Brief* 56: 12 July.

Cook, D. (1989) *Rich Law, Poor Law: Different responses to tax and supplementary benefit fraud*, Milton Keynes: Open University Press.

Coopers and Lybrand (1994) *Preventive Strategy for Young People in Trouble*, London: Prince's Trust.

Corbett, J. (1990) *Uneasy Transitions: Disaffection in Post-Compulsory Education and Training*, Basingstoke: Falmer Press.

Corbett, J. and Barton, L. (1992) *A Struggle for Choice: Students with special educational needs in transition to adulthood*, London: Routledge.

Cornford, J. (1992) 'Policy Issues and the Underclass Debate', in D. Smith (ed.) *Understanding the Underclass*, London: Policy Studies Institute.

Corrigan, P. (1976) 'Doing nothing', in S. Hall and T. Jefferson (eds) *Resistance through Rituals*, London: Hutchinson.

Courtnay, G. and McAleese, I. (1993) *England and Wales Youth Cohort Study, Cohort 5: aged 16–17 years old in 1991, Report on Sweep 1*, Research and Development, Youth Cohort Series 22, Sheffield: Employment Department.

—— (1994) *England and Wales Youth Cohort Study, Cohort 4: aged 17–18 years old in 1990, Report on Sweep 2*, Research and Development, Youth Cohort Series 27, Sheffield: Employment Department.

Craig, G. (1991) *Fit For Nothing: Young People, Benefits and Youth Training*, London: Children's Society.

Craine, S. F. (1988) 'The hoisters: survival crime and informal community networks', paper presented at Group for Anthropology in Policy and Practice Conference 'Ethnography of the North West', 16 January 1988, University of Manchester.

—— (1994) *Beggars Can't be Choosers: An Ethnography of Youth Transitions in a High Unemployment Area*, unpublished PhD thesis, Salford: University of Salford.

Craine, S. F. and Coles, B. (1995) 'Alternative careers: youth transitions and young people's involvement with crime', *Youth and Policy* 48: 6–27.

Bibliography

Crompton, R. (1996) 'The fragmentation of class analysis', *British Journal of Sociology* 47: 56–67.
Crompton, R. and Brown, P. (1994) 'Introduction', in P. Brown and R. Crompton (eds) *A New Europe? Economic Restructuring and Social Exclusion*, London: University College London Press.
Crow, I. (1982) 'The Unemployment/Crime Link', *Unemployment Unit Bulletin* 4 (July): 4–5.
Crow, I., Richardson, P. and Riddington, C. (1989) *Unemployment, Crime and Offenders*, London: Routledge.
Dahrendorf, R. (1987) *The Underclass and the Future of Britain*, 10th Annual Lecture, Windsor: St. George's House.
—— (1992) 'Footnotes to the discussion', in D. Smith (ed.) *Understanding the Underclass*, London: Policy Studies Institute.
Daniel, W. W. (1990) *The Unemployed Flow*, London: Policy Studies Institute.
Daniel, W. W. and Stilgoe, E. (1977) *Where are They Now?*, London: Political and Economic Planning.
David, M. (1994) 'Fundamentally Flawed', in Murray, C. *Underclass: The Crisis Deepens*, London: Institute for Economic Affairs.
Davies, B. (1986) *Threatening Youth: Towards a National Youth Policy*, Milton Keynes: Open University Press.
Davies, J. (ed.) (1993) *The Family: Is it just another Lifestyle Choice?*, London: Institute of Economic Affairs.
Davis, J. (1990) *Youth and the Condition of Britain: Images of Adolescent Conflict*, London: Athlone.
Davis, M. (1990) *City of Quartz*, London: Vintage.
Dawes, L. (1993) *Long-Term Unemployment and Labour Market Flexibility*, Leicester: Centre for Labour Market Studies, University of Leicester.
Deakin, B. M. (1996) *The Youth Labour Market in Britain: The Role of Intervention*, Cambridge: Cambridge University Press.
Deakin, N. (1990) 'Mr. Murray's Ark', in C. Murray *The Emerging British Underclass*, London: Institute for Economic Affairs.
Dean, H. (1991) 'In search of the underclass', in P. Brown and R. Scase (eds) *Poor Work: Disadvantage and the Division of Labour*, Buckingham: Open University Press.
Dean, H. and Melrose, M. (1995) *Manageable Discord: Citizenship and welfare fraud*, Economic Beliefs and Behaviour Programme Discussion Paper No. 6, Canterbury: Economic and Social Research Council.
—— (1996) 'Unravelling citizenship: the significance of social security benefit fraud', *Critical Social Policy* 48(16): 3–32.
Dean, H. and Taylor-Gooby, P. (1992) *Dependency Culture: The explosion of a myth*, Hemel Hempstead: Harvester Wheatsheaf.
Dench, S. (1993) 'What types of people are employers seeking to employ?', paper presented to Employment Department/Policy Studies Institute Conference on 'Unemployment in Focus', Rotherham.
Dennis, N. (1993) *Rising Crime and the Dismembered Family*, London: Institute of Economic Affairs.
Dennis, N. and Erdos, G. (1992) *Families Without Fatherhood*, London: Institute of Economic Affairs.

Department for Education (1994) *Code of Practice and the Identification and Assessment of Special Educational Needs*, London: Department for Education.

Department of Education and Science (1978) *Special educational needs: Report of the committee of enquiry into the education of handicapped children and young people*, London: DES.

—— (1992) *The Further and Higher Education Act*, London: DES.

—— (1993) *The Education Act*, London: DES.

Department of Employment (1981) *A New Training Initiative: A Programme for Action*, London: HMSO.

—— (1988) *Employment for the 1990s*, London: HMSO.

—— (1988) *The Education Reform Act*, London: DES.

Department of Health (1991) *The Children Act 1989: Guidance and Regulations* (1–9), London: HMSO.

Department of Health and Social Security (1986) *The Disabled Persons Act (Services, Consultation and Representation)*, London: DHSS.

Dronkers, J. (1994) 'The changing effects of lone-parent families on the educational attainment of their children in a European welfare state', *Sociology* 28: 171–91.

Eager, W. (1953) *Making Men*, London: University of London Press.

Edgell, S. and Duke, V. (1991) *A Measure of Thatcherism*, London: Harper-Collins.

Edin, K. (1991) 'Surviving the Welfare System: how AFDC recipients make ends meet in Chicago', *Social Problems* 38(4): 462–74.

Elder, G. H. (1974) *Children of the Great Depression*, Chicago: University of Chicago Press.

Employment Department (1991) 'Into work', *Skills and Enterprise Briefing* 15/91 (October), London: Employment Department.

—— (1994) *Labour Market and Skill Trends 1995/96*, London: Employment Department.

Evason, E. and Woods, R. (1995) 'Poverty, deregulation of the labour market and benefit fraud', *Social Policy and Administration* 29(1): 40–54.

Fainstein, N. (1993) 'Race, class and segregation: discourses about African Americans', in *International Journal of Urban and Regional Research* 17(3): 384–403.

Farmer, E. and Parker, R. (1991) *Trials and Tribulations: Returning Children from Local Authority Care to their Families*, London: HMSO.

Farrington, D. P., Gallagher, B., Morley, L., St Ledger, R. J. and West, D. J. (1986) 'Unemployment, school leaving, and crime', *British Journal of Criminology* 26(4): 335–56.

Fergusson, R. and Unwin, L. (1993) 'Staying power', in *Guardian Education*, 9 November 1993: 4.

Field, F. (1989) *Losing Out: The Emergence of Britain's Underclass*, Oxford: Blackwell.

—— (1990) 'Britain's Underclass: Countering the Growth', in C. Murray *The Emerging British Underclass*, London: Institute for Economic Affairs.

—— (1993) *An Agenda For Britain*, London: HarperCollins.

Foster, J. (1990) *Villains*, London: Routledge and Kegan Paul.

Foucault, M. (1977) *Discipline and Punish*, London: Penguin.

Franklin, B. (ed.) (1986) *The Rights of Children*, Oxford: Blackwell.

Fraser, S. (1995) (ed.) *The Bell Curve Wars: Race, Intelligence and the Future of America*, New York: HarperCollins.

Fryer, D. (1986) 'Employment deprivation and personal agency during unemployment', *Social Behaviour* 1(1): 3–23.

Fukuyama, F. (1992) *The End of History and the Last Man*, New York: Free Press.

Full Employment UK (1990) *Britain's New Underclass: Challenges for the Employment Services*, London: Full Employment UK.

Furlong, A. (1992) *Growing Up in a Classless Society? School to Work Transitions*, Edinburgh: University of Edinburgh Press.

Furlong, A. and Spearman, M. (1989) 'Psychological well-being and the transition from school to work', *British Journal of Education and Work* 3(1): 49–55

Galbraith, K. (1992) *The Culture of Contentment*, London: Penguin.

Gallie, D. (1988) 'Employment, unemployment and social stratification', in D. Gallie (ed.) *Employment in Britain*, Oxford: Basil Blackwell.

—— (1994) 'Are the unemployed an underclass? Some evidence from the social change and economic life initiative', *Sociology* 28(3):737–57.

Gallie, D. and White, M. (1993), *Employee Commitment and the Skills Revolution*, London: Policy Studies Institute.

Gans, H. (1990) 'Deconstructing the underclass', *American Planning Association Journal* 52: 271–7.

—— (1993) 'From "underclass" to "undercaste": some observations about the future of the postindustrial economy and its major victims', *International Journal of Urban and Regional Research* 17(3): 327–35.

—— (1995) *The War Against the Poor: The Underclass and Anti-Poverty Policy*, New York: Basic Books.

Garnett, L. (1992) *Leaving Care and After*, London: National Children's Bureau.

Geertz, C. (1973) *The Interpretation of Cultures*, London: Hutchinson.

Gibson, B. (1995) 'Young people, bad news, enduring principles', *Youth and Policy* 48: 64–70.

Giddens, A. (1973) *The Class Structure of the Advanced Societies*, London: Hutchinson.

—— (1991) *Modernity and Self-Identity: Self and Society in the Late Modern Age*, Cambridge: Polity Press.

—— (1994) 'Living in a post-traditional society', in U. Beck, A. Giddens and S. Lash (eds) *Reflexive Modernisation*, Cambridge: Polity Press.

Gilchrist, R. and Jeffs, T. (1995) 'Foyers: housing solution or folly?', *Youth and Policy* 50: 1–14.

Gillis, J. R. (1974) *Youth and History*, New York: Academic Press.

Giroux, H. (1996) *Fugitive Cultures: Race, Violence and Youth*, New York: Routledge.

Gittins, D. (1993) *The Family in Question: Changing Households and Familiar Ideologies*, 2nd edition, Basingstoke: Macmillan.

Glasgow, A. (1981) *The Black Underclass*, New York: Vintage Books.

Goetschius, G. and Tash, J. (1967) *Working With Unattached Youth*, London: RKP.

Gofton, C. and Gofton, L. (1984) 'Making out in Giro City', *New Society* 22 November 1984: 280–2.

Golding, P. and Middleton, S. (1982) *Images of Welfare*, Oxford: Martin Robertson.

Goldthorpe, J. H., Llewellyn, C. and Payne, C. (1987) *Social Mobility and Class Structure in Modern Britain*, Oxford: Clarendon Press.

Goldthorpe, J. H., Lockwood, D., Platt, J. and Bechoffer, F. (1968) *The Affluent Worker in the Class Structure*, Cambridge: Cambridge University Press.

Gray, J. (1992) 'What's driving the recent increases in post-16 staying on rates? Some propositions for review and debate', ESRC Research Seminar on 'Participation in Education and Training: Age Group 16–19', June 1992.

Gray, J., Jesson, D. and Tranmer, M. (1993) *England and Wales Youth Cohort Study. Boosting Post-16 Participation in Full-time Education: A study of some key factors*, Research Series, Youth Cohort Report 20, Sheffield: Employment Department.

Green, D. (1992) 'Liberty, policy and the underclass', in D. Smith (ed.) *Understanding the Underclass*, London: Policy Studies Institute.

—— (1993) *Reinventing Civil Society*, London: Institute of Economic Affairs.

Griffin, C. (1986) 'Broken transitions: from school to the scrap heap', paper presented to 'British Sociological Association Conference', University of Loughborough, March 1986.

—— (1993) *Representations of Youth*, Cambridge: Polity Press.

Hakim, C. (1987) 'Trends in the flexible workforce', *Employment Gazette* 95(11): 549–60.

—— (1989) 'Workforce restructuring, social insurance coverage and the Black Economy', *Journal of Social Policy* 18(4): 471–503.

—— (1990) 'Core and periphery in employers' workforce strategies: evidence from the 1987 ELUS survey', *Work, Employment and Society* 4(2): 157–88.

Hall, P. (1952) *The Social Services of Modern England*, London: RKP.

Hall, S. (1995) 'Grasping at straws: the idealisation of the material in liberal conceptions of youth crime', *Youth and Policy* 48: 49–64.

Hall, S. and Jefferson, T. (eds) (1976) *Resistance through Rituals*, London: Hutchinson.

Hamburg, D. A. (1992) *Today's Children: Creating a Future for a Generation in Crisis*, New York: Times Books.

Harding, P. and Jenkins, R. (1989) *The Myth of the Hidden Economy*, Milton Keynes: Open University Press.

Haskey, J. (1994) 'Stepfamilies and stepchildren in Great Britain', *Population Trends* 76: 17–28.

Hayek, F. (1976) *Law, Legislation and Liberty: Volume 2 – The Mirage of Social Justice*, London: Routledge and Kegan Paul.

Hayes, J. and Nutman, P. (1981) *Understanding the Unemployed*, London: Tavistock.

Heath, A. (1992) 'The attitudes of the underclass', in D. Smith (ed.) *Understanding the Underclass*, London: Policy Studies Institute.

Hebdige, D. (1988) *Hiding in the Light*, London: Routledge.

Hendricks, H. (1990) *Images of Youth: Age, Class and the Male Youth Problem 1880–1920*, Oxford: Oxford University Press.

—— (1994) *Child Welfare: England 1872–1989*, London: Routledge.

Hendry, L., Love, J., Craik, I. and Mack, J. (1994) *Measuring the Benefits of Youth Work*, Edinburgh: Scottish Office Education Department.

Herrnstein, R. J. and Murray, C. (1994) *The Bell Curve*, New York: Free Press.

Hessing, D., Elffers, H., Robben, H. and Webley, P. (1993) 'Needy or greedy? The social psychology of individuals who fraudulently claim unemployment benefits', *Journal of Applied Social Psychology* 23(3): 226–43.

Hirsch, D. (1983) *Youth Unemployment: A Background Paper*, London: Youthaid.

Hirst, M. and Baldwin, S. (1994) *Unequal Opportunities: Growing Up Disabled*, London: HMSO.

HMSO (1992) *Households Below Average Income: A Statistical Analysis 1979–1988/89*, London: HMSO.

—— (1996) *Social Trends 26*, London: Central Statistical Office.

Hobbs, D. (1989) *Doing the Business*, Oxford: Oxford University Press.

—— (1994) 'Mannish boys', in T. Newburn and E. Stanko (eds) *Just Boys Doing Business? Men, Maculinities and Crime*, London: Routledge.

Holland, G. (1977) *Young People and Work*, London: Manpower Services Commission.

Holland, J., Ramazanoglu, C. and Sharpe, S. (1993) 'Wimp or Gladiator', *WRAP/MRAP* (9), London: Tufnell Press.

Hollands, R. G. (1990) *The Long Transition: Class Culture and Youth Training*, Basingstoke: Macmillan.

—— (1995) *Friday Night, Saturday Night: Youth Cultural Identification in the Post-industrial City*, Newcastle: University of Newcastle upon Tyne.

Holman, B. (1994/5) 'Urban youth – not an underclass', *Youth and Policy* 47: 69–78.

Home Office (1989) *Bulletin: Criminal Careers of those born in 1953 and 1963*, London: Home Office Research and Statistics Department 27/89.

Honess, T. H. (1989) 'A longitudinal study of school-leavers' employment experiences, time structuring and self-attributions as a function of local opportunity structure', *British Journal of Psychology* 80: 45–77.

Hopkins, M. (1947) *Hannah More and Her Circle*, New York: Longman, Green.

Horton, C. (1985) *Nothing Like a Job*, London: Youthaid.

Howe, L. (1994) 'Ideology, domination and unemployment', *Sociological Review* 42: 315–40.

Hudson, R. (1989) 'Labour market changes and new forms of work in old industrial regions: maybe flexibility for some but not flexible accumulation', *Environment and Planning D: Society and Space* 7: 5–30.

Humphries, S. (1981) *Hooligans or Rebels? An Oral History of Working Class Childhood and Youth 1889–1939*, Oxford: Blackwell.

Hunt, J. and Small, P. (1981) *Employing Young People* (Scottish Council for Research), in S. Hutson and R. Jenkins (1989) *Taking the Strain*, Milton Keynes: Open University Press.

Hutson, S. and Liddiard, M. (1994) *Youth Homelessness*, Basingstoke: Macmillan.

Hutton, W. (1995) *The State We're In*, London: Cape.

—— (1996) 'Churning in and out of poverty in Tory Britain', *Observer*, 20 October 1996.

Industrial Relations Services (1996) 'Recruiting and training school-leavers: the 1996 IRS Survey', *Employee Development Bulletin* June: 6–13.

Inniss, L. and Feagin, J. R. (1989) 'The "black underclass": ideology in race relations analysis', *Social Justice* 16(4): 13–34.

Inter-Departmental Committee on Physical Deterioration (1904) *Report Cmnd 2175*, London: HMSO.

Istance, D., Rees, G. and Williamson, H. (1994) *Young People Not in Education, Training or Employment in South Glamorgan*, Cardiff: South Glamorgan Training and Enterprise Council/University of Wales, Cardiff.

Jacoby, R. and Glauberman, N. (eds) (1995) *The Bell Curve Debate: History, Documents, Opinions*, New York: Times Books.

Jahoda, M. (1979) 'The impact of unemployment in the 1930s and the 1970s', *Bulletin of the British Psychological Society* 32: 309–14.

—— (1981) 'Work, employment and unemployment', *American Psychologist* 36(2): 184–91.

—— (1982) *Employment and Unemployment: A Social Psychological Analysis*, Cambridge: Cambridge University Press.

James, O. (1990) 'Crime and the American mind', *Independent*, 21 May 1990.

—— (1995) *Juvenile Violence in a Winner–Loser Culture*, London: Free Association.

Jeffs, T. (1979) *Young People and the Youth Service*, London: Routledge.

—— (1987) 'Youth and community work and the community school', in G. Allen (ed.) *Community Education: An Agenda for Educational Reform*, Milton Keynes: Open University Press.

—— (1994) 'Children's rights, schools and recent legislation', in B. Franklin (ed.) *Children's Rights: A handbook of comparative policy and practice*, London: Routledge.

Jeffs, T. and Smith, M. (1990a) 'Youth work, youth service and the next few years', *Youth and Policy* 31: 15–28.

—— (1990b) *Using Informal Education*, Milton Keynes: Open University Press.

—— (1993) 'Getting the job done: training for youth work', *Youth and Policy* 40: 10–32.

—— (1994) 'Young people, youth work and a new authoritarianism', *Youth and Policy* 46: 17–32.

—— (1995) 'Youth', *Developments in Sociology* (11), Lancashire: Causeway Press.

—— (1996a) 'Getting the dirtbags off the streets', *Youth and Policy* 53: 1–14.

—— (1996b) *Informal Education*, Ticknall, Derbyshire: Education Now Books.

Jencks, C. and Peterson, P. E. (eds) (1991) *The Urban Underclass*, New York: Brookings.

Jenkins, R. (1982) 'Acceptability, suitability and the search for the habituated worker: how ethnic minorities and women lose out', paper presented to workshop on The Management and Mismanagement of Labour, Loughborough University.

—— (1983) *Lads, Citizens and Ordinary Kids*, London: Routledge and Kegan Paul.

Jephcott, P. (1943) *Clubs For Girls*, London: Faber.

Jones, G. (1995a) *Leaving Home*, Buckingham: Open University Press.

—— (1995b) *Family Support for Young People*, London: Family Policy Studies Centre and Joseph Rowntree Foundation.

Jones, G. and Stevens, C. (1993) 'Young people in and out of the housing market: About the project', *Project Working Paper 5*, Centre for Educational Sociology, University of Edinburgh.

Jones, G. and Wallace, C. (1992) *Youth, Family and Citizenship*, Buckingham: Open University Press.

Jones, J. (1992) *The Dispossessed: America's Underclass from the Civil War to the Present*, New York: Basic Books.

Jones, M. G. (1952) *Hannah More*, Cambridge: Cambridge University Press.

Jones, P., Williamson, H., Payne, J. and Smith, G. (1983) *Out of School: A Case Study of the Role of Government Schemes at a Time of Growing Unemployment*, Sheffield: Manpower Services Commission.

Jordan, B. and Redley, P. (1994) 'Polarisation, the underclass and the welfare state', *Work, Employment and Society* 8(2): 153–76.

Jordan, B., James, S., Kay, H. and Redley, P. (1992) *Trapped in Poverty? Labour market decisions in low income households*, London: Routledge.

Joseph Rowntree Foundation (1995a) *Single Lone Mothers*, Social Policy Research Findings 84, York: JRF.

—— (1995b) *Progress and Polarisation on Twenty Council Estates*, Housing Research Findings 151, York: JRF.

Jowell, R., Curtice, J., Brook, L. and Ahrendt, D. (eds) (1994) *British Social Attitudes: The 11th Report*, Aldershot: SCPR/Dartmouth.

Kamin, L. (1995) 'Lies, damned lies and statistics', in R. Jacoby and N. Glauberman (eds) *The Bell Curve: History, Documents, Opinions*, New York: Random House.

Kanter, R. M. (1990) *When Giants Learn to Dance*, London: Unwin Hyman.

Kaplan, H. B. (1980) *Deviant Behaviour in Defence of Self*, New York: Academic Press.

Katz, M. (ed.) (1993) *The 'Underclass' Debate: Views from History*, Princeton NJ: Princeton University Press.

Keep, E. and Mayhew, K. (1994) 'UK Training Policy – Assumptions and Reality', in A. Booth and D. J. Snower (eds) *The Skills Gap and Economic Activity*, Cambridge: Cambridge University Press.

Kelvin, P. and Jarrett, J. (1985) *Unemployment: Its Social Psychological Effects*, Cambridge: Cambridge University Press.

Kelvin, P., Dewberry, C. and Morley-Bunker, N. (1984) *Unemployment and Leisure*, London: University College.

Kempson, E., Rollinson, K. and Bryson, A. (1994) *Hard Times: How Poor Families Make Ends Meet*, London: Policy Studies Institute.

Kendrick, A. and Rioch, C. (1995) 'Knowing the back roads', *Youth and Policy* 51: 46–57.

Kiernan, K. (1992) 'The impact of family disruption in childhood on transitions made in young adult life', *Population Studies* 46(2): 525–49.

Kingdom, J. (1991) *Local Government and Politics in Britain*, Hemel Hempstead: Phillip Allan.

Kinsey, R. (1993) 'Innocent underclass', in *New Statesman and Society*, 5 March 1993: 16–17.

Kroll, B. and Barrett, D. (1995) 'Troublesome children: failure and moral liability', in H. Dean (ed.) *Parents' Duties, Children's Debts*, Aldershot: Arena.

Labour Market Quarterly Report (1996) 'Youth Training/Youth Credits Outcomes', *Labour Market Quarterly Report* May 1996.

Lash, S. (1994) 'The making of an underclass; neo-liberalism versus corporatism', in P. Brown and R. Crompton (eds) *A New Europe? Economic Restructuring and Social Exclusion*, London: University College London Press.

Lawrence, E. (1982) 'Just plain common sense: the "roots" of racism', in Centre for Contemporary Studies (eds) *The Empire Stikes Back: Race and racism in '70s Britain*, London: Hutchinson.

Lee, D., Marsden, D., Rickman, P. and Dunscombe, J. (1990) *Scheming for Youth: A Study of YTS in the Enterprise Culture*, Buckingham: Open University Press.

Lerner, R. M. (1995) *America's Youth in Crisis*, Thousand Oaks CA: Sage.

Lewis, O. (1966) *La Vida*, New York: Random House.

Liddiard, M. and Hutson, S. (1991) 'Homeless young people and runaways – agency definitions and processes', *Journal of Social Policy* 20(3): 365–88.

Lilley, P. (1992) 'The something for nothing society', speech to the Conservative Party Conference, Blackpool, 1992.

Lipsitz, G. (1994) 'We know what time it is: race, class and youth culture in the nineties', in A. Ross and T. Rose (eds) *Microphone Fiends: Youth Music and Youth Culture*, New York: Routledge.

Lister, R. (1990) *The Exclusive Society: Citizenship and the Poor*, London: Child Poverty Action Group.

Little, M. (1990) *Young Men in Prison: The Criminal Identity Explored Through the Rules of Behaviour*, Aldershot: Dartmouth.

Loader, I. (1996) *Youth, Policing and Democracy*, London: Macmillan.

Lucas, N. (1973) *Britain's Gangland*, London: Westwood.

MacDonald, R. (1991) 'Youth, Class and Locality in Rural England', *Youth and Policy* 33: 17–27.

—— (1994) 'Fiddly jobs, undeclared working and the "something for nothing" society', *Work, Employment and Society* 8(4): 507–30.

—— (1996a) 'Labours of love: voluntary working in a depressed local economy', *Journal of Social Policy* 25(1): 19–38.

—— (1996b) 'Welfare dependency, the enterprise culture and self-employed survival', *Work, Employment and Society* 10(3): 431–47.

—— (1996c) 'Nouveaux modeles de transition et d'exclusion sociale de la jeunesse au Royaume-Uni', *Agora: debats/jeunesses* 5: 37–49.

—— (1997) 'Informal work, survival strategies and the idea of an underclass', in R. Brown (ed.) *The Changing Shape of Work*, London: Macmillan.

MacDonald, R. and Coffield, F. (1991) *Risky Business? Youth and the Enterprise Culture*, Basingstoke: Falmer Press.

Maclagan, I. (1992) *A Broken Promise: The Failure of Youth Training Policy*, London: Youthaid.

—— (1993) *Four Years' Severe Hardship*, London: Youthaid/Barnardo's.

—— (1996a) 'How successful are modern apprenticeships?', *Working Brief* 72 (March): 14–16.

—— (1996b) 'Only half of YT leavers get jobs or qualifications, survey reveals', *Working Brief* 72 (March): 9–11.

Maclagan, I. and Convery, P. (1994) 'Income Support overtakes YT allowance', *Working Brief* 53: 16.

Macleod, J. (1987) *Ain't No Makin' It: Levelled Aspirations in a Low Income Neighbourhood*, London: Tavistock.

McCluskey, J. (1994) *Acting in Isolation*, London: CHAR.

McLaughlin, E. (1994) 'Flexibility or Polarisation?', in M. White (ed.) *Unemployment and Public Policy in a Changing Labour Market*, London: Policy Studies Institute.

McLaughlin, E., Millar, J. and Cooke, K. (1989) *Work and Welfare Benefits*, Aldershot: Avebury.

Macnicol, J. (1987) 'In pursuit of the underclass', *Journal of Social Policy* 16(3): 293–318.

—— (1994a) 'Is there an underclass? The lessons from America', in M. White (ed.) *Unemployment and Public Policy in a Changing Labour Market*, London: Policy Studies Institute.

—— (1994b) Review of M. Katz (ed.) *The 'Underclass' Debate: Views from History*, in *Journal of Social Policy* 23(1): 103–4.

McRae, H. (1994) 'Too young and too precious to waste', *Independent*, 12 May 1994.

Maizels, J. (1970) *Adolescent Needs and the Transition from School to Work*, London: Athlone.

Malthus, T. R. [1806] (1989) *An Essay on the Principle of Population* Vol. 2, P. James (ed.), Cambridge: Cambridge University Press.

Manchester City Council (1985) *Manchester: A Picture of Ill Health*, Social Studies Group: Planning Department, Research Paper 11.

—— (1986) *Poverty in Manchester*, Report by Officers from Manchester City Council, and Staff from Manchester Polytechnic and the University of Manchester.

Mann, K. (1992) *The Making of an English 'Underclass'?: The Social Divisions of Welfare and Labour*, Milton Keynes: Open University Press.

—— (1994) 'Watching the defectives: observers of the underclass in the USA, Britain and Australia', *Critical Social Policy* 41: 79–99

Manpower Services Commission (1981) *A New Training Initiative: An Agenda for Action*, London: Manpower Services Commission.

Marsh, C. (1988) 'Unemployment in Britain', in D. Gallie (ed.) *Employment in Britain*, Oxford: Blackwell.

Marshall, G., Roberts, S. and Burgoyne, C. (1996) 'Social class and underclass in Britain and the USA', *British Journal of Sociology* 47: 22–44.

Marshall, T. H. (1950) 'Citizenship and social class', reprinted in T. H. Marshall and T. Bottomore (1992) *Citizenship and Social Class*, London: Pluto Press.

Marsland, D. (1996) 'From Cradle to Grave Mistake', *Times Higher Educational Supplement*, 17 May 1996.

Marx, K. and Engels, F. [1848] (1971) *The Manifesto of the Communist Party*, Moscow: Progress.

Mattera, P. (1985) *Off the Books*, London: Pluto.

Matza, D. (1964) *Delinquency and Drift*, New York: Wiley.

—— (1969) *Becoming Deviant*, New Jersey: Prentice Hall.

May, M. (1973) 'Innocence and experience: the evolution of the concept of juvenile delinquency in the mid-nineteenth century', *Victorian Studies*17: 7–29.

Mayhew, H. [1861] (1950) *London's Underworld*, P. Quennell (ed.), London: Spring Books.

Mead, L. (1986) *Beyond Entitlement: The Social Obligations of Citizenship*, New York: Free Press.

Measham, F., Newcombe, R. and Parker, H. (1994) 'The normalisation of recreational drug use among young people in North-West England', *British Journal of Sociology* 44: 187–312.

Mercer, K. (1990) 'Welcome to the jungle: identity and diversity in postmodern politics', in J. Rutherford (ed.) *Identity: Community, Culture, Difference*, London: Lawrence and Wishart.

Merton, R. (1938) 'Social Structure and Anomie', *American Sociological Review* 3: 672–82.

Middleton, L. (1992) *Children First – Working with Children and Disability*, Birmingham: Venture Press.

Mingione, E. (1993) 'The new urban poverty and the underclass', *International Journal of Urban and Regional Research* 17(3): 2–4.

Mitchell, W. (1996) 'Young people growing up in and outside the care system: an ethnographic approach to social policy issues', DPhil thesis, unpublished draft chapters, Department of Social Policy and Social Work, University of York.

Mizen, P. (1995) *The State, Young People and Youth Training*, London: Mansell.

Montague, C. J. [1904] (1969) *Sixty Years of Waifdom*, London: Woburn Press.

Morgan, P. (1978) *Delinquent Fantasies*, London: Temple Smith.

—— (1995) *Farewell to the Family?*, London: Institute of Economic Affairs.

MORI (1991) *A Survey of 16 and 17 year old Applicants for Severe Hardship Payments*, London: Department of Social Security.

Morris, A., Giller, H., Szwed, E. and Geach, H. (1980) *Justice for Children*, Basingstoke: Macmillan.

Morris, L. (1992) 'Social segregation and the long-term unemployed in Hartlepool', *Sociological Review* 40: 344–69.

—— (1993) 'Is there a British underclass?', *International Journal of Urban and Regional Research* 17(3): 404–13.

—— (1994) *Dangerous Classes: the Underclass and Social Citizenship*, London: Routledge.

Morris, L. and Irwin, S. (1992) 'Employment histories and the concept of an underclass', *Sociology* 26: 401–20.

Morris, L. and Scott, J. (1996) 'The attenuation of class analysis', *British Journal of Sociology* 47: 45–55.

Morse, M. (1965) *The Unattached*, Harmondsworth: Penguin.

Muncie, J. (1984) *The Trouble with Kids Today: Youth and Crime in Post-War Britain*, London: Hutchinson.

Mungham, G. (1982) 'Workless youth as a "moral panic"', in T. L. Rees and P. Atkinson (eds) *Youth Unemployment and State Intervention*, London: Routledge and Kegan Paul.

Murray, C. (1984) *Losing Ground: American Social Policy 1950–1980*, New York: Basic Books.

—— (1989) 'Underclass: a disaster in the making', *Sunday Times Magazine*, 26 November 1989: 26–46.

—— (1990) *The Emerging British Underclass*, London: Institute of Economic Affairs.

—— (1993) 'The coming white underclass', *Wall Street Journal*, 29 October 1993.

—— (1994) *Underclass: The Crisis Deepens*, London: Institute of Economic Affairs.

Myrdal, G. (1962) *Challenge to Affluence*, New York: Pantheon.

National Children's Homes (1993) *A Lost Generation? A Survey of the Problems Faced by Vulnerable Young People Living on their Own*, London: National Children's Homes.

National Institute of Adult Continuing Education and the Norah Fry Research Centre (1996) 'Further education for people with learning difficulties', *Findings, Social Care Research 85*, York: Joseph Rowntree Foundation.

Newburn, T. and Stanko, E. (1994) 'Men, masculinities and crime', in T. Newburn and E. Stanko (eds) *Just Boys Doing Business?*, London: Routledge.

Nicholaus, M. (1968) 'Fat cat sociology', remarks made at *American Sociology Conference*, August 1968.

Nozick, R. (1974) *Anarchy, State and Utopia*, Oxford: Blackwell.

Observer (1996) 'Wasted Generation, Wasted Billions', 3 November 1996: 1.

OFSTED/Social Science Inspectorate (1995) *The Education of Young People Who Are Looked After*, London: HMSO.

Oliver, M. (1990) *The Politics of Disablement*, London: Macmillan.

Packman, J. (1986) *Who Needs Care?*, London: Blackwell.

Pahl, R. (1984) *Divisions of Labour*, London: Blackwell.

Pain, R. (1995) 'Local contexts and the fear of crime: elderly people in the north-east of England', *Northern Economic Review* 24 (Winter): 96–111.

Palmer, V. (1928) *Field Studies in Sociology: A Student's Manual*, Chicago: University of Chicago Press.

Paneth, M. (1944) *Branch Street*, London: George Allen and Unwin.

Parker, H., Bakx, K. and Newcombe, R. (1988) *Living with Heroin: The Impact of a Drugs Epidemic on an English Community*, Milton Keynes: Open University Press.

Parker, H. J. (1974) *View From the Boys*, Newton Abbot: David and Charles.

Parker, H., Measham, F. and Aldridge, J. (1995) *Drug Futures: Changing Patterns of Drug Use amongst English Youth*, London: Institute for the Study of Drug Dependence.

Paterson, A. (1911) *Across the Bridges*, London: Macmillan.

Paton, J. (1908) *Cleansing Our Cities*, London: Macmillan.

Patrick, J. (1973) *A Glasgow Gang Observed*, London: Eyre–Methuen.

Paylore, I. and Smith, D. (1995) 'The needs and problems of young seasonal workers in South Lakeland', *Youth and Policy* 51: 11–20.

Payne, J. (1987) 'Does unemployment run in families?', *Sociology* 21: 199–214.

Payne, J. and Payne, C. (1994) 'Recession, restructuring and the fate of the unemployed: evidence in the underclass debate', *Sociology* 28(1): 1–21.

Pearson, G. (1975) *The Deviant Imagination*, London: Macmillan.

—— (1983) *Hooligan: A History of Respectable Fears*, London: Macmillan.

—— (1994) 'Youth, crime and society', in M. Maguire, R. Morgan and R. Reiner (eds) *Oxford Handbook of Criminology*, Oxford: Clarendon Press.

Peck, C. J. and Emmerich, M. (1992) *Recession, Restructuring and the Greater Manchester Labour Market*, SPA Working Paper 17, Manchester: School of Geography, University of Manchester.

Pelham, T. (1890) *Boys' Clubs*, London: James Nisbet.

Penhale, B. (1989) 'Associations between unemployment and fertility among young women in the early 1980s', *Working Paper 60*, London: City University, Social Statistics Research Unit.

Perfect, M. and Renshaw, J. (1996) *Misspent Youth: Young People and Crime*, London: Audit Commission, HMSO.

Pethick, E. (1898) 'Working Girls' Clubs', in W. Reason (ed.) *University and Social Settlements*, London: Methuen.

Philips, M. (1994) 'Where are the New Victorians?', in C. Murray *Underclass: The Crisis Deepens*, London: Institute for Economic Affairs.

Piachaud, D. (1991) *Unemployment and Poverty*, London: Campaign for Work.

Pickvance, C. and Pickvance, K. (1994) 'Towards a strategic approach to housing behaviour: a study of young people's housing strategies in South-East England', *Sociology* 28(3): 657–77.

Pilkington, A. (1992) 'The underclass thesis and race', presented at British Sociological Association Conference, University of Kent, Canterbury.

Piore, M. J. and Sabel, C. F. (1984) *The Second Industrial Divide*, New York: Basic Books.

Pitts, J. (1988) *The Politics of Juvenile Crime*, London: Sage.

—— (1990) *Working With Young Offenders*, London: Macmillan.

Platt, J. (1976) *Realities of Social Research: An Empirical Study of British Sociologists*, London: Chatto and Windus.

Platt, T. and Takagi, P. (1981) 'Intellectuals for law and order: a critique of the new "realists" ', in T. Platt and P. Takagi (eds) *Crime and Social Justice*, London: Macmillan.

Plotkin, A. L. and Elias, G. (1977) 'The Curfew Bill as it relates to the juvenile and his family', *Adolescence* 12: 48–59.

Pollock, G. (1996) 'Unemployed and under 18', *Youth and Policy* 54: 38–53.

Polsky, N. [1967] (1971) *Hustlers, Beats and Others*, Harmondsworth: Penguin.

Popple, K. (1995) *Analysing Community Work: Its Theory and Practice*, Buckingham: Open University Press.

Porter, M. (1990) *The Competitive Advantage of Nations*, London: Macmillan.

Prothrow-Stith, D. (1991) *Deadly Consequences: How Violence is Destroying Our Teenage Population*, New York: Harper.

Pryce, K. (1979) *Endless Pressure*, Harmondsworth: Penguin.

Pyle, D. (1987) 'The fight against crime', *Social Studies Review* 2(3): 17–21.

Raffe, D. (1987) 'The context of the Youth Training Scheme: an analysis of its strategy and development', *British Journal of Education and Work* 1(1): 1–31.

—— (1992) *Participation of 16–18 year olds in education and training*, National Commission on Education Briefing, 3 May 1992.

Redhead, S. (ed.) (1991) *Rave Off!*, Aldershot: Avebury.

Reed, B. (1950) *Eighty Thousand Adolescents: A Study of Young People in Birmingham*, London: Allen and Unwin.

Rees, T. and Atkinson, P. (eds) (1982) *Youth Unemployment and State Intervention*, London: Routledge and Kegan Paul.

Rex, J. and Tomlinson, S. (1979) *Colonial Immigrants in a British City*, London: Routledge.

Riseborough, G. (1993) 'GBH – The Gobbo Barmy Harmy', in I. Bates and G. Riseborough (eds) *Youth and Inequality*, Buckingham: Open University Press.

Roberts, K. (1968) 'The entry into employment: an approach towards a general theory', *Sociological Review* 16: 2.

—— (1987) 'ESRC – Young People in Society', *Youth and Policy* 22: 15–24.

—— (1993) 'Career trajectories and the mirage of increased social mobility', in I. Bates and G. Riseborough (eds) *Youth and Inequality*, Buckingham: Open University Press.

—— (1995) *Youth and Employment in Modern Britain*, Oxford: Oxford University Press.

Roberts, K. and Jung, B. (1995) *Poland's First Post-Communist Generation*, Aldershot: Avebury.

Roberts, K. and Parsell, G. (1989) *The Stratification of Youth Training*, Occasional Paper 11, ESRC 16–19 Initiative, London: City University.

Roberts, K., Dench, S. and Richardson, D. (1987) *The Changing Structure of Youth Labour Markets*, London: Department of Employment Research Paper 59.

Roberts, K., Duggan, J. and Noble, M. (1981) *Unregistered Youth Unemployment and Outreach Careers Work*, London: Department of Employment Research Paper 31.

Roberts, K., Noble, M. and Duggan, J. (1982a) 'Youth unemployment: an old problem or a new life-style?', *Leisure Studies* 1: 171–82.

Roberts, K., Duggan, J. and Noble, M. (1982b) 'Out of school youth in high unemployment areas: an empirical investigation', *British Journal of Guidance and Counselling* 10(1): 1–11.

Robins, D. (1992) *Tarnished Vision: Crime and Conflict in the Inner City*, Oxford: Oxford University Press.

Robinson, F. and Gregson, N. (1992) 'The "underclass": a class apart?', *Critical Social Policy* 34 (Summer): 38–51.

Roche, M. (1993) *Rethinking Citizenship: Welfare, ideology and change in modern society*, Cambridge: Polity Press.

Rosenberg, F. and Rosenberg, M. (1978) 'Self-esteem and delinquency', *Journal of Youth and Adolescence* 7: 279–91.

Rosenberger, L. R. (1996) *America's Drug War Debacle*, Aldershot: Avebury.

Rowe, J., Hundleby, M. and Garnett, L. (1989) *Child Care Now: A Survey of Placement Patterns*, London: BAAF.

Ruefle, W. and Reynolds, K. M. (1995) 'Curfews and delinquency in major American cities', *Crime and Delinquency* 41(3): 347–63.

Runcimann, W. G. (1990) 'How many classes are there in contemporary British society?', *Sociology* 24: 378–96.

Russell, C. and Russell, L. (1932) *Lads' Clubs: Their History, Organisation and Management*, London: A. C. Black.

Rutter, M. and Madge, N. (1976) *Cycles of Disadvantage*, London: Heinemann.

Salaman, G. (1992) 'Work design and corporate strategies', in J. Allen, P. Braham and P. Lewis (eds) *Political and Economic Forms of Modernity*, Cambridge: Open University Press.

Sarup, M. (1993) *Post-structuralism and Postmodernism*, Hemel Hempstead: Harvester Wheatsheaf.

Sayers, S. (1988) 'The need to work: a perspective from philosophy', in R. E. Pahl (ed.) *On Work*, Oxford: Blackwell.

Schorr, L. B. (1988) *Within Our Reach: Breaking the cycle of disadvantage*, New York: Doubleday Books.

Scott, A. F. (1975) *Every One a Witness*, London: Purnell.

Scott-Clark, C. and Byrne, C. (1995) 'A Degree of Dismay', *Sunday Times*, 28 May 1995.

Seabrook, J. (1987) 'Surviving', in S. Fineman (ed.) *Unemployment: Personal and Social Consequences*, London: Tavistock.

Secretan, H. (1931) *London Below Bridges*, London: Godfrey Bles.

Sennett, R. and Cobb, J. (1977) *The Hidden Injuries of Class*, Cambridge: Cambridge University Press.

Shakespeare, J. (1995) *Images of Want*, Manchester: Church Action on Poverty.

Short, J. F. (1996) 'Personal, gang and community careers', in C. R. Huff (ed.) *Gangs In America*, Thousand Oaks CA: Sage.

Sibley, D. (1995) *Geographies of Exclusion*, London: Routledge.

Sieber, J. E. (ed.) (1982) *The Ethics of Social Research: Fieldwork Regulation and Publication*, New York: Springer.

Silver, H. (1993) 'National conceptions of the new urban poverty', *International Journal of Urban and Regional Research* 17(3): 336–50.

Skilbeck, M., Connell, H., Lowe, N. and Tait, K. (1994) *The Vocational Quest: New Directions in Education and Training*, London: Routledge.

Slipman, S. (1994) 'Would you take one home with you?', in C. Murray *Underclass: The Crisis Deepens*, London: Institute for Economic Affairs.

Smith, D. (ed.) (1992a) *Understanding the Underclass*, London: Policy Studies Institute.

—— (1992b) 'The future of the underclass', in D. Smith (ed.) *Understanding the Underclass*, London: Policy Studies Institute.

Smith, D. and Paylore, I. (1996) 'Reluctant heroes: youth work and crime prevention', *Youth and Policy* 52: 14–23.

Smith, David J. (1995) 'Youth crime and conduct disorders: trends, patterns, and causal explanations', in M. Rutter and D. J. Smith (eds) *Psychosocial Disorders in Young People: Time Trends and Their Causes*, Chichester: John Wiley.

Smith, M. (1988) *Developing Youth Work*, Milton Keynes: Open University Press.

Social Services Inspectorate (1991) *Corporate Parents*, London: HMSO.

Springhall, J. (1977) *Youth, Empire and Society*, London: Croom Helm.

Springhall, J., Fraser, B. and Hoare, M. (1983) *Sure and Steadfast: A History of the Boys' Brigade*, London: Collins.

Spruit, E. and de Goede, M. (1995) 'Changing family structures and adolescent well-being', paper presented to Second European Sociological Association Conference, Budapest.

Stacey, J. (1988) 'Can there be a feminist ethnography?', *Women's Studies International Forum* 11(1): 21–7.

Stager, S. F. (1983) 'Determinants of self esteem among labelled adolescents', *Social Psycyhology Quarterley* 46(1): 3–10.

Stanley, M. (1890) *Clubs for Working Girls*, London: Macmillan.

Stedman-Jones, G. (1971) *Outcast London: A Study in the Relationship between Classes in Victorian Society*, Harmondsworth: Penguin.

Stein, M. and Carey, K. (1986) *Leaving Care*, London: Blackwell.

Stenson, K. and Factor, F. (1995) 'Governing youth: new directions for the youth service', in J. Baldock and M. May (eds) *Social Policy Review 7*, Canterbury: Social Policy Association.

Stephens, P. (1992) 'Urban underclass is challenge', *Financial Times*, 25 November 1996.

Strickland, S. (1995) 'Bringing it all back home', *Guardian*, 11 April 1995.

Swann, W. (1988) 'Trends in special school placement to 1986: measuring, assessing and explaining segregation', *Oxford Review of Education* 14(2) (quoted in Barnes, C. 1991).

Sykes, G. and Matza, D. (1957) 'Techniques of neutralisation: a theory of delinquency', *American Sociological Review* 22: 664–70.

Tarling, R. (1993) *Analysing Offending*, London: HMSO.

Taylor, T. (1987) 'Youth workers as character builders: constructing a socialist alternative', in T. Jeffs and M. Smith (eds) *Youth Work*, London: Macmillan.

Teesside Training and Enterprise Council (1995a) *Labour Market Assessment*, Middlesbrough.

—— (1995b) Personal communication, Middlesbrough.

Thatcher, M. (1987) Interview with Douglas Keay, *Woman's Own*, 31 October 1987.

Therborn, G. (1986) *Why Some Peoples are More Unemployed than Others*, London: Verso.

Thomas, P. (1995) 'The young and the violent', *Washington Post National Weekly*, 24 September 1995.

Thompson, E. P. and Yeo, E. (eds) (1973) *The Unknown Mayhew*, Harmondsworth: Penguin.

Thomson, G. and Ward, K. (1994) *Patterns and Pathways: Individuals with disabilities in transition to adulthood*, A Report to the Leverhulme Trust and The Scottish Office Education Department, Department for Education: University of Edinburgh.

Thornton, S. (1995) *Club Cultures*, Cambridge: Polity Press.

Tisdall, K. (1996) 'Are young disabled people being sufficiently involved in their post school planning? Case studies of Scotland's Future Needs Assessment and Ontario's Educational–Vocational Meetings', *European Journal of Special Needs Education* 11(1): 17–32.

Todd, S. (1995) 'Preludes to secrecy: handling the transition of young people from a special school', in S. Salisbury and S. Delamont (eds) *Qualitative Studies and Education*, Aldershot: Avebury.

Tomlinson, S. (1982) *The Sociology of Special Education*, London: Routledge and Kegan Paul.

Tomlinson, S. and Colquhoun, R. F. (1995) 'The political economy of special education need in Britain', *Disability and Society* 10(2): 191–202.

Townsend, P., Davidson, N. and Whitehead, M. (1988) *Inequalities in Health*, London: Penguin.

Travers, P. (1986) 'Contingent and non-contingent effects of unemployment', *Sociology* 20: 192–206.

Tucker, S. (1994) 'Changing times, changing roles: an examination of contemporary youth and community practice', *Youth and Policy* 46: 5–16.

Turner, R., Boyston, A. and Wight, D. (1985) 'The work ethic in a Scottish town with declining employment', in B. Roberts, R. Finnegan and D. Gallie (eds) *New Approaches to Economic Life*, Manchester: Manchester University Press.

Ullah, P. (1987) 'Unemployed black youths in a northern city', in D. Fryer and P. Ullah (eds) *Unemployed People: Social and Psychological Perspectives*, Milton Keynes: Open University Press.

Unwin, L. (1993) *Dropping Out in the 1990s: A Study of Post-16*

Destination Patterns in Derbyshire 1987–1992, ESRC Seminar Group: Issues Paper, September 1993.

Urwick, E. (1904) *Studies of Boy Life in Our Cities*, London: Dent.

Utting, W. (1991) *Children in the Public Care* (The Utting Report), London: Department of Health and Social Service Inspectorate.

Valentine, C. (1968) *Culture and Poverty*, Chicago: University of Chicago Press.

Veness, T. (1962) *School Leavers*, London: Methuen.

Wacquant, L. (1991) 'From "black metropolis" to "hyperghetto": race, state and economy in the post-Fordist era', paper presented to Working Conference on Poverty, Immigration and Urban Marginality in the Advanced Societies, Paris.

Wainwright, H. (1994) *Arguments for a New Left*, Oxford: Blackwell.

Walker, A. (1990) 'Blaming the Victims', in C. Murray *The Emerging British Underclass*, London: Institute for Economic Affairs.

Wallace, C. (1986) 'From generation to generation: the effects of employment and unemployment upon the domestic life cycle of young adults', paper presented at the British Sociological Association Conference, University of Loughborough, March 1986.

—— (1987) *For Richer For Poorer: Growing Up In and Out of Work*, London: Tavistock.

Ward, K., Riddell, S., Dyer, M. and Thompson, G. (1991) *The Transition to Adulthood of Young People with Recorded Special Educational Needs*, Scottish Office Education Department: Department of Education at the Universities of Edinburgh and Stirling.

Warnock, M. W. (1978) *Special Educational Needs: Report of the Committee of Enquiry into the Education of Handicapped Children and Young People*, cmnd 7212, London: HMSO.

Warr, P. (1983) 'Work, jobs and unemployment', *Bulletin of the British Psychological Society* 36: 305–11.

Warren, C. (1988) *Gender Issues in Field Research*, London: Sage University Paper, Qualitative Research Methods Series, No. 9.

Wellman, D. (1994) 'Constituting ethnographic authority: the work process of field research, an ethnographic account', *Cultural Studies* 8(3): 569–83.

Westergaard, J. (1992) 'About and beyond the underclass: some notes on influences of social climate on British Sociology', *Sociology* 26: 575–87.

White, M. and McRae, S. (1989) *Young Adults and Long Term Unemployment*, London: Policy Studies Institute.

Wiener, M. (1981) *English Culture and the Decline of the Industrial Spirit*, Cambridge: Cambridge University Press.

Wilkinson, C. (1995) *The Drop Out Society: Young People at the Margin*, Leicester: Youth Work Press.

Wilkinson, H. and Mulgan, G. (1995) *Freedom's Children*, London: Demos.

Williams, F. (1989) *Social Policy: A Critical Introduction*, Cambridge: Polity Press.

Williams, J. E. (1906) *The Life of George Williams*, London: Armstrong.

Williamson, H. (1978) 'Choosing to be a delinquent', *New Society*, 7 November 1978.

—— (1993) 'Youth policy in the United Kingdom and the marginalisation of young people', *Youth and Policy* 40: 33–48.

—— (1994) 'Status Zer0 16 and 17 year olds: identification, cultures and policy implications', paper presented at 4th Nordic Youth Research Symposium, Stockholm.

Willis, P. (1977) *Learning to Labour*, London: Saxon House.

—— (1982) *Male school counterculture*, V203 Popular Culture, Block 7, Unit 30, Milton Keynes: Open University Press.

—— (1984) 'Youth unemployment 2: ways of living', *New Society*, 5 April 1984: 13–15.

—— (1990) *Common Culture: Symbolic Work at Play in the Everyday Cultures of the Young*, Milton Keynes: Open University Press.

Wilson, R. A. and Webb, T. (1995) *Review of the Economy and Employment: Occupational Assessment*, Coventry: University of Warwick, Institute for Employment Research.

Wilson, W. J. (1978) *The Declining Significance of Race*, Chicago: University of Chicago Press.

—— (1987) *The Truly Disadvantaged*, Chicago: University of Chicago Press.

—— (1991) 'Studying inner-city social dislocations', *American Sociological Review* 56: 1–14

—— (1992) 'Another look at The Truly Disadvantaged', *Political Science Quarterly* 106: 639–56.

Wintour, P. (1996) 'Think you're safe when you've finally got a job?', *Observer*, 1 September 1996.

Wood, S. (ed.) *The Transformation of Work?*, London: Unwin Hyman.

Wooden, W. S. (1995) *Renegade Kids, Suburban Outlaws: From Youth Culture to Delinquency*, Belmont CA: Wadsworth.

Wright, D. (1994) *Workers not Wasters*, Edinburgh: Edinburgh University Press.

Young, J. (1992) *The Rise in Crime in England and Wales 1979–1990*, Middlesex: Centre for Criminology, Middlesex Polytechnic.

—— (1994) 'Incessant chatter: recent paradigms in criminology', in M. Maguire, R. Morgan and R. Reiner (eds) *Oxford Handbook of Criminology*, Oxford: Clarendon Press.

—— (1995) 'Social breakdown as a causative factor of youth crime', paper given at conference entitled 'A Clockwork Orange: Deprived or Depraved?', Newcastle: Newcastle Playhouse.

Index

Note: Page numbers in italic type refer to tables. Page numbers followed by 'N' refer to notes.